Capitalism Hates You

CAPITALISM HATES YOU

Marxism and the New Horror Film

Joshua Gooch

UNIVERSITY OF MINNESOTA PRESS
MINNEAPOLIS | LONDON

Copyright 2025 by the Regents of the University of Minnesota

All rights reserved. No part of this publication may be reproduced, stored in a retrieval system, utilized for purposes of training artificial intelligence technologies, or transmitted, in any form or by any means, electronic, mechanical, photocopying, recording, or otherwise, without the prior written permission of the publisher.

Published by the University of Minnesota Press
111 Third Avenue South, Suite 290
Minneapolis, MN 55401-2520
http://www.upress.umn.edu

ISBN 978-1-5179-1796-8 (hc)
ISBN 978-1-5179-1797-5 (pb)

A Cataloging-in-Publication record for this book is available from the Library of Congress.

Printed in the United States of America on acid-free paper

The University of Minnesota is an equal-opportunity educator and employer.

CONTENTS

INTRODUCTION   1

1. Work Hates You: Antiwork Horror and Value Theory   25

2. Love Hates You: Feminist Anticapitalist Horror and Social Reproduction Theory   43

3. Nature Hates You: Psychedelic Eco-horror and Ecological Marxism   67

4. The Neighborhood Hates You: New Black Horror and Uneven Development   93

5. Commodities Hate You: Mass-Culture Horror and Commodity Forms   123

6. The Family Hates You: Elevated Horror and Family Abolition   147

7. Feelings Hate You: Therapeutic Horror and Emotion Work   173

CONCLUSION   199

ACKNOWLEDGMENTS   209

FILMOGRAPHY   211

NOTES   217

INDEX   253

INTRODUCTION

"I feel like I'm leaving the movie theater after seeing *The Witch* or *Hereditary*," *Maintenance Phase* cohost Aubrey Gordon said after describing the little-understood and harmful effects of sugar alcohols widely used by the food industry. "This feels bad in a very large-scale kind of way."[1] It's no mistake that when Gordon needed a filmgoing experience to describe a systemic problem, she turned to horror. Perhaps more than any other contemporary film genre, horror captures how our conjuncture makes us feel about hard-to-localize, large-scale problems. Fans of the genre see these anxiety-inducing feelings as part of horror's appeal. Watching horror today can often seem less like a transgressive act than a therapy session. In *Screaming for Pleasure: How Horror Makes You Happy and Healthy*, horror fan and host of the podcast *Hellbent for Horror* S. A. Bradley describes the genre's salutary effects in therapeutic terms:

> You may have noticed a few recurring themes that come up when I talk about the influence horror can have on a person: coping with trauma and tragedy, renewing a passion for life, indulging playfulness, and finding a sense of belonging in a community. No matter who you are, if you have those things, life is happier and healthier.[2]

Bradley isn't the only person who sees the genre as mood adjusting. In *Vice*, Abby Moss discusses "self-medicating with horror movies," a practice that combines exposure therapy with the idea that horror is a safe space to confront terror.[3] To support her claims, Moss turns to the work of horror scholar and evolutionary psychology proponent Mathias Clasen. For Clasen, people turn to horror because it induces anxious feelings deeply rooted in their nervous systems and the experience teaches them how to control those feelings. During the Covid-19 pandemic, Clasen released a coauthored study, "Pandemic Practice: Horror Fans and Morbidly Curious Individuals Are More Psychologically Resilient during the COVID-19 Pandemic," that made the sudden upsurge in horror viewing a therapeutic activity.[4] *National Geographic* and *Psychology Today* wrote stories about horror's therapeutic potential, and the *Washington Post* framed a feature on horror with the Clasen-esque lead: "A horror film? In these times? It may seem counterintuitive, but sometimes it's helpful to channel real-life fears into fictional stories."[5]

In this book, I approach horror not as therapy but as diagnosis. I argue that horror, by harnessing the negative thoughts and feelings that imbue our political economic moment, lets us grapple with an often unstated yet overwhelming intuition: *Capitalism hates us*. As we'll see, horror gives affective shape to what we know, however imprecisely, about our domination by capital. It doesn't offer viewers the promise of catharsis or relief. It isn't therapeutic. What it does is give form to the negative feelings that imbue our historical moment. These feelings are social and political. In *The Cultural Politics of Emotion*, Sara Ahmed describes how the emotions most tightly bound up with horror—hate, fear, and disgust—can create and reinforce social and cultural divisions.[6] Yet if feeling keeps people apart, it can also bring them together. Marxist political philosopher Frédéric Lordon emphasizes affect's dual role in constituting and dividing political groups. Affect is important to creating groups, but it isn't, Lordon argues, strong enough to hold together emancipatory political projects. For Lordon, we need reason to create "durable" political bodies; only reason can overcome the ways in which affects create boundaries or dissolve them.[7] From this perspective, horror can articulate negative feelings about our moment in ways that may bring people together or split them apart. To create a durable political analysis out of horror's feelings, we need reason. We will find this reason in Marxist thought. Marxism, I maintain, can help us understand how capitalism works and the ideas that maintain its hegemony, while also deepening our understanding of the new horror film.[8]

Horror certainly isn't foreign to Marxist thought. Marx littered the first volume of *Capital* with vampires, necromancers, werewolves, and specters. Some readers may be tempted to take Marx's use of these elements as rhetorical or literary. Critics have connected Marx's style and form to his analysis of capitalism, sometimes to reinforce Marx's points and sometimes to deconstruct them.[9] The vampire is likely the most recognizable of Marx's Gothic tropes. Critics sometimes take it as a figure for capitalism's limitless desire for accumulation or its social parasitism.[10] Yet as Mark Neocleous rightly notes, Marx doesn't turn to the vampire as "a rhetorical device" but "to illustrate one of the central dynamics of capitalist production—the distinction between living and dead labor."[11] The importance of the vampire in Marx is, I think, dwarfed by the ghostly. The idea of undead, spectral agency provides Marx with a way to describe an economic system of impersonal social domination that is indifferent to human needs. It takes center stage in Marx's account of commodity fetishism. English translations of *Capital* render Marx's explanation of the commodity fetish as "the fantastic form of a relation between things."[12] In German, however, Marx's phrase is "*phantasmagorische Form*"—that is, a phantasmagoric form, not a fantastic one.[13] In eighteenth- and nineteenth-century Britain, the phantasmagoria was a popular show that thrilled patrons with specters projected on clouds of smoke.[14] For Marx, these ghostly performances provide a way to describe how immaterial objects can nonetheless produce real effects in people, as Michael Heinrich notes.[15] For Marx, the phantasmagoria captures a crucial quality of abstract value, what he calls "*gepenstige Gegenständlichkeit*," and Ben Brewster translates as "phantom-like objectivity."[16] However, Alexander Locasio offers a better translation: "spectral objectivity."[17] Value is a ghost with agency in the world. It may be immaterial, but it has real effects. Most importantly, it determines whether your labor gets counted as part of what Marx calls the aggregate of social labor. It doesn't do that while you work. Value is ghostly because it isn't present during your laboring time or what Marx calls concrete labor. In purely economic terms, it determines whether you're hired or fired. That isn't to say it makes those decisions. What it does is force your employer to decide whether your work is likely to produce value in exchange. Of course, your employer can't be sure, either. Value is present enough to matter but not enough to tell anyone exactly what to do. It is the ghost that makes everyone guess about what everyone else needs or wants or will buy. If the product you worked on or the service you provide sells, then value retroactively determines that your labor was productive. If not, it was not. Value spiritualizes some material activities through the act of commodity exchange and casts others out.

Prior Marxist accounts of horror have been more interested in the body than value, and for good reasons. The body has long been the crucial site for political interpretations of horror. For feminist critics, the feminine body is the genre's primary locus for evocations of fear, disgust, and terror.[18] Horror, they argue, subjects female bodies to sadistic violence, treats them as abject, and uses their sexualization to make bodily permeability and penetration into the stuff of (male) terror. Other critics highlight the centrality of racialized bodies. From this perspective, horror's irrational, animalized, and foreign monstrosities represent racialized bodies to be destroyed in imaginary pogroms of social purification.[19] Still others read the genre's focus on the body as transgressive, rather than repressive. By evoking bodily otherness, horror makes the body into a site where norms can be contested. Horror's physical deformations thus undercut physiological notions of bodily coherence and autonomy, attack socially constructed ideas of normality, and thwart ideas of good taste.[20] For Marxist critics, the body in horror captures the violence that capitalism directs at workers. Perhaps the key passage in Marx for these readings is his comparison in *Capital* of abstract labor to *Gallerte*, a jelly-like product of boiled meat, bone, and cartilage.[21] In essence, capitalism consists of a set of forms that mean to reduce us to meat jelly. For Mark Steven, "splatter" or "gore" films, a genre that includes the so-called meat movies of the 1970s, gross-out horror, and torture porn, dramatize capitalism's reduction of workers to meat.[22] In Steven's account, horror's violence enacts exploitation's violence, and cycles of splatter films mark shifts in regimes of global capital accumulation, from the rise of finance in the 1970s with early culturally resistant films like *The Texas Chainsaw Massacre* and *Dawn of the Dead*, to finance capital's consolidation of political economic power in the 1980s with reactionary body horrors like *Videodrome* and *Hellraiser*. David McNally also focuses on the violence directed at workers' bodies in his analysis of the Gothic. For McNally, Gothic tales such as Mary Shelley's *Frankenstein* present body panics that reflect capitalism's dismemberment of workers. Importantly, though, McNally also insists capitalism's violence can't be reduced to the violence of production; it also includes the violence of primitive accumulation, which pervades rather than precedes capitalism.[23]

While the body is indeed a powerful figure for displaying the violence capitalism aims at workers, we miss something crucial about horror and capitalism if we reduce both to violence against bodies. We'll return to value in chapter 1. For the moment, we need to address the fact that capitalism is oppressive but doesn't rely solely on negative affects. As Jules Joanne Gleeson and Elle O'Rourke argue, it is also "productive of affects, attachments, fierce passions, commitments, and hatreds."[24] In short, capitalism offers pleasures and attachments as well as violence. And the same holds true for horror. Early feminist critics treated the genre as an expression of male sadism created by castration anxiety and the need to make the feminine monstrous and abject.[25] Other critics focus on horror's unpleasant affects. In *The Philosophy of Horror*, Noel Carroll offers an analytic definition of horror as a feeling of agitation caused by something threatening, impure, or repulsive.[26] When Xavier Aldana Reyes crafts his affective approach to the Gothic, he centers feelings evoked by physical threats: "Gothic affect, as I understand it, hinges on the human self-preservation instinct, and, thus, relies on notions of external threat, whether these are ominous and shapeless, or embodied."[27] Clasen takes this position further, using evolutionary psychology to argue that horror relies on innate responses to feelings of threats and disgust. "Horror fiction," Clasen writes, "works by throwing a live wire into ancient structures in the audience's central nervous system."[28] Marxist accounts tend to be less determinist but just as focused on evocations of threat and disgust. The result is a picture of the genre defined by violence, gore, and images meant to repulse. From the twenty-first century, this understanding of horror seems tightly bound to a particular era of film production, the era of Steven's splatter capitalism, and leaves little room for the new kinds of horror we find in the 2020s. As we will see, films like Prano Bailey-Bond's *Censor*, Jane Schoenbrun's *We're All Going to the World's Fair*, and Amy Seimetz's *She Dies Tomorrow* use horror and its affects quite differently than *The Texas Chainsaw Massacre*.

We need to reconsider, then, what horror is and why viewers seek it out. In the past, critics explained audiences' attraction to images of violence as the result of masochism. For Carol Clover, it explains why horror's ideal spectator, an adolescent man, enjoys identifying with vulnerable women. In effect, Clover's argument combines Laura Mulvey's description of female spectatorship as a form of masochism with Teresa de Lauretis's account of female spectatorship as a kind of double identification.[29] Male spectators, Clover explains, work through their Oedipal troubles by holding their gendered identifications at a distance. They "take it in the eye."[30] The pleasure of a horror film is an experience of vulnerability and control, of being the killer and the final girl. By contrast, Marco Abel argues that masochism allows viewers to approach painful images as a source of critical pleasure. By seeking out violent images, spectators undertake what Abel styles a kind of critical pedagogy. Encounters with violent images force masochists to withhold judgment, Abel explains, and thus "defer the advent of pleasure that criticism clearly derives from the moment at which the critic gets to articulate his judgment of violence, or certainty."[31] In essence, the masochist is a critic and the critic a masochist, both forced to examine without coming to conclusions.

These masochistic accounts of horror have much in common with Immanuel Kant's notion of the sublime. For Kant, the sublime's evocation of the infinite offers viewers cognitive pleasure in their subjective ability to hold the vast and unimaginable in their minds. In masochist accounts of horror, masochists do something similar, expanding their range of identifications or withholding judgment for aesthetic contemplation. However, we uncover a different sense of horror's appeal if we consider instead the sublime of Edmund Burke. For Burke, the sublime describes how pain, fear, and terror produce astonishment and delight when evoked without threatening a spectator with actual harm. As spectators realize their proximity to and distance from what causes pain, they're filled with delight.[32] While this may suggest horror as a safe space to encounter terror, Burke's sublime doesn't make the encounter with terror a way to work out individual fears or develop an appreciation for our cognitive capacities. For Burke, the sublime is a kind of physical "exercise or labor" that revitalizes "the nerves," what Tom Furniss calls "the eighteenth-century equivalent to a work-out."[33] In effect, Burke's sublime is a kind of aesthetic strength training that means to save spectators from any dangerously "languid inactive state" that could lead to "melancholy, dejection, despair, and often-self-murder."[34] From this perspective, horror wouldn't help us work through traumas, take pleasure in them, or learn from them. It offers us a physical, affective reworking in response to the sheer vastness of a terrifying system. Here we might reframe what Clasen sees as horror's focus on fight-or-flight responses as instead the aesthetic production of heightened sensory experiences that mean to shock and energize.[35] Andrew Schopp approaches the Burkean sublime in his account of the pleasure fear makes possible. It's a kind of thrill-seeking "catharsis," a charge "predicated on experiencing a fear directly connected to the potential for real danger."[36] If Schopp's example, *The Blair Witch Project* (1999), doesn't offer viewers much in the way of cathartic relief, beyond the fact that the film ends, what it does offer is a series of jolts or energizing encounters with fear.

Burke thought such encounters could unleash energies that might lead to political reconciliation; I would argue that isn't why people seek out these experiences, nor does it make reconciliation a given.[37] We can better understand people's attraction to the genre through the work of horror scholar Jeffrey Andrew Weinstock. Weinstock argues that people come to horror out of a "desire for wonder" that originates in "deep-seated desires for and fascination with the prospect of another world governed by different laws."[38] Weinstock sees this desire as rooted in a fascination with the Freudian stuff of magical thinking. When we analyze the genre through Marxism, this desire for wonder gains new contours. People are attracted to the experience of energizing fright, I would argue, because it reveals a world in which the oppressive laws that govern our lives take on a more immediate form. What horror offers spectators is the prospect of a world in which the hidden conflicts of a vast antagonistic system become suddenly, horrifyingly, tangible. At last there's something to fight or to flee.

Still, is that enough to make these experiences pleasurable? Sianne Ngai's work on the zany can help us to understand how genre has remade the oppressions of capitalism into revitalizing delights. For Ngai, the aesthetic category that best captures and recasts the stresses and desperation of twentieth- and twenty-first-century capitalism isn't horror but the zany. It turns the joylessness of capitalism's new forms of work—immaterial labor, social reproduction, and the so-called feminization of labor—into something "playful, [and] hypercharismatic."[39] Horror does something similar. Where zaniness turns work's oppressions into something joyful, horror turns them into something terrifying, reshaping capitalism's intensities into generic forms that allow us to feel the horrors of our historical moment. As we will see, the affects and effects of the new horror film draw on capitalism's oppressions now: the shift to knowledge work and the feminization of labor, the destruction of the biosphere and the uneven development of the built environment, the changing face of commodification, the exploitation of reproductive labor, and the demand for feeling management.[40]

The pleasure of horror comes not from remaking work so much as the shared aesthetic judgment that coheres a genre through recognition. In her discussion of the zany, Ngai admits that even though our moment is deeply marked by capitalism's exploitation of immaterial labor, social reproduction, and the feminization of labor, the zany now has little cultural purchase. Ngai's explanation for our contemporary lack of zaniness is that people have come to prefer aesthetic categories that require "universal agreement on a judgment of value based solely on feelings of pleasure and displeasure."[41] The cute, the interesting, and the gimmicky are, Ngai asserts, more popular aesthetic categories at the moment because they demand universal judgments from viewers. Indeed, the gimmick asks them to create judgments about (capitalist) value itself. However, the zany, which relies on subjective judgments, does not.[42] And here's where horror comes in. Horror *does*. If Ngai is right that our aesthetic categories and our conjuncture are deeply entwined—and I think she is—then we might say that horror fills a gap in contemporary culture, an aesthetic category able to remediate the horrors of our economic system into something pleasurable.[43] It is no mistake that, as Johanna Isaacson argues, a new generation of filmmakers has reshaped the genre around the concerns of living in an era of so-called feminized labor.[44] The pleasure audiences can find in horror has less to do with attacks on feminized and racialized bodies or the embrace of transgression than with audiences' shared judgments about the terrors of their historical moment. The nature of those judgments are always up for grabs. Societies sliding into fascism may tend toward terrors of monstrous others, whether racial, sexual, or whatever.[45] The shared rejection of specific social norms may encourage judgments that the norms themselves are monstrous.[46] The pressures of global warming and inequality may encourage judgments about norms of consumption, production, and so on. Horror gives affective shape to the negative feelings of our time, but it doesn't give those feelings a politics. It only gives them a new valence of pleasure, one that comes from shared judgments about what we find unpleasurable.

Gender and Genre in Our Conjuncture

We can see what these kinds of shared judgments look like in Linda Williams's study of the distribution and reception of Hitchcock's *Psycho*.[47] Building on her claim that women refuse to look at horror films, Williams analyzes photos of audience reactions to *Psycho*. Following Clover, Williams maintains that the men in these photos could look directly at the film's violence because they retained a gendered distance from the female bodies that Hitchcock makes the object of screen violence, while the women look away to avoid direct identification with these objects. Yet, Williams argues, these photos also reveal how women learned to take pleasure in horror. By performing their fear and terror for other women in the audience, they made their performance of these responses the pleasure of being part of an audience. In other words, the female audience members realized they were linked through shared judgments about displeasure.

What this means, I think, is that horror is, at its core not about being scared but about being scared *with other people*. Evolutionary psychological and therapeutic interpretations of horror misunderstand the genre because they center their analyses on individuals. Horror is communal. Like any genre, horror consists of a set of social judgments. Genres aren't stable but "open categories," as Ralph Cohen explains, and "each member alters the genre by adding, contradicting, or changing constituents."[48] But genres aren't just a matter of what's in a text. They're made, as Rick Altman shows, through the continued interactions of writers, directors, producers, studios, distributors, audiences, critics, and academics—in short, by all the institutions and agents involved in the making, distribution, sale, and reception of genre texts.[49] This collective work of genre-making includes, but is not limited to, the aesthetic judgments of audiences and fans, as the entertainment industry has learned and exploited.[50] When we understand horror as created collectively and aimed at creating collective affective experiences, we can more fully recognize the importance of changes in who makes and watches horror. As more women, trans, and BIPOC people create horror, the more shared judgments about what is unpleasurable will alter the genre. While it is tempting to treat what came before as defining a genre, the collective work of genre-making reveals such claims to be at best historically descriptive and at worst blindly prescriptive. Horror is and will be what the collective work of genre-making agrees it is at a given moment in time.[51] The collective work of genre creation, then, is subject to continual contestation. In this sense, the question of what makes a text recognizably part of a genre should be understood as a struggle for hegemony. As Stuart Hall explains, hegemony is "the *process* by which a historical bloc of social forces is constructed and the ascendency of that bloc secured."[52] Genres, like hegemony, aren't given for all time, but are the subject of continued and constant struggle. One knows when hegemony has been achieved when it takes on the form of common sense, and that's certainly the case for genre definitions.

This affects my approach to interpretation and analysis. Marxist criticism often begins with formalist analyses of individual texts. However, the labor of genre construction indicates that we would better focus our attention on sets of texts with shared elements and narrative structures if we wish to understand how horror captures capitalism's terrors. I focus on texts in close historical proximity to show how shared elements and structures may indicate shared aesthetic judgments about what is terrifying. Those judgments often take me outside the films themselves to examine the forces of capitalism at work in our conjuncture, rather than, as often happens in formalist Marxist criticism, reducing texts to their formal properties or drawing isomorphisms between narrative structures and claims about what capitalism is or does.[53] This isn't to reject Marxist criticism's use of formalism. Formalist analyses can help test and verify what texts mean to communicate and what they may say in spite of those aims. Yet we misunderstand capitalism's cultural productions if we treat them as produced and received individually. Culture is conjunctural and every text appears in the midst of others, not just as individuals but as genres. What a text says or does interests me most for what it says and does in its generic and conjunctural context, not simply in itself.

What, then, is horror now? Horror has long been cheap to produce, whether pre-sold films like the inexpensive Italian horror films of the 1960s or the independently produced American slasher and exploitation films of the 1970s and 1980s. In the 2010s and '20s, the genre became what the *Los Angeles Times* calls "a rare bulwark against the takeover of

Hollywood by superhero films and other tentpole action movies."[54] As screenwriter C. Robert Cargill explains, "Horror is the last remaining genre that doesn't require IP to be successful and doesn't require big names or big budgets . . . It circumvents all the problems that Hollywood usually has with making films and getting them in front of audiences."[55] This isn't to say the genre exists outside the forces of corporate consolidation that mark cultural production in the twenty-first century.[56] Over the last decade, streaming companies have pumped money into the production of their own media and purchased other media to entice a newly nonlinear viewing audience into monthly subscriptions.[57] Even low-budget independent horror is caught up in the processes of financialization and proletarianization unleashed by streaming. As media scholar Colin Jon Mark Crawford explains, streaming giant Netflix "views its titles as enterprising investments—risks—of varying sizes and its content library as a portfolio, all of which serve to project the Netflix brand."[58] Other media companies have followed the Netflix model, expanding production to increase their subscriber numbers and rake in stock-market gains, even as they keep actual viewership numbers and earnings under wraps to undercut worker claims to compensation. Still, the so-called golden age of streaming saw significant changes in the kinds of projects that received funding. "One of the best things about the boom," entertainment journalists Josef Adalian and Lane Brown note, "was that it created space for stories and voices that had usually been marginalized."[59] Women's roles in media expanded during this era, with 2022 seeing twice as many female directors as 1998, and slightly lower increases in roles for women as writers and executive producers.[60] Adding to this new representational space was the corporate response to the Black Lives Matter movement. After worldwide protests over George Floyd's murder, Netflix, HBO, Amazon, and Hulu announced commitments to expanded representation in their hiring and offerings.[61]

Horror was deeply affected by these changes. It saw productions by a more diverse set of creators, whether for horror-specific streaming services such as Shudder and Screambox, major streaming services like Netflix and Amazon, or studios and their streaming services. The shift in genre voices occurred alongside a shift in aesthetics. The entertainment industry's changing economic model overlapped with a cycle of art horror widely referred to as elevated horror. Although this cycle began in the 2000s with films more tentatively connected to the genre, such as

AntiChrist (2009), *Under the Skin* (2013), and *It Follows* (2014), it cohered into a recognizable cycle and horror subgenre with the successes of two films from A24 studios: Robert Eggers's *The Witch* (2015) and Ari Aster's *Hereditary* (2018). Elevated horror combines art-house attention to cinematography, acting, and production values; character-driven narratives borrowed from melodrama and the women's film; and horror elements to produce films that are equal parts horror and critical allegory.[62] The rise of streaming and the success of elevated horror expanded the market for smaller budget films like Ali Abbasi's *Shelley* (2016), Alice Lowe's *Prevenge* (2016), Rose Glass's *Saint Maud* (2019), Gillian Wallace Horvat's *I Blame Society* (2020), Jonathan Cuartas's *My Heart Can't Beat Unless You Tell It To* (2020), Amy Seimetz's *She Dies Tomorrow* (2020), Prano Bailey-Bond's *Censor* (2021), Jane Schoenbrun's *We Are All Going to the World's Fair* (2021), and Mariame Diallo's *Master* (2022). Elevated horror plays to the desire of critics and audiences to separate this wave of horror from slashers, gross-out, and splatter films. As David Church explains, "Professional critics less often valorize [these] films according to what they are (part of the larger history of art-horror cinema), than what they are not (the mainstream horror film as 'bad object')."[63] Almost unnoticed in this shift toward art horror is that many of its key elements—the focus on character development, emotion, tension and suspense, strong acting, and high production values—feature prominently in Brigid Cherry's sociological study of horror's female viewers.[64] Cherry's account counters Linda Williams's claim that women experience horror films as an assault, as does the critical work collected in Alison Pierse's *Women Make Horror*.[65] At the very least, one can see in contemporary horror that market-driven shifts in who makes horror and who watches it have altered the genre to make room for films that fit the preferences of viewers like those in Cherry's study, including inexpensive high-concept horror films like *Slaxx*, *In Fabric*, and *Mayhem*, which offer the camp and unrealistic gore that Cherry notes appeals to female viewers.

Given the uncertainties of streaming as an economic model, there's no telling what horror will or will not look like in the future. In 2022, when the streaming era's bull market entered a phase of crisis and decline, investment in more diverse productions slowed.[66] And after the 2023 strikes by the Writers Guild of America and the Screen Actors Guild, some writers believed this new diversity was under threat.[67] What we can say is that the 2010s and 2020s show us a conjunctural contestation of genre that made room for different perspectives and kinds of horror. A key to this shift was renewed emphasis on critique. Elevated horror's chief narrative strategy is to use fantastic elements to create metaphors and allegories for social problems. By juxtaposing monsters, uncanny objects, and the supernatural and realistic depictions of the contemporary world, critical horror makes its terrors from the defects of its time. Michael Löwy usefully terms this narrative mode "critical irrealism."[68] However, as Löwy describes in his discussion of nineteenth- and early twentieth-century irrealist tales, critical irrealist texts shouldn't be mistaken for Marxist ones. Critical irrealism doesn't offer systemic critiques of capitalism so much as express a broader "Romantic opposition to capitalist-industrial modernity."[69] And the same holds true for twenty-first century critical horror, though its critiques have little to do with Romantic opposition to modernity. Instead, they focus on social inequities of race, class, and gender. That's perhaps clearest in the films associated with what Sheri-Marie Harrison calls "the New Black Gothic," such as *Get Out*, *Candyman*, and *Master*; but we will see this approach across films of the 2010s and 2020s, from the feminist anticapitalist horrors discussed in chapter 2 to the antitherapy horrors of chapter 7.[70] As a genre, horror offers creators a strategy to comment on social injustices and represent anticapitalist feelings. For this reason, horror can help us to locate the pieces of common sense that keep capitalism going: *Work is punishment, but you should love it anyway. Humanity is responsible for global warming, not capitalism. You can't stop gentrification. Everything will get commodified eventually. The family is our sole protection from the market. You have to manage your feelings as a worker.* Horror evokes the dread and terror of capitalism's forms of common sense, but only Marxism can help us understand how capitalism affects our work, the biosphere, our built environment, the goods and services we produce, our relationships, and our minds.

Capitalism Hates You

Let's talk about Marxism, then. For a Marxist project, it may seem odd to say that "capitalism hates you." A properly Marxist perspective would hold that we shouldn't personalize or personify economic processes. In *Capital*, Marx insists that capitalism is a system, not a set of personal feelings: "Under free competition, the immanent laws of capitalist production confront the individual capitalist as a coercive force external to him."[71] To claim a system is actively hostile to you—that's what hate means, after all—is to risk turning it into a monster, and from there we're one wrong step from falling down a slippery slope of *ad hominems* into a morass of conspiracy theory, antisemitism, and xenophobia. Hateful systems encourage us to find others to hate. Still, we shouldn't take this to mean that Marx thought capitalists were benign people. His point was that the structure of the market and the dictates of the accumulation of capital don't compel individuals to be personally hateful. As a system, capitalism coerces them to act as they do. We could qualify the statement, then. As a system, capitalism—with its drive to find new zones of appropriation and new ways to extract surplus value—is actively hostile to you.

In other words, capitalism hates you.

One reason I'm so insistent that we should view what capitalism does as hateful has to do with what capitalism is doing right now: attacking the biosphere by dumping carbon into the atmosphere and destroying local ecosystems in the search for cheap resources, food, and energy. Capitalism may be an impersonal system, but it is one that is inimical to the continued existence of life on Earth. Twenty-first century investment banks may trumpet their commitments to climate policy in PR announcements, but the people who run their so-called responsible investing units can't help but show how little they care about this destruction. In a 2022 conference presentation, the head of responsible investing for HSBC's asset management unit said: "Climate change is not a financial risk that we need to worry about . . . Who cares if Miami is six meters underwater in 100 years, Amsterdam's been six meters underwater for ages, and that's a really nice place. We will cope with it."[72] Left unsaid is who is going to be able to cope with *it* and who isn't. The way that capitalism apportions wealth and life is fundamentally unequal and will certainly doom vast swathes of humanity to climate-induced deaths, if not all of it.

When we begin with capitalism's active hostility to life, we recognize the importance of what eco-feminists term *appropriation*, an idea we'll explore throughout the book. Appropriation and its violence are as central to capitalism as exploitation. This matters because exploitation in capitalism often seems like a bloodless accounting trick. You exchange your abstract capacity to work with an employer as simply one more commodity to be consumed in production, but your concrete labor produces more than its price as a commodity. The difference? Surplus-value. When we pay attention to appropriation, though, we see that capitalism isn't simply an economic system but a violent social, political, cultural, and economic system.[73] This is somewhat of a break with Marx, who saw appropriation as horrific but prior to capitalism as a mode of production. In *Capital*, Marx describes a period of "primitive accumulation," a time when people violently appropriated resources, including colonial conquests abroad and the enclosure of the commons in Europe.[74] Capitalism, Marx writes, emerges from this period of primitive accumulation "dripping from head to toe, from every pore, with blood and dirt."[75] For Marx, this period is capitalism's necessary precondition. The production process needs wealth to buy materials and labor and to sustain the capitalist through the production cycle. Primitive accumulation's appropriations provided this wealth. However, recent work by feminist and ecological Marxists, among others, demonstrates that capitalism never manages to shower off this blood and dirt without getting more on itself. It has always relied on the violence of colonialism, imperialism, and slavery, and it brings to bear the power of economic, political, and sociocultural forces, including the power of the state, to seize what it wants. Marx understood this when he discussed how capitalism robbed the earth of its resources. There, Marx explains that surplus-value comes from nature as much as labor.[76] Ecological Marxists have shown that capitalism relies on cheap food, cheap energy, cheap natural resources, and cheap and unpaid labor. Capitalism can't exist without the destructive extraction of un- or underpaid resources from people and the planet.[77]

Appropriation lets us see that capitalism constructs more than one structural class of the oppressed. It also uses racialized differences to create populations for distinct forms of domination. As Cedric Robinson shows, capitalism relies on these racialized populations to justify its use of more or less harsh forms of work-discipline, to rationalize its appropriation of land and resources, and to divide workers from one another. In this respect, capitalism is less a break with European feudalism than an intensification of its use of race to distinguish and subjugate laborers, soldiers, and other subject peoples. Appropriation helps us to see that capitalism must be understood as racial capitalism, a social, political, and economic system that relies on what Robinson calls a "tendency of European civilization . . . to differentiate—to exaggerate racialized, subcultural, and dialectical differences into 'racial' ones."[78] If people don't recognize racial capitalism's violence from day to day, that isn't because it's hidden. We see it every day as racism. As Ruth Wilson Gilmore explains, racism is "the state-sanctioned and/or extralegal production and exploitation of group-differentiated vulnerability to premature death."[79] The exposure to premature death is an effect of racial capitalism's creation of particular populations and geographies. Nothing makes this clearer than what Gilmore calls racial capitalism's "organized abandonment" of Black communities in the global North during the neoliberal era.[80]

We can also see capitalism's violence in its uneven development, whether regional disinvestment in developed economies or investments in resource-intensive, dangerous, or environmentally destructive ventures in underdeveloped ones. We see its violence in the ways it uses patriarchy to control women's economic, reproductive, and sexual labor, as Maria Mies, Claudia von Werlhof, Silvia Federici, Leopoldina Fortunati, and others argue.[81] And we see it in the ways that capitalism uses sexuality and sexual identity to divide and control workers, as Christopher Chitty demonstrates with capital's use of homosexuality to control segments of the working-class population during capitalism's emergence.[82] To be clear, this is not to reduce racism, patriarchy, gender, and sexuality to mere effects of capitalism. Each has its own distinct history of practices and discourses. Capitalism acts as what Louis Althusser calls a "structure in dominance."[83] It affects and acts on each of these sociocultural hierarchies in order to maintain capital accumulation. Each retains partial autonomy, free but hemmed in by capital's demands, acting within capitalism and, as Étienne Balibar puts it, on another scene.[84]

As a result, capitalism's violence shapes us as human beings. Every day, we negotiate its demands and the hierarchies and vulnerabilities it creates. Those negotiations are acts of subjectivation, or, more simply, how we discover ourselves as subjects in capitalism. Maurizio Lazzarato focuses on the violence of capitalism's production of subjectivity in *Capitalism Hates Everyone*. For Lazarrato, capitalist production is premised on war, a result of the development of transnational logistics to supply the front and the violent repression of the working class at home and abroad. Lazzarato argues that violence is the necessary precondition to the state's control of life through policy and consent, or what Michel Foucault called biopower and governmentality. Lazzarato highlights our conjuncture's imbrication of finance, capital, and the state. The state and capital work together to privatize social services and force workers into debt as they navigate the basic demands of social reproduction such as education, health care, and so on. Debt, backed by the threat of state violence, becomes part of a process of subjectivation, producing new indebted subjects who are more pliable to capital's demands. Capitalism, Lazzarato insists, needs these new flexible subjects as much as it needs to accumulate value. Revising Marx's take on the vampire, he explains that "capital needs to suck up subjectivity like the vampire sucks blood."[85] It isn't enough for capital to threaten or even use violence to extract value. It needs subjects suited to the violence of its appropriation and exploitation. One might say that capitalism lives on its capacity to produce violence.

All of which is to say, capitalism hates you. And it relies on hatred—of race, gender, sexuality, and class—to do its work of accumulation.

Still, some might object that capitalism isn't *actively* hostile so much as indifferent. To a degree, that's right. Moishe Postone knew what he was talking about when he described capitalism as a system of impersonal social domination.[86] Capitalism *is* indifferent, and not only to the needs of working people but to those of capitalists. For Postone, like many of the other theorists who inform this book such as Michael Heinrich, Jarius Banaji, and Alfred Sohn-Rethel, everyone in capitalism is driven by the same coercive force: value. This is true whether you're a waged or unwaged worker, a capitalist, or even someone torn between waged work and limited levels of institutional power.[87] And that's not hard to understand when we remember that capitalism has more forms for value than what Marx calls abstract labor. As we'll see in chapter one, abstract labor is important, but the value-form that rules us all in capitalism is easier to recognize. It's *money*.[88] It's tempting to say that our domination by money is passive. Sacks of cash don't come to your house and rough you up. But if you can't pay your rent, your landlord or a representative of the state might, and, at the very least, they'll remove you and your possessions from your home, likely damaging both in the process. While money doesn't literally drag your carcass to work every day, your need for it to buy the commodified goods and services that support your existence in a capitalist society does. Capitalism exerts a unique power on us, one that Søren Mau shows isn't based on coercion or consent. Its unique form of economic power exploits, in Mau's words, "the gap between life and its conditions."[89] It is a form of "mute compulsion." Mau explains, that "only works because the *worker wants to live*."[90] This helps us to see that capitalism isn't reducible to market logics; it is inseparable from the people who act within it. As Nancy Fraser puts it, we don't live in a capitalist economy, but "a capitalist *society*."[91] Capitalism consists of a particular set of social, historical, political, and economic activities and systems that humans have created to organize the reproduction of social life. The power it exerts on us is unique and structural, but it requires our activity too. Capitalism can't destroy our lives, our social relations, and our biosphere on its own. The destructive power of this system of impersonal domination is the result of real people making real decisions, even if those decisions are structurally determined.

Horror can help us to see what capitalism's active and passive hatred looks and feels like. Consider Sam Raimi's *Drag Me to Hell* (2009). We could focus on the racism of its conceit, a Roma curse that drags people to hell, but we should place its division of the population alongside the ire and violence the film launches at the financial system. The plot follows a banker, Christine, after she is cursed by Mrs. Ganush, an elderly Roma woman, for refusing to refinance her mortgage. A riff on the predatory mortgage lending that precipitated the 2008 financial crisis, the plot of *Drag Me to Hell* asks whether Christine can evade personal responsibility for the destructive indifference of the system that she works in. The answer is no, but that doesn't stop Christine from trying, leaving a path of death and destruction in her wake. She sacrifices her kitten, leads a medium to her death, and exhumes and desecrates Mrs. Ganush's corpse to shake off the curse. Until the earth opens under her feet, Christine insists that it wasn't her fault; it was the system's. And the film encourages audiences to side with her. Mrs. Ganush is a grotesque, racialized Other, portrayed as poor, disorganized, and disgusting compared to the young, thin, blonde, and business-minded Christine. Christine didn't refinance Mrs. Ganush's mortgage, but, audiences can rationalize, her manager made it clear she wouldn't get her promotion if she did. Once Mrs. Ganush attacks her in the parking garage, her refusal seems inconsequential. After all, Christine didn't attack her physically. The film elides Mrs. Ganush's eviction and focuses instead on the gross indignities the curse visits on Christine. She swallows flies, gets doused with embalming fluid from a corpse's mouth, and flounders in a watery grave (Figure 1). The continued evocations of disgust keep audiences from noticing what these indignities mean: Christine will put up with anything to evade responsibility for what she's done. Right up to the end, it seems like she will succeed. Certain she's ended the spell by shoving her cursed button down the throat of Mrs. Ganush's corpse, Christine stands happily on a train platform at Union Station with her boyfriend only to realize that she hadn't given him a rare quarter she found at the bank but her cursed button. In shock, she falls onto the tracks as the curse comes due. The ground opens beneath her, and she's dragged to hell.

We could read *Drag Me to Hell* not as a critique of capitalism as a system but as a way to blame and punish individuals. What I want to draw out here is how the film lets us see and feel the activity that capitalism's impersonal domination demands from people like Christine. She uses its racialized divisions of the population to expose some people more easily to death than others, and she is rewarded for this violence. Structural determination can make it easy for people to shrug off their role in the system's brutality. This isn't to say that individuals should bear all the blame for systemic failings—the system remains the problem—

Figure 1. Christine stands in an open grave, desperate to remove Mrs. Ganush's curse. *Drag Me to Hell*, directed by Sam Raimi. Universal, 2009.

but the system also doesn't work without our activity, whether we give it enthusiastically or not. The value-form needs us to keep it moving, and it offers powerful incentives to do so. Christine wants more money, more power, more expensive clothes, and a better job. The structure of capitalism rewards her for the violence she aims at Mrs. Ganush in defense of her social, political, and economic position. She calls in the police to drag the woman away and takes matters into her own hands when the curse's effects begin. Christine's violence is hers *and* the system's. The confusion of the button for a quarter reveals to Christine for the first time what money actually is: a form that capitalism inserts between people and their ability to live. In its final moments, the film redirects disgust from Mrs. Ganush to *money*, encouraging audiences to feel the revulsion of money's separation of life from the means of reproduction.

Drag Me to Hell, then, helps us see how the value-form in capitalism produces the kinds of feelings that we associate with horror. Disgust, shock, and terror let audiences take on their structural determination by the value-form and deflect its violence onto a legitimate target or at least someone else. Horror helps us to discover in the value-form capitalism's structural hatred of life itself. In its use of abstract labor and money, value creates equivalences, reducing workers and nature to mere inputs in production. The dream of capitalism, a tendency never to be fully realized yet still oppressively real, is to create value without use-values. Capital fantasizes being free from the constraints imposed by the needs of actual human beings or nature. It is in this fantasy of accumulation freed from human or ecological needs that we discover what capitalism's hatred means. Hatred is more than active hostility. We might better understand it through Spinoza's account of hate. For Spinoza, hate is the result of "pain accompanied by the idea of an external cause" and the desire "to remove and destroy" that cause.[92] For capitalism, humanity and nature are the external causes of its pain. "Capital," Marx writes, is the endless and limitless drive to go beyond

> its limiting barrier. Every boundary is and has to be a barrier for it. Else it would cease to be capital—money as self-reproduction. If ever it perceived a certain boundary not as a barrier, but became comfortable within it as a boundary, it would have declined from exchange value to use value.[93]

Capitalism dreams of being free from the desires and limits of actual life, of being able to produce value for value's sake. From tulips and South Sea Company stock to collateralized debt obligations, credit-derivative swaps, and nonfungible tokens, capitalism fantasizes about multiplying money into more money without the bother of use-values that could serve the flourishing of human or nonhuman life. This is why it engages in a constant series of what Nancy Fraser calls "boundary struggles," fights to commodify and reorganize social reproduction, politics, and nature.[94] Capitalism lives parasitically on what is outside its control, and it hates what it can't control. Capital wants to consume its exterior entirely, but it can't without destroying itself. Why does capitalism hate you? Because you, and the rest of social, political, and ecological life, make persistent demands to exist regardless of capital's insistence that all that matters is value.

In the chapters that follow, I trace how horror captures that hatred. Each chapter focuses on a piece of common sense, traces its role in a horror subgenre, and uses a line of Marxist thought to analyze it. Chapter 1 highlights perhaps the most widespread piece of common sense in capitalism: *We hate work*. Using Joe Lynch's horror-comedy *Mayhem* (2017), "Work Hates You: Antiwork Horror and Value Theory" offers an account of Marx's understanding of work using value-form theory. A Marxist interpretation of *Mayhem* uncovers how twenty-first century capitalism encourages feelings of cynicism. Chapter 2 turns to a countervailing piece of common sense, the demand to love your work. Using the insights of social reproduction theory, "Love Hates You: Feminist Anticapitalist Horror and Social Reproduction Theory" examines four films made by and about women in the workplace, *I Blame Society* (2021), *The Power* (2020), *Censor* (2020), and *Saint Maud* (2019). These feminist anticapitalist horrors show how meaningfulness naturalizes increased exploitation. The women in these films become possessed by their work, revealing the violence hidden in the demand to find personal meaning through employment.

Chapter 3, "Nature Hates You: Psychedelic Eco-Horror and Ecological Marxism," examines a piece of common sense that sustains capitalism in an age of climate disasters: It's humanity's fault, not capitalism's. I argue that the Anthropocene is really, as Jason W. Moore puts it, the Capitalocene and trace how a recent set of psychedelic ecological horrors,

Gaia (2021), *In the Earth* (2021), and *She Dies Tomorrow* (2020), focus our attention on impersonal systems and the environment. Using the work of John Bellamy Foster, Paul Burkett, and Kate Soper, I argue that capitalism's ecological assaults reveal its reliance on appropriation, and point toward de-accumulation as a Marxist way to reimagine the future. Psychedelic eco-horror captures the importance of appropriation and de-growth in its use of the fungal to figure impersonal counterpowers. Chapter 4, "Your Neighborhood Hates You: New Black Horror and Uneven Development," shifts our attention to the built environment. At the local level, uneven development takes the form of gentrification. The common sense of gentrification casts it as inescapable. Following the work of radical geographers like Neil Smith, David Harvey, and Leslie Kern, this chapter argues that who gets to be where is a political-economic question, not an unchangeable natural market process. Horror helps us to see that capitalism's effects on the built environment are inseparable from what George Lipsitz calls "the racialization of space and the spatialization of race."[95] No subgenre captures this better than new Black horror. Jordan Peele's *Get Out* (2017) and *Us* (2019), Mariame Diallo's *Master* (2022), Jenna Cato Bass's *Good Madam* (2021), and Nia DaCosta's *Candyman* (2021) reveal gentrification's common sense for what it is, an attempt to reduce us to a state of terrified helplessness in the face of a seemingly inescapable process. Drawing on the work of Katherine McKittrick, Ruth Wilson Gilmore, and Frank Wilderson, I examine how gentrification provides Black creators with a metaphor that allows them to craft critiques of anti-Blackness and to reflect on their own fraught position as culture industry storytellers. Chapter 5, "Commodities Hate You: Mass-Culture Horror and Commodity Forms," takes on the common sense that capitalism commodifies everything. While much of western Marxism treats commodification as the creation of passive consumers, I follow value-form theorists to argue that commodification is a form of spectral objectivity. Value searches out masks to wear as it extracts value from production and circulation. As a result, commodification relies on the activity of different kinds of masks and mask wearers, not passive consumption. Using the work of Luc Boltanski and Pierre Esquerre and twenty-first century mass-culture horror, I describe these different commodity-form masks and their effects on workers. We see the standard form commodity in *In Fabric* (2018); the collection form commodity in *Personal Shopper* (2016); the trend form commodity in *Slaxx* (2020); and the asset form commodity in *Murder Party* (2007). The feeling of horror in these films comes not from experiences of passive determination but from those of persistent activity. Mass-culture horror shows that we aren't passively consumed by objects but actively engaged in the process of our destruction.

Capitalism's violence becomes more intimate in the final two chapters. In chapter 6, I study the violence it exerts through the family. Using the work of materialist feminists like M. E. O'Brien, Sophie Lewis, and Audre Lorde, "The Family Hates You: Elevated Horror and Family Abolition" argues that capitalism's exploitation of reproductive labor is inextricable from its use of racialization and gender norms to maintain class power. Elevated horrors such as *The Witch* (2015), *Hereditary* (2017), *Shelley* (2016), and *Prevenge* (2016) show that the protections allegedly offered by the family merely naturalize the appropriation of reproductive labor by pregnant people and caregivers. Elevated family horror captures the family's terrors in an aesthetics of coldness and distance, and crafts its feelings to reflect what it shows: an indifferent world of dread punctuated by moments of terror and disgust. The final chapter takes on capitalism's demands that we manage and deaden our feelings as we navigate the oppressions of the market. "Feelings Hate You: Therapeutic Horror and Emotion Work" concentrates on elevated horror's use of metaphors to represent difficult emotions. Drawing on feminist film theory, Marxist work on intellectual and manual labor, and sociological work on emotion work, I argue that films like *The Babadook* (2014), *The Vigil* (2019), and *Men* (2022) constitute a subgenre of therapeutic horror films and reveal capitalism's demand to manage our unwieldy emotions. This cycle of therapeutic horror opens space for a countercycle of films about the refusal to manage our feelings with films like *A Banquet* (2021), *Hatching* (2022), and *We Are All Going to the World's Fair* (2021). I conclude by insisting Marxism needs horror just as much as horror needs Marxism. To address the problems of capitalism that we find in the new horror film, we must draw on an array of concepts from disparate lines of Marxist thought. In this way, horror can renew our sense of the vitality and openness of Marxism. And we need that. Horror lets us feel what it means to live under a political economic system bent on our destruction. Marxism can help us to imagine one that isn't.

1

WORK HATES YOU
Antiwork Horror and Value Theory

For most people, work is proof enough that capitalism hates us. The early days of the Covid-19 pandemic brought that home as the r/antiwork forum on Reddit saw its number of subscribers leap into the millions. At the time, media coverage attributed the jump to the so-called Great Resignation, when millions of workers left or changed jobs and employers complained they couldn't hire at their usual miserable wages. Later macroeconomic developments show there was no sustained drop in workforce participation, only an immediate drop associated with the onset of the pandemic and pandemic-induced layoffs.[1] Nonetheless, media coverage of r/antiwork and the Great Resignation allowed U.S. popular culture to encounter one of the central tenets of Italian Marxism: the refusal of work. Kathi Weeks sums up the refusal best: "Rather than a simple act of disengagement that one completes, the refusal is, in this sense, a process, a theoretical and practical movement that aims to effect a separation through which we can pursue alternative practices and relationships."[2] Unfortunately, the posters on r/antiwork were not as antiwork as media coverage suggested. "To me, and I think the majority of people [on r/antiwork]," one poster explained in an interview, "when I see them talk about antiwork, it's just that, like, we're not opposed to work, we just want fair work . . . We want to give our labor and get compensated fairly, and we want to have some input into the process, into how we're giving our labor."[3] Another poster offered a similar outlook but with a sizable dose of what social theorist Mark Fisher calls capitalist realism, the idea that there is no outside or end to capitalism.[4] "I appreciate the ideals that a lot of these people have about us not having to work, and frankly that should be the case due to all the advancements that the world has been through," this poster told the interviewer, "but, unfortunately, that's probably not going to be happening any time soon. Realistically, I think that things like a four-day work week, better treatment, better wages, that's something achievable in the short-term."[5]

Being against work, then, doesn't mean you need a Marxist analysis of work. Common sense has long viewed work as a form of punishment. In the Bible, work is God's punishment of Adam and Eve for eating the apple: "In the sweat of thy face shalt thou eat bread, till thou return unto the ground; for out of it wast thou taken: for dust thou art, and unto dust shalt thou return."[6] In the nineteenth century, economists polished up this Biblical injunction with a bit of utilitarian calculus. Working, William Stanley Jevons said, means "undertaking every action of which the resulting pleasure exceeds the pain which is undergone."[7] In other words, wages should offer enough pleasure to counter work's pains. Max Weber's account of capitalism's emergence from the Protestant work ethic underscored work's value as a sign that its practitioners were among God's elect, but it never suggested that work was pleasurable or subjectively rewarding.[8] Capitalism simply doesn't need to conceive of work as pleasurable in economic terms.[9] In the next chapter, we'll see how it reconceives of work as meaningful using noneconomic measures. For the moment, we simply need to recognize in r/antiwork's pleas for fair work the view that work is necessarily punishing. Instead of reimagining what work is or could be, the participants in the subreddit focus on ensuring people are compensated fairly for the pain that work causes. There's nothing wrong with that—far from it—but it shows us that capitalism doesn't care whether we view our work as punishment or not.

Horror can help us to see how this view of work reveals domination's role in capitalism. I begin by examining how horror engages with work and domination in adaptations of *Dracula*, then turn to Joe Lynch's horror-comedy office slasher *Mayhem* (2017). Lynch's film uses an irreal element to launch its critique of work culture: A rage virus allows an unjustly fired lawyer and a woman with her house in foreclosure to kill their way to the top. *Mayhem* reveals the violence that lurks in capitalism's uniquely impersonal forms of domination and helps us to understand how this domination affects the ways we think and feel about work. To start, then, we need to understand what work means for Marx. To do that, we have to take on the crux of Marx's thought, the theory of value.

From Marx's Theory of Value to Gothic Domination

When Marxists talk about work, they're talking about, as Kathi Weeks writes, "the primary means by which individuals are integrated not only into the economic system, but also into social, political, and familial modes of cooperation."[10] Marx understood work to be necessary for human social life, not an existential punishment. While work is a transhistorical necessity, the work we do is always conjunctural, historically located. Our work always takes place with a particular set of resources, tools, technologies, and knowledges. The conjunctural specificity of work doesn't tell us much about work's overall role in capitalism, though. What Marx wants us to see about work in capitalism is that capitalism subordinates all the conjunctural factors that define how we work—our tools, our resources, our knowledge, and so on—to its drive to accumulate value. To understand work's role in capitalism, then, we have to understand value, specifically Marx's theory of value. Note that I did not write "the labor theory of value." The labor theory of value maintains that only labor creates value. Marx's theory of value doesn't. If you want to read about how value is the result of your labor, read John Locke.[11] Marx's theory of value doesn't describe individual bodies producing individual values; it describes the forms of social domination specific to capitalism.

Domination is pivotal to Marx's theory of value, his political project, and his understanding of work's role in capitalism.[12] We can see this first as a question of surplus value, that extra bit of value that seems to come from nowhere. Prior modes of production extracted surplus labor from workers directly. For example, in some forms of feudalism, landowners extracted surplus labor from workers using the *corvée*, a set number of days they had to labor unpaid on the owner's land. Capitalism doesn't extract surplus labor through this sort of direct personal domination. It relies on exchange. There's one difficulty, though. A simple exchange of equivalents can't produce a surplus; it only moves around equivalent amounts of one thing or another. A surface reading of Marx would say this is where surplus labor comes in: Capitalists extract more labor from workers than they pay for, and this extra labor produces surplus value. This is why some Marxists mistakenly insist that labor produces all value, a position that ignores the role of nature in value's production and obscures what makes value in capitalism so strange. Marx doesn't claim that labor produces all value or even all surplus value, as we will see in chapter 3. In capitalism, value is produced through a series of dynamic interactions between labor and capital in production, exchange, and consumption.

What is value, then? We can't understand it without Marx's concept of "abstract labor."[13] As Diane Elson shows, in Marx, abstract labor "is the concept of the unity or similarity of human labor, differentiated simply in terms of quantity, duration."[14] Abstract labor is what makes actual labor into something countable, whether in pieces made or time worked. While work is a transhistorical phenomenon, abstract labor isn't. It's unique to capitalism.[15] As an economic system, capitalism needs this conceptualization of labor to translate actual concrete labor into an abstract commodity that can be quantified and sold. Abstract labor is crucial for shifting capitalism's domination from the personal to the impersonal, and thus for extracting surplus labor from workers. In capitalism, workers don't sell their actual or "concrete" labor, only their *capacity* to labor, what Marx calls "labor-power." Labor-power is an abstract and exchangeable commodity and capitalists consume it in the production process like any other commodity. What makes labor-power unique, Marx emphasizes, is that it ceases to be an abstraction during the production process. In its concrete form, labor-power produces more than its cost as an abstract form. As Marx explains, labor-power is the only commodity in capitalism with a use-value that can produce more use-values than it consumes. Capitalism's domination is the result of this translation between abstract and concrete labor-power. Why? Because the use-values that labor-power produce belong to the capitalist who purchased it. In capitalism, the surplus that capitalists seize isn't theft, at least according to its rules of private property. They pay for what they take. And this is why Marx's theory of value reveals capitalism to be, as Elson puts it, "the domination of abstract labor."[16]

Abstract labor and surplus value show us the basic forms of capitalism's domination, but we're still missing an important aspect of what makes capitalism a system of *impersonal* domination. Abstract labor's domination isn't isolated within production, though capitalists would like to pretend it is. From their perspective, everything should look like a simple exchange of equivalents. Money buys commodities, including abstract labor-power, and directs them into production where they combine to create more value. Yet for workers and the natural world, these exchanges aren't as simple or equal as they appear. Capitalism presents them as exchanges of equivalent amounts of monetary value, but these abstract and contractually equal exchanges mask materially unequal ones that take more in real terms from workers and the natural world than they give back. These unequal exchanges don't just happen in production. They're all around us as a result of capitalism's market system. We see this most clearly in the cost of abstract labor. Labor-power's cost isn't determined by workers' actual needs but by the market-determined costs of their commodified means of subsistence. "The value of labor-power," Marx explains, "is the value of the means of subsistence."[17] This cost isn't given or set. It's the result of the forces and relations of food production. If changes in production make them cheaper as market commodities, then labor-power's value declines too. This is why capitalism's history is inseparable from the search for and development of cheap food. The only countervailing force to the devaluing of labor-power is class struggle. Workers can raise the cost of labor-power by forcing employers to increase wages through organization and struggle. Otherwise, the market costs of the means of subsistence determine wages, not anyone's actual needs.

Capitalists, too, are at the market's mercy, albeit for different reasons. They can't get value directly out of the production process. To realize the value and surplus value in their commodities, they have to sell them. This act reveals a crucial problem. In capitalism, labor and the actual production processes are inherently private affairs, undertaken by individual firms with no promise of buyers or of social necessity. Successful exchange socializes these private labors and marks them as what Marx calls "socially necessary labor"—that is, labor that creates a use-value "under the conditions of production normal for a given society and with the average degree of skill and intensity of labor prevalent in that society."[18] While some readers take this for a description of a society's level of technological development, this misses what Marx sees as unique to capitalism: the unity of exchange and production.[19] Socially necessary labor time isn't just about society's productive capacities but about paying demand. Michael Heinrich explains the link between the two:

> To see how the "labor time socially necessary for production" asserts itself, both aspects have to be considered: the necessary labor-time as determined by the conditions of production and the labor-time needed to cover the paying demand. Both magnitudes are unknown to producers in advance. Only on the market is the individual producer informed about whether his conditions of production correspond to the social average and whether his branch as a whole has produced too many products.[20]

Only the market decides, through unknown and inconsistent processes, what constitutes socially necessary labor. Makoto Itoh puts it succinctly: "the representative condition of production, which determines market value, is only defined through an anarchic process of intra-sectoral market competition."[21] Individual capitalists can never know whether their commodities are socially necessary until after they have been sold. If they remain unsold, the market has deemed the conditions of production and labor-power used to create them to be socially unnecessary. Under this system, no one can know for certain what may be socially productive at a given time. All capitalists can do is invest in production and hope it will allow the value they've invested to be realized as socially necessary. This is what it means to say that everyone in capitalism is dominated by abstract labor. Without it, the anarchy of the market wouldn't be able to determine what is socially necessary labor time and what isn't.

Marx's theory of value, then, shows us how work in capitalism makes up one facet of a system where domination is abstract, impersonal, and social. Workers must sell their labor-power as a commodity to buy their means of subsistence on the market, and capitalists must continually reorganize production to produce goods and services in quantities and at prices they hope will sell. This should help us better understand Marx's term for capitalism's formal domination: commodity fetishism. Too often, people take commodity fetishism for a description of false consciousness. From this perspective, people misrecognize how capitalism works. Instead of seeing the labor that goes into production, people captured by the commodity fetish pay more attention to what is being exchanged. That's not the point. Commodity fetishism isn't about how people think but how they *act*. Alfred Sohn-Rethel gets at this idea when he calls commodity fetishism a real abstraction, an abstract relation with real effects.[22] *Pace* Slavoj Žižek, commodity fetishism doesn't depend on whether we know or don't know what we're doing.[23] We live in and enact these historically situated relations of domination *whether we know about them or not*. Commodity fetishism isn't about what we know but about how we must act to survive. This is what makes capitalism's domination impersonal. It's a system, as Søren Mau explains, of "mute compulsion."[24] That's what makes capitalism unique. Its economic operations can function without coercion, consent, or knowledge. Its decentralization of production and exchange means we're all dominated by value, whether we need it to pay for the means of subsistence or to revolutionize production.

But what does all this have to do with horror? Domination has been a central thematic concern for the genre since the Gothic. At first glance, the villainous aristocrats of the eighteenth-century Gothic suggest feudalism's personal domination rather than capitalism's impersonal one. Manfred of Horace Walpole's *Castle of Otranto* and Signor Montoni of Ann Radcliffe's *Mysteries of Udolpho* do what they please to whomever they please. Yet the villainy of the Gothic's unaccountable aristocrats isn't one of a pure will-to-power. Like the tyrants of Plato's *Republic*, Gothic aristocrats are enslaved by their passions.[25] Tyranny and domination go together in the Gothic to create a state of total domination, one in which people are tyrannized by the tyrant and the tyrant by his or her passions. That's certainly the case in Bram Stoker's 1897 novel, *Dracula*. The Count may seem like a rational businessman, but he's dominated by his passions, the result of what Van Helsing calls a "selfish child-brain."[26] This selfishness not only leads to the Count's defeat; it also shows us one way the genre represents work. The novel's fearless vampire hunters are mostly professional workers—a solicitor, two doctors, and a secretary—and their collective knowledge work overcomes the passions-driven Count. In the process, the novel shows us how the young solicitor, Jonathan Harker, becomes an empowered knowledge worker by drawing a parallel between the Count and Harker's first employer, Mr. Hawkins. Just as the Count controls Mina telepathically, Hawkins commands Harker from a distance. Thematically, Hawkins and the Count block Harker's access to maturity. As Hawkins's poor clerk, Harker can't marry, and the Count and his coterie of vampires rob Harker of his sexual potency. Harker doesn't so much overcome his dominators as take on their tyrannical powers. He gains Hawkins's wealth and status as a solicitor upon the man's death, and his hunt for the Count sees him use the law to his own ends. To his wife Mina, the results prove Harker to be "never so resolute, never so strong, never so full of volcanic energy."[27] This changes again when the Count assaults Mina and puts her under his spell, but Harker reasserts his potency after chopping off the vampire's head with an extremely phallic "great knife."[28] No surprise, then, that the novel ends with Harker a successful solicitor and a new father.

Screen adaptations of Stoker's tale develop the link between Hawkins's economic domination and the Count's telepathic and sexual domination. F. W. Murnau's *Nosferatu* (1922) condenses Hawkins and Renfield into Jonathan's employer, Knock, an estate agent. The Count's domination of Jonathan becomes inseparable from Jonathan's domination by work.[29] Subsequent adaptations increasingly emphasize a relationship between professional work and domination. The rise of the managerial class in the twentieth century occurred alongside adaptations that gave Van Helsing, the autonomous knowledge worker, increasingly superhuman qualities. Unlike the impotent Professor Bulwer of Murnau's *Nosferatu* or Doctor Martin Hesselius, the feckless precursor to Stoker's character in Sheridan Le Fanu's short story "Green Tea," Van Helsing the professional uses his knowledge to counterbalance the vampire's tyranny. The professional knowledge worker's heroic trajectory reaches its nadir in *Van Helsing* (2004). In a fantasy of muscular technocracy, a buff Van Helsing physically and intellectually dominates the film's vampires, who, unlike the virile protagonist, are having trouble reproducing. Yet no adaptations capture the interactions between professional work and domination as well as the comedic ones. A *Simpsons* parody of Francis Ford Coppola's *Bram Stoker's Dracula* puts Homer Simpson in the role of Harker and Mr. Burns, Homer's boss, as the Count. Realizing he must kill the head vampire to save his family, Homer muses, "Kill my boss? Do I dare live out the American dream?"[30] He does, only to discover there's no freedom from domination in capitalism. He's got to make his peace with becoming a vampire anyway. The television series *What We Do in the Shadows* makes the professional worker's embrace of domination even more explicit. A vampire workplace comedy, the show includes a long-running subplot in which a familiar, Guillermo, discovers he's one of Van Helsing's descendants. Caught between his desire to be a vampire, his unstated love for his master, and his skill as a vampire killer,

Guillermo tries to escape his domination by embracing it, first as his boss's bodyguard, then by becoming a vampire himself.

Mayhem: Antiwork Horror

This Gothic drive to escape work's domination by embracing its violence takes on a different form in Joe Lynch's antiwork horror *Mayhem*. Lynch's film is useful not only for its thematic focus on work but for its prominent place in the promotion of contemporary horror. AMC's digital horror subscription service Shudder prominently featured *Mayhem* in its long-running banner ad on Amazon (Figure 2). The banner evokes different kinds of horror and promotes AMC-affiliated or -owned intellectual properties: a woman in peril for the series *Creepshow*, an intense-looking Steven Yeun with one red eye for *Mayhem*, and a creepy clown mask for the film *Haunt*. Yeun is the banner's face of male violence, a figure on a saturated red background that matches his eye and stands in contrast to the black background of the other images. It conjures threat and evokes the gore associated with Asian horror films like *Battle Royale (Batoru Rowaiaru)* (2000) and *Ichi the Killer (Koroshiya 1)* (2001).

Yet *Mayhem* isn't an Asian horror, it's an American horror-comedy. Yeun plays Derek, a nerdy but successful lawyer who gets fired after his manager, Kara, blames him for her mistakes. An outbreak of a rage virus puts the firm's building on lockdown, and Derek uses the resulting legal limbo to become, like Jonathan Harker, an empowered man, wielding violence against his enemies to save a woman in distress. Like elevated horrors, *Mayhem* uses an irreal element to unleash the workplace's hidden

Figure 2. Shudder's promotional banner on Amazon circa 2020–23.

violence, allowing Derek to reject his domination and claw his way to the top of the corporate ladder.[31] Yet *Mayhem* is not an elevated horror. Its aesthetics aren't arthouse but grindhouse *à la* Frank Miller, Quentin Tarantino, and Robert Rodriguez's *Sin City* (2005), and its tone isn't quiet or contemplative but loud and fast. The film's frenetic violence purposefully recalls the fast-paced slaughter of zombie films. That's not just because the rage virus is like the viruses in zombie movies such as *28 Days Later* (2002), *28 Weeks Later* (2007), and *The Sadness (Ku bei)* (2021). Yeun starred in the popular zombie series *The Walking Dead*, and the series' production company, Wide Circle of Confusion, produced *Mayhem*. *Mayhem* turns the near constant stream of zombie killings of a horror-comedy like *Zombieland* (2009) into a near constant stream of murdered coworkers and bosses. Interweaving jokes about work and violence with representations of violence, a formula pioneered by gory horror-comedies like Sam Raimi's *Evil Dead 2* (1987), *Mayhem* takes the edge off its bloodshed by making it all a joke. It helps, as Derek explains, that the virus suspends the law.

If all this sounds more troubling than comedic, it is. Yet *Mayhem* is but one entry in a subgenre of antiwork horror comedies. One of the key difficulties such films confront, at least for American audiences, is that office killing sprees aren't unusual or funny. That's likely why the plots in these films don't turn on traumatized workers attacking their colleagues. Instead, they combine moral judgments about particular kinds of work with horror elements and narrative structures that allow colleagues and bosses to become acceptable objects for violence. Consider *Severance* (2006), a British film about office workers for a weapons manufacturer. The film relies on a basic cabin-in-the-woods structure for its narrative. A group on a work retreat finds itself hunted by war criminals their firm illegally armed. Patrik Eklund's *The Conference (Konferensen)* (2023) follows a similar conceit. A group of regional development bureaucrats are hunted on their work retreat by the man whose land their company seized. In both films, the company's unethical actions make its characters acceptable targets, and those who oppose these acts escape unharmed. *Mayhem* follows the same pattern. The building quarantine provides the physical and legal isolation necessary to exact retribution, and the unethical acts of the law firm justify Derek's violence.

The moral judgments in these films are deeply conjunctural. *Severance*, made during the Global War on Terror, has arms manufacturers in its sights, and *The Conference*, fake development deals. *Mayhem* targets those who profited off the 2008 financial crisis. The film introduces Derek kicking a woman out of her house, and reveals *Mayhem*'s central thematic concern, *responsibility*. Who is responsible for the decisions made in an impersonal system, the film asks. Derek tells Melanie that her foreclosure isn't his decision; it's his boss's. Her reply captures the film's understanding of capitalism's impersonal domination: "My mother used to say that no one raindrop ever thought it caused the flood." Whether people choose to recognize their responsibility or not, *Mayhem* insists, they are responsible for what they do. And that isn't wrong, at least not quite. We might say that what matters to the value form, from a structural perspective, is what you do.

But that's not quite what *Mayhem* means. In its eyes, responsibility matters. Let's contrast this with the film discussed in the introduction. *Drag Me to Hell* makes the foreclosure Christine's decision. She could have decided otherwise, didn't, and gets punished for it. In *Mayhem*, Derek can't do a thing. He tells the woman in foreclosure, Melanie, that he couldn't stop her foreclosure even if he wanted to. What the film does with violence, then, is try to put a finger on *who* did *what* to *whom*. For *Mayhem*, to take responsibility means to step forward and receive the violence that your work has directed at others. We see this when Derek confronts Lester, the human resources director who fired him. He repeats Melanie's words. Lester, too, pleads that it wasn't his decision; it was the firm's. Derek asks where the firm is, adding, "I would love to kick the firm's ass." Exasperated, Lester replies, "You can't kick a firm's ass. That's the point." "Well," says Derek, raising his weapon, "then that brings us back to you."

The film's focus on responsibility calls into question the rules that allow knowledge workers to shrug off the violence of their work, but it does so by attacking the individuals who benefit from this domination, not the forms of domination themselves. This slippage helps us to understand why Derek's resistance to capitalism's impersonal domination has less to do with the forms that keep capitalism going than with his ability to manipulate rules. *Mayhem* is a cynical film, and its cynicism reflects the role that cynicism plays in contemporary economic life. Paolo Virno helps us to understand what such cynicism means in his analysis of the affects of post-Fordism (a cognate for neoliberalism and postmodernity). For Virno, the affective matters because of the extreme disunity of capitalism's current mode of production. If there is a mode of production to post-Fordism, Virno argues, it is one defined by a lack of a dominant set of material productive forces. Claims to the era as one of multitude, of cognitive work, of care work, do not hold. What unites workers in the contemporary world's highly dispersed and uneven mode of production, Virno claims, "are their emotional tonalities, their inclinations, their mentalities, and their expectations."[32] A disunited mode of production, Virno maintains, is connected only through hazier experiences of affect, in particular cynicism, fear, and opportunism. Virno argues that these affects are the result of the emergence of what Marx called "the general intellect," a term used in the *Grundrisse* to describe the accumulation of scientific knowledge, technology, and social cooperation. This abstract body of codes, rules, and technological know-how, Marx suggested, would increase productivity for capitalism, free people from work, and make communism possible. Virno rightly notes that the end of the twentieth century revealed the general intellect's ability to increase productivity yet didn't bring a hint of liberation from work. While the growth of the general intellect increased capital's productive capacities, it lowered its demand for labor. Abstract labor, socially necessary labor, and the commodity fetish are still operative, but workers are now also subject to increased precarity as the productive power of the general intellect diminishes capital's demand for labor-power.

The result has made work more affectively fraught. Capitalism has long relied on the fear of hunger to make people work. This fear exists outside the work-relation. The increased precarity produced by the general intellect, however, moves fear into the work-relation. Fear forces workers to develop their so-called human capital and accept more and more flexibilized working conditions. It encourages opportunism. Instead of building trustworthy relationships, workers must constantly watch for whatever might get them ahead. Unlike fear and opportunism, cynicism isn't produced by precarity but by the changed working conditions created by the general intellect. With the rise of knowledge work, workers become adepts of codes, rules, and know-how. They learn, Virno explains, "rules rather than 'facts.'"[33] And this focus on rules creates cynicism:

> Intimacy with the rules becomes a process of adaptation to an essentially abstract environment. From the a priori conditions and paradigms that structure action, cynicism picks up only the minimum of signals needed to orient its struggle for survival. It is no accident, therefore, that the most brazen cynicism is accompanied by unrestrained sentimentalism. The vital contents of emotion—excluded from the inventories of an experience that is above all else an experience of formalisms and abstractions—secretly returns, simplified and unelaborated, as arrogant as they are puerile.[34]

What makes *Mayhem* a film about the horrors of work in capitalism now is the way it links impersonal domination to a focus on *rules*. Derek understands his job as a lawyer to be not about maintaining or enforcing laws but about manipulating them. When Melanie asks what he does, he says, "Loopholes. It's my specialty." The film's comedy comes from its cynicism. For all its discussions of responsibility, *Mayhem* has no problem with Derek manipulating rules to his benefit. His murderous ascent through the building is a cynical manipulation of the rules to get what he wants. The only rule is "fuck you," as one office drone scrawls on the back of his shirt.

Consider Derek's confrontation with Kara, the cutthroat manager who got him fired and the film's one Black character. Kara knows that Derek wants her keycard to the top floor of the building, so she gives it to her assistant, Meg, a young white woman Kara spends most of the film abusing. When Derek confronts Kara, he gives her a choice: her keycard or her life. Kara tells Meg to hand it over, only for Meg to reveal she destroyed it. The firm's partners thought Kara would sell them out and offered Meg a promotion to protect them. The film doesn't comment on the implicit racism here, but it is clear that Kara and Derek must both compete for status in a white-dominated hierarchy that is only too eager to sell them out. When an angry Kara begins to demean Meg again, Meg kills her with a pair of scissors while Derek and Melanie look on (Figure 3). Everything is negotiable in the cutthroat world of business. Another sequence makes a similar point. Derek lures the partner responsible for foreclosures, Irene, to a lower-level conference room by hacking her computer. He offers to exchange her data for her key card. All she has to do is sign paperwork to stop Melanie's foreclosure. Irene agrees but tells them she will file a petition that she wasn't in her right mind to restart the foreclosure. In retaliation, Melanie destroys Irene's computer. Irene then makes Derek an offer. Give her Melanie and she will give him the card. And Derek agrees. Rules, you see, are negotiable. And that means Derek, too, can change them whenever he wants. As the elevator doors close to take him to the top floor, he reveals to Irene that he untied Melanie and gave her a gun.

Cynicism also helps us better understand how the film uses the office building as a metaphor for class structure. There's an entire subgenre of class-structure horror: J. G. Ballard's 1975 novel *High-Rise*, Bong Jo Hoon's *Snowpiercer* (2013), Ben Wheatley's adaptation of Ballard's novel (2015), the Spanish-language Netflix film *The Platform (El Hoyo)* (2019), and Gauillaume Nicloux's *Lockdown Tower (La Tour)* (2022). In those films, the built environment *is* the class structure. Both are all-encompassing. Characters may traverse this environment, but they can no more escape it than we can escape the social structure itself. That's the trade-off these allegories make. If the built environment is a metaphor for class structure, then the world outside becomes a literal no-man's land. This is why the outside of the building is an inescapable void in *Lockdown Tower* and why the two survivors of *Snowpiercer* wander into an empty and unlivable landscape after their train/society goes off the rails. *Mayhem*, however, refuses to follow these rules. The building is a metaphor for social structure, but it isn't all-encompassing. The possibility of

Figure 3. Kara and Meg argue about who's responsible, while Derek and Melanie look on. *Mayhem*, directed by Joe Lynch. RLJE Films, 2017.

escape always remains. The rules that govern the building during quarantine are different from those outside, and they will change once quarantine ends. This sense of an exterior to the social structure affects the way the film conceptualizes rules. Every rule is negotiable. There's always another system besides this one.

The film shows us, then, how people deal with their domination by work and the commonsense understanding of work as punishment: *Use cynicism, not fear.* Fear shows you don't understand how to manipulate codes and rules. Cynicism shows you do. Derek's story demonstrates how successful cynicism can be. In other films, viruses throw characters into the grips of violent irrational psychoses. In *Mayhem*, the virus authorizes Derek's fantasy of class mobility and sexual agency. Throughout, he makes rational decisions based on his legal immunity, most especially limiting his brutality to quarantine. His climactic fight with the firm's head ends just as the clock runs out and his boss hits the concrete ten stories below. The other partners take this as evidence of Derek's savviness and offer him the firm's top job. He takes it, cancels Melanie's foreclosure, and quits. Why? The solution that *Mayhem* offers to the punishment of work is not to attack the forms of its oppression but to manipulate its rules to get what you want. For all the antagonisms of work, the film does not see a coherent system of oppression, only an array of manipulable systems. You can always play one set of rules against another. This refusal of work isn't a form of exodus from capitalism's domination.[35] For Derek, quitting alters the rules. As he glibly explains: "I didn't have a job. The job had me. I was just another fucking slave to the grind." That is, until he wasn't. This also explains the conclusion's sudden shift in tone. Where other class-structure horrors often turn bleak in the final reel, *Mayhem* offers viewers what Virno calls the "simple and unelaborated" emotions of sentimentality. The possibility of another system means that Derek can leave the law to take up a lost interest, art. The film's final sequence shows Derek and Melanie painting and flirting as Derek offers cliché-laden pathos in voice-over: "But they do say everything happens for a reason. I'm starting to believe it. Here's one more pro tip. Paint your own path to success in work, love, and life before it's too fucking late."

It may seem strange that a movie about murdering your boss and coworkers ends with language people hang on the walls of vacation rentals. It's not far from *Paint your own path to success in work, love, and life!*

to *Live, laugh, love!* But as we'll see in the next chapter, what Derek invokes here is another piece of common sense about work in twenty-first-century capitalism: *Do what you love, and you'll never work a day in your life.* The idea that work should be rewarding is more diffuse, social, and fraught with concerns about gender roles and social-reproduction work than the economic sense that work is punishment. To the degree *Mayhem* says anything about gender and social reproduction, it appears in the way this sentimental turn to the good life intersects with the film's attempts to subvert stereotypes about Asian American men. Derek's journey from emasculated nerd to empowered man seems engineered to reverse American cultural stereotypes of Asian American men as nerdy and emasculated. For all Derek's legal abilities, he is unable to navigate the office's cutthroat politics until he gets infected with the rage virus. The virus allows him to take on characteristics that Tiffany Besana, Dalal Katsiaficas, and Aerika Brittian Loyd identify as "stereotype-resisting" for Asian American men: bravery, loyalty, and mischievousness.[36] This shift removes Derek's emasculation—he and Melanie have sex in the midst of all their murders—and sets up the film's sentimental turn. When he quits the firm, he displays another stereotype-resistant quality, what Besana, Katsiaficas, and Loyd describe as "[consciousness] of the valuable things in life that do not require money such as love."[37]

A Marxist reading of the film helps us to see that Derek's subversions of these stereotypes rely on his cynicism. If Derek discovers love and meaning by the film's end, it is because he has embraced the cynicism created by twenty-first century knowledge work. Derek's seeming rejection of capitalism's impersonal domination is in fact his reintegration into capitalist society. When cynicism fails, try love. These two pieces of common sense work hand in hand. Think back to what those r/antiwork posters said: They weren't talking about refusing work but about changing the rules. We can make work fairer, get more input into how it's organized, and get more money. What we can't do is change the form of our domination. To be clear, there's nothing wrong with reforming the rules of work. My point is that these reforms illustrate how cynicism and the promise of meaningful work keep us lumbering through the awfulness of capitalism. Instead of fighting to extract what we can from the domination of abstract labor—that is, to decommodify what we need to survive—we get male fantasies of violence and sexual potency like those we find in *Mayhem* and the many iterations of *Dracula*. These fantasies may evoke the felt indignities wrought by capitalism's impersonal economic domination, but they can just as easily become a search for scapegoats. Everyone in *Mayhem* is trying to get ahead by finding someone to blame. As Lester says, you can't kick a firm's ass. Marx's theory of value may not be able to change that, but it can help us to identify and understand the forms of capitalism's impersonal domination without falling prey to these violent fictions.

2

LOVE HATES YOU

Feminist Anticapitalist Horror and
Social Reproduction Theory

Work should be meaningful. On its face, the statement seems inarguable. Better meaningful work than meaningless drudgery. Yet if we want to understand why capitalism hates us, we have to understand how this piece of common sense supports capitalism as a system of impersonal social domination. We can see how this idea helps to construct hegemony if we look at its most used form: *Do what you love, and you'll never work a day in your life.* Media commentators tried to attribute the so-called Great Resignation of 2021–22 and the accompanying increase of antiwork sentiments to workers suddenly questioning whether their work was meaningful. Writing for *Fortune*, Sam Allen described the Great Resignation as driven by "a desire for more meaningful, more impactful, purpose-driven work—work that might actually change the world."[1] Even when writers questioned whether meaningful work was possible, they turned to sociologists who could translate the idea into the language of meaning and value. In "What If the New Dream Job Is No Job at All?" Olivia Harrison interviewed sociologist Erin Cech, who imagines workers asking themselves: *"What do I really value? What's really important to me? How do I align my decision-making with that?"*[2] The idea of meaningful work makes the refusal of work in capitalism unimaginable. "You can't reject work altogether," the voice of reason proclaims. "You have to work to survive." This insistence that we be realistic about work—not as a transhistorical need but as it currently exists under capitalism—eviscerates the refusal of work's radical meaning. To refuse work in this sense simply means to search for more money or more meaning. People quit their jobs to get more value or better values, not because they want to live outside the constraints of a system organized by value.[3]

This idea that work should be meaningful didn't emerge from the pandemic. People often treat it as an expression of neoliberal ideology. It is no mistake that Sarah Jaffe titled her study of the problems of contemporary labor *Work Won't Love You Back*.[4] Without a doubt, people have begun to feel the demand to love their work as precisely that, a demand. But where does that demand come from? Who does it serve? What makes it "neoliberal"? One of the most interesting accounts of the idea comes from French philosopher and economist Frédéric Lordon. For Lordon, the demand is a response to regulatory shifts of the post-Fordist or neoliberal era. During the Fordist era (1918–1970), state policies limited capital's mobility to foster employment and growth inside nations. In the post-Fordist or neoliberal era, states removed those policies, allowing capital to become more mobile and flee one region for another in search of the highest rate of profit. The neoliberal era's increased capital mobility set off deindustrialization, public disinvestment, and increased precarity throughout the global North. Lordon offers an analysis of the affects of this shift that dovetails nicely with Paolo Virno's account of post-Fordism's affects, discussed in the previous chapter. For Lordon, work's affective tenor during the Fordist era was essentially sad. People endured work to experience the joys of consumerism available outside of work. Capital's unrestrained movement in the neoliberal era changes the relation between work and affect as employment became more precarious. As Virno argues, precarity produces fear, opportunism, and cynicism. Lordon shows how precarity fundamentally reorganizes work's affects. In the neoliberal era, workers don't look for joy outside of work. Instead, they must discover "'fulfilment' and 'self-realization' in and through work."[5] Lordon points out that the joy workers are supposed to find in work isn't really theirs. Precarity's demand to find fulfillment in work forces workers to align their pleasures and desires with those of their employer. From this perspective, questions like "What do I really value? What's really important to me? How do I align my decision-making with that?" aren't so much expressions of workers searching for personal meaning as attempts to come to terms with what other people want them to want.

Several recent horror films can help us see the violence produced by the demand to love your work. Gillian Wallace Horvat's *I Blame Society* (2020), Corinna Faith's *The Power* (2021), Prano Bailey-Bond's *Censor*

(2021), and Rose Glass's *Saint Maud* (2019) aim their critiques at women's exploitation on the job. Each presents a variation on the idea of a woman possessed by her work. In *I Blame Society*, a filmmaker becomes a serial killer to prove her professional bona fides; in *The Power*, a nurse is possessed by the victim of a sexual predator; in *Censor*, a film censor loses her grip on reality when she cannot separate herself from her work; and in *Saint Maud*, a carer sacrifices herself in a desperate bid for meaningful work. This focus on how work exploits women through their commitments and doubts suggests these films should be placed in the emerging genre of feminist anticapitalist horror that Patricia Stuelke identifies in literature. "These works," Stuelke explains, "repurpose horror conventions in order to confront the entangled forces of environmental destruction, financialization and extraction, and the exploitation of women's labor."[6] In chapter 7, we will see how filmmakers draw on the woman's film to bring women's elided experiences into horror.[7] Here, I want to focus on how horror films from female filmmakers can help us better understand one of the crucial insights of materialist feminism and social reproduction theory: Capitalism uses meaningfulness to make women's unpaid labor seem like a natural expression of their being. As Silvia Federici explains,

> To have a wage means to be part of a social contract . . . you work, not because you like it, or because it comes naturally to you, but because it is the only condition under which you are allowed to live. But exploited as you might be, *you are not that work*. . . . In the case of housework the situation is qualitatively different. Housework had to be transformed into a natural attribute rather than be recognized as a social contract because from the beginning of capital's scheme for women this work was destined to be unwaged. *Capital had to convince us that it is a natural, unavoidable, and even fulfilling activity to make us accept working without a wage*. In turn, the unwaged condition of housework has been the most powerful weapon in reinforcing the common assumption that *housework is not work*, thus preventing women from struggling against it.[8]

Like other theorists associated with the Wages for Housework movement of the 1970s, Federici had in mind the mid-twentieth-century heteronormative family, an institution supported by a male head of household earning a family wage. (We'll talk about the family at length in chapter 6.) The point is that if women thought the work of maintaining the family was "natural, unavoidable, and even fulfilling," they wouldn't understand that capital exploited them indirectly through the family wage, and men wouldn't recognize patriarchy as another form of work discipline.

The Wages for Housework movement aimed to denaturalize women's work at home to build solidarity between the sexes.[9] However, the economic changes of the neoliberal era fundamentally altered the situation of domestic labor in the global North. Capital's increased mobility meant an end to the family wage with the North's deindustrialization, which led to a shift in so-called developed economies toward services—in essence, a shift to FIRE (finance, insurance, real estate), intellectual production (arts and intellectual property), and care work (e.g., health care, education, elder care, childcare). The loss of the family wage saw the mass entrance of women into the workforce, most especially in the service sector. Capitalism's turn to services posed a problem for how Marxists thought about exploitation and the proletariat. In the early twenty-first century, Michael Hardt and Antonio Negri argued that the rise of services meant capitalism had entered a new and potentially revolutionary era. Capitalism's attempts to extract value from people's immaterial labor, they said, could constitute a new transnational revolutionary class.[10] Well, that hasn't happened. As we have learned, capitalism is more than capable of exploiting work in services. Marx himself said as much.[11] If Marx didn't discuss services at length, it was because he didn't believe service workers like educators or nurses were likely to be subject to mass exploitation. Unlike industrial production, services are notoriously resistant to technological increases in labor productivity.[12] Even now, capitalism's technological revolutionizing of production hasn't managed to increase labor productivity in services.[13] It is no coincidence that the neoliberal era is the era of the demand to love your work. Much of service work remains gendered, especially in terms of care work. The naturalization of exploitation through gendered norms can rationalize low wages and bad working conditions. The call to love your work is a technology to increase labor productivity. What that old saw really means is *Love what you do, and you'll work every day of your life.*

Social Reproduction Theory, Original Accumulation, and Appropriation

Social reproduction theory forces us to alter how we understand capitalism. Gender norms naturalize women's unpaid domestic labor, social reproduction theorists argue, because capitalism *needs* the value that their labor creates. This claim constitutes a challenge to Marx's theory of value. For Marx, unpaid concrete labor like domestic labor that women did in the nineteenth century can't produce value. That's not because this labor doesn't matter. It's that it isn't sold as a commodity to a capitalist and thus isn't consumed like a commodity in the production process. If labor isn't abstracted, sold, and consumed as a commodity, then capital can't pocket the difference between its abstract value and its concrete production. In other words, it can't produce surplus value. From a classically Marxist perspective, unpaid labor should be treated as a historical remnant, either of feudalism and its direct coercion of labor or of the period that Marx called *ursprünglich Akkumulation*, the violent pre-capitalist stage in which people, land, and resources were expropriated by Europeans. In either case, classical Marxism views violent coercion and appropriation of work without pay as outside capitalism's history. In the 1970s, debates over capitalism's origins renewed discussion about the role of violence and state power. The debates' victors, Robert Brenner and Ellen Meiksins Wood, pushed violence and state coercion outside capitalism. Brenner argued that because capitalism relies on the continual revolutionizing of production, not violent appropriation, primitive accumulation's violence was external to its operations.[14] And Wood, who offers likely the summative account of capitalism's origins, described it as a system of "appropriation without coercion."[15]

Social reproduction theorists relied on a different account of capitalism's origins. Instead of Brenner and Wood, they turned to the work of world-systems theorist Immanuel Wallerstein. Wallerstein held that the violence of primitive accumulation wasn't limited to a prior period; it ran all through capitalism's development and continues to underpin the unequal exchanges between the core and periphery of modern capitalism.[16] German Marxists such as Maria Mies, Claudia von Werlhof, and Veronika Bennholdt-Thomsen, as well as American and Italian Marxists like Federici and Mariarosa Dalla Costa, drew on Wallerstein's work to argue that capitalism appropriates women's unpaid labor in the same fashion.[17] The continued appropriation of women's unpaid work, they argue, shows the centrality of unequal exchange and violence to capitalism's production of value. Importantly, they draw links between the appropriation of women's unpaid domestic labor, colonization's appropriation of land and natural resources, and slavery's appropriation of people's bodies. Instead of maintaining that these processes are outside capitalism because they don't follow the dynamics of wage exploitation, social reproduction theorists insist that these processes of appropriation are crucial mechanisms for capitalism's production of value.

What social reproduction theory helps us to do, then, is to push Marxism beyond a simple account of labor and exploitation. It remakes Marxism into a theory able to account for capitalism's reliance on material dispossession *and* its exploitation of waged work. Capitalism isn't simply an expansive system of exploitation focused on the accumulation of value; it's a system that accumulates value through the appropriation of the earth, the bodies of enslaved peoples, and unpaid domestic and reproductive labor.[18] If we aren't used to seeing appropriation as part of capitalism, it is because its acts of appropriation have been naturalized culturally through ideas about gender, race, and nation, as well as in the affective demand to love our work.

I Blame Society: The Destructive Search for Meaning

Horror helps us to see how this form of common sense differs from how gender norms naturalize appropriation. Where gender norms rely on the assertion of what a person is, the demand to love what you do relies on doubts about your abilities. Workers measure themselves against an unknown and unknowable standard: Is my work good enough to be meaningful? Capitalism answers this question with value—that is, money. It can't recognize work as work unless someone has bought it. The problem is that, in an era defined by precarity and stagnation, workers face flat or falling wages. A lack of worker organization makes it difficult for workers to address capitalism's failings as structural issues. For employers, it's much better if workers treat this structural problem as a personal one. Instead of economic precarity, workers confront questions of personal capacity: *Good workers get paid more and they don't get fired, right?* Personalization can't resolve structural issues, but it can generate doubts about workers' capacities and commitment: *Maybe I'm just not good enough.* To escape these doubts, workers can respond by intensifying their commitment to work: *If I work harder, I'll show everybody how good my work is and how worthy I am of it.* In essence, they fall under the sway of another person's idea of what they should do, as Lordon explained, and continually try to align themselves with whatever they think their work should be. In short, they become possessed by their work.

Although each of these films involves possession by work, none of them are exorcism stories, nor do they resemble past horror films about characters possessed by work. Likely the most explicit subgenre of films in which work subsumes workers are Hollywood's representations of Haitian zombis. In *White Zombie* (1931) and *I Walked with a Zombie* (1943), to be possessed by work is to be physically enslaved. Crucially, the zombi is an enslaved body, not an enslaved mind.[19] That's fitting for the zombi's fraught position, as Sarah Juliet Lauro explains, between colonial slavery and the possibility of slave revolts.[20] *White Zombie* shows how capitalism's impersonal domination literally reduces people to abstract labor-power. Zombis lumber along in silence, indifferent to whether they're loading sugar cane or themselves into a thresher. That isn't the case in these films. Here, possession starts not with physical but mental control as the characters in these films internalize the ideas that they want to embrace. It is the intensity of this internalization and the doubts it produces that reveal the violence in the demand to love your work.

Consider Gillian Wallace Horvat's *I Blame Society*. In Horvat's film, Gillian, an out-of-work documentary filmmaker, is driven mad by doubt in her search for meaningful work. Horvat, the film's writer, director, and star, plays a fictionalized version of herself. For genre audiences, *I Blame Society* appears to be a found-footage serial-killer film akin to *Creep* (2014). However, *I Blame Society* is less engaged with the terrors of serial killing than with the desires and doubts of filmmaking. For Gillian, meaningful work is moviemaking, but her career has stalled. As the film opens, her manager/agent drops her. He can't place her scripts, he says, because she won't write strong, likable female leads. Full of doubts about her career, Gillian returns to an abandoned project, a personal documentary about a backhanded compliment that she would make a great murderer. Based on a project that Horvat abandoned, Gillian's film interpolates interview footage that Horvat shot of friends and family members before shifting into a fictional mode as Gillian becomes a killer.

The plot of this fictional project hinges on Gillian remaking herself to be what everyone tells her they want: a strong female lead. The conversation with her agent introduces the idea, but Gillian's possession begins in earnest when she lands a meeting with two male producers. They talk about championing women in the industry, and say they want to make films from diverse voices that feature strong, likable female leads. When Gillian pitches her project, they express passing interest but quickly turn to the meeting's real purpose. They want her to make a pitch-deck for a male director's already finished project. It would look better to have a woman's name on it. Annoyed, Gillian agrees. She isn't interested in the pitch deck, though. She thinks they'll buy her film, if she can finish it. The key is to give them what they say they want. It isn't enough to talk about how she would make a great murderer. To be a strong female lead, she has to show that she *is* a great murderer.

It's no mistake the film's title is *I Blame Society*. It's about how external ideas affect Gillian's thoughts and actions. Gillian's descent into serial murder is the result of her naturalization of other peoples' ideas about how women should be represented on film, so much so that she walks around with a camera mounted on her forehead (Figure 4). Johanna Isaacson describes Gillian's interactions with these men as a form of emotional labor, specifically the emotional labor of putting up with their misogyny masquerading as feminism. Gillian's turn to serial killing is a kind of "smile strike," Isaacson argues, because it withholds positive emotional labor.[21] Gillian isn't striking, though. She is *working*, performing the industry's stated desires, albeit in the most perverse fashion. She's building a reel. The film's comedic premise is that Gillian understands what these men want better than they do. She knows that when they say they want a "diversity of voices," they mean clichéd characters representing different demographic groups. Her victims come from a cross-section of society, and she gives them fake suicide notes full of stereotypical problems: A young woman complains about beauty standards, an old man about generational differences, and so on. She knows that when the producers say they want a strong, likable female lead, what they mean is they want a woman who will objectify herself. Before she starts killing, Gillian films herself having sex with her unwitting (and later angry) partner, and while her murders begin with women, she quickly moves to male victims to give them a pattern of screwing and killing. We might better say that the film encourages smile strikes, but Gillian is working the entire time.

The tragedy of Gillian's possession by these ideas about who and what she should be is that her success as a murderer has nothing to do with the norms she's adopting. It's due to her skill as a filmmaker. As Horvat shows, both tasks require the same planning, preparation, and improvisation. Each murder forces Gillian to deal with casting, location scouting, set preparations, and staging. During her crimes, Gillian has to elicit convincing performances from her victims and capture them on camera. Yet even after all her efforts to remake herself into the kind of person the industry claims to want, Gillian still can't get recognition. No one can figure out that she is the serial killer. "I'm so good at murdering," she tells one of her victims. "It just sucks that I can't get the credit for it." As a worker in a field that relies on freelance and gig work, Gillian sees the link between selling her film and getting credit for her

Figure 4. Gillian carries the film industry's standards with her like the camera strapped to her head. *I Blame Society*, directed by Gillian Wallace Horvat. Cranked Up Films, 2020.

spree. All of her work takes place outside a formal wage relation, so unless she sells her film, she's not even getting paid in exposure—no one knows it's her! When she returns to the producers to sell her film, they're aghast, but not because Gillian's film reveals her crimes. They're angry she didn't finish the pitch deck, and their annoyance brings out their misogyny. The film is all wrong, they say. A female killer? Unbelievable, embarrassing. The lead is strong, but she's not likable—except, one qualifies, when she takes off her top. It's clear that they find the very idea of a female director ridiculous. Gillian responds by slaughtering them. Moments before she slits the second producer's throat, he asks in terror who she is. She replies, "I'm a strong female lead."

The Power and *Censor*: Meaningful Work and the Neoliberal Past

I Blame Society shows the doubts the search for meaningful work can create in the twenty-first century. Corinna Faith's *The Power* and Prano Bailey-Bond's *Censor* subject these doubts to a sort of historical analysis. Both films are set during the United Kingdom's entrance into the neoliberal era, *The Power* in the years before Margaret Thatcher's Tory government came to power and *Censor* in the midst of it. Unlike the unwaged Gillian, the main characters of these films are waged workers, but doubt remains the basis for their total appropriation by work.

The Power is about who has social, political, and economic power, and its historical setting reframes its main character's appropriation by work as a metaphor for solidarity. Set during the 1974 National Union of Mineworkers' (NUM) strike, *The Power* uses the strike's rolling blackouts as the backdrop to a young nurse's hellish first night of training. Valerie starts her day listening to a labor militant on the radio declare, "This strike is for everyone at the bottom of the pile." That describes Valerie. An orphan, Valerie was sexually assaulted by a priest when she was a child. Although she registered a complaint, the nuns and police forced her to recant, leaving her with the reputation of a sexually promiscuous liar. What Valerie wants is to help other poor young people. She explains to the head matron, a dour West Indian woman, that she chose the East London Royal Infirmary for her training because it is in London's poorest neighborhood, before admitting it is also her own.[22]

The matron's snide response indicates how little class consciousness matters to those with power: "Back to serve your community. How noble." Stung, Valerie replies, "I thought I'd be most useful here." The matron isn't interested. "Ideals are fine," she says, "but what I require is discipline." The other nurses are equally hard, unwilling to recognize humanity or suffering in their patients. Everything in the hospital is discipline, as the film's orderly formal compositions of beds and hallways underscore. Only a pediatric doctor, Dr. Franklyn, appears to be an exception to the hospital's strict regulation. When Valerie recognizes him from a public lecture on the slum's health problems, he responds warmly and offers to move her to the pediatric wing. The film uses the frame to reveal how this seemingly positive encounter is also shot through with power. Like everyone else in the hospital, Franklyn looks down on Valerie (Figure 5). Although neither she nor the audience realize it, this visual composition indicates the danger Valerie is in. It's no mistake that his warm response gets her in trouble with the matron. She puts Valerie on the night shift, where she will be easy prey for Franklyn, a murderer and rapist who stalks the hospital's patients. The strike's scheduled blackouts are the perfect time for him to attack.

Valerie is saved by the intercession of the ghost of one of Franklin's victims, a little girl named Gail. Gail doesn't work on her own, though. She possesses Valerie, taking control of her body. Valerie doesn't understand what is happening. She's riddled with doubts about her abilities,

Figure 5. The Power intimates Franklyn's violence by making him look down at Valerie in this American two shot. *The Power*, directed by Corinna Faith. RLJE Films, 2021.

her knowledge, and her sanity. It doesn't help that her reputation has followed her to the hospital. No one believes her when she sees unexplained things, let alone when Gail takes control of her body. Everyone treats Valerie as a crazy woman who makes up stories. After Gail wreaks mayhem during the night, Valerie is dismissed from her position and nearly institutionalized. Only once she stops doubting Gail's motives does she understand what is happening. Gail chose Valerie for much the same reason that Valerie became a nurse: her experience means she should understand what's happening. Gail's violence wasn't meaningless. She used Valerie's appropriated body to take revenge on those who overlooked her suffering at Franklyn's hands. Once she's overcome her doubts, Valerie helps others overcome theirs. When the matron sees the state Valerie is in the next morning, she realizes that Franklyn has been abusing Valerie and another patient, Saba, and helps them escape. However, Franklyn corners them in the basement with the aim of murdering and incinerating them, just as he did Gail. All but rubbing his hands in glee, Franklyn tells them to shut up. At this moment, Valerie, Saba, and Gail respond in unison: No, he will hear them. Valerie levitates and her superior visual position shows who has the power now (Figure 6). The three women scream and immolate Franklyn in a flash of light. Power, the film avers, comes from the collective. Like the NUM strike, working together turns it on or off.

Figure 6. The Power reverses the power dynamic with this low-angle shot of Valerie confronting Franklyn. *The Power*, directed by Corinna Faith. RLJE Films, 2021.

Valerie's search for meaningful work is a plea for solidarity, but attention to the demand to love your work reveals another, less savory, implication. The search for meaningful work can draw you, wittingly or not, into doing terrible things. Valerie's unconscious destruction of the hospital staff while possessed isn't all that different from their unwitting role in Gail's abuse. Valerie is possessed by her search for meaningful work, but she doesn't know the meaning of the work she actually does.

Thematically, *The Power* wants to avoid this ambivalence almost as much as the ambivalence of its historical situation. The NUM strike of 1974 was the last major labor action before the neoliberal era began. The NUM were fighting a Tory government for wage increases to address inflation, and the strike's blackouts demonstrated their electrical and electoral power. The Tories were pushed out of office in October 1974. The new Labour government gave workers the wage increase they demanded and another a few years later. However, in the winter of 1978–79, after other trade unions pushed for wage increases and truck drivers led a major strike, the Labour government collapsed with a vote of no confidence. With the Tories returned to power, the era of what William Davies calls "combative neoliberalism" began in earnest.[23] In 1984, the NUM launched another industrial action, and their defeat by Thatcher the next year broke the labor movement in the United Kingdom. *The Power* may end on a jubilant note of solidarity, but Valerie, Saba, and Gail are running into a future where labor's collective power dramatically fails.

It's telling, then, that Prano Bailey-Bond's *Censor* includes an early scene of Thatcher speaking after the defeat of NUM's 1985 strike. There's no solidarity in *Censor*; only personal responsibility. Instead of labor action, the film approaches the era through moral panic around so-called "video nasties," a term for horror films distributed on VHS such as *The Evil Dead* (1981), *Zombie (Zombi 2)* (1979), *Inferno* (1980), and *The Texas Chainsaw Massacre* (1974). The film's main character, Enid, works as a censor for the British Board of Film Classification (BBFC), a non-governmental institution created by the British film industry in 1912 to classify and censor theatrical films. Like the American Production Code Administration, the BBFC was an institution of self-regulation until 1984, when Thatcher's conservative Parliament placed home-video releases under its purview with the 1984 Video Recordings Act. Conservative outrage over video nasties drove the passage of the VRA, which gave the

BBFC formal legal authority to classify and censor home video releases. Films that had been rejected or not passed by the BBFC were not simply unrated but illegal. Video stores could be (and were) raided by the police, tapes seized, and so on.[24] Enid works the tip of the spear in this conservative culture war, studying horror films with humorless assiduity. For her, work is no space for doubt but a great responsibility, and she derives real meaning from it. Enid is only interested in "getting it right," as she tells a colleague. "Don't think of anything else."

The problem is that no one can really say what "getting it right" means when it comes to censorship. How do you edit a film like *Cannibal Holocaust* (1980) for moral value? To come to any conclusions about what a horror film should or shouldn't include, you would have to approach horror as an aesthetic project. That certainly wasn't the case in 1980s Britain. As British film historian and critic Julian Petley explains, critics held horror in contempt, routinely condemning films for genre conventions, and ignoring their narrative, audio, and visual construction. "Critical disdain for the horror film," Petley writes, "meant that when the video nasty bomb dropped in the early 1980s, not one mainstream film critic saw fit to defend in print any of the films in question, nor to take issue with the distorted and ludicrous nonsense [in their publications]."[25] If critics supplanted critical judgment with moral condemnation first, the state and the BBFC were not far behind. Conservative politicians and media figures offered a simplistic rationale for censorship: Watching violent videos leads to acts of violence. The media hammered the point home, linking a series of shocking crimes to film violence. The 1987 Hungerford Massacre was attributed to the influence of the *Rambo* series, and the murders of James Bulger and Suzanne Capper to the violence in *Child's Play 3* (1991). Petley argued at the time that these claims were Conservatives' attempts to distract voters from the destructive social and economic effects of their neoliberal policies. In 1994, Petley wrote in the *British Journalism Review*:

> Examine the brutalizing, impoverishing, and destructive effects of policies carried out in the spirit of the dogma that "there is no such thing as society"? Not on your life! So step forward the scapegoats: sixties "permissiveness," "trendy" teachers, single mothers, the "underclass" and, of course, the ever-reliable video nasty.[26]

While attacks on video nasties were undoubtedly a political distraction, the controversy and its role in *Censor* help reveal some of the common sense that holds the neoliberal era together.

In modern discourse, people use the word *neoliberalism* as shorthand for attacks on the welfare state, most especially the replacement of social benefits with so-called market solutions. It's tempting to treat neoliberalism as a coherent political program. From this perspective, neoliberalism was launched in the 1970s by conservatives across the globe in response to the wage-price spiral. To return the world to capitalist rationality from the supposed economic deformations of state intervention, neoliberal politicians hiked interest rates to increase unemployment and lower wages, limited the state's regulatory power over industries, and passed laws that allowed new forms of capital mobility.[27] The problem with this account is that neoliberalism isn't a coherent political project. It's a series of ad-hoc assaults on any and all policies that aren't market based.[28] For neoliberals, every problem has one solution, *capitalism*. Once we recognize neoliberalism as a defense of capitalism, we can make sense of its policies' fundamental incoherence. In the neoliberal era, market-based programs are constantly promoted as better than state-run ones. If neoliberalism were about a political return to economic rationality, it would matter when market-based solutions cost more or produce worse outcomes, which they often do. Market failures in sectors such as housing, health care, and education would be taken as signs that the market can't solve every problem. But in the neoliberal era, outcomes don't matter. What matters is the *rightness* of capitalism. Only the market apportions resources properly.[29] Who are you going to believe, the neoliberal asks, me or your lying eyes?

The promoters of neoliberal ideas believe society can't solve its own problems. Why not? Because, as Thatcher famously proclaimed, "there is no such thing as society." For neoliberals, society is a ruse. It's just an idea that allows individuals to become dependent on social welfare programs instead of taking responsibility for themselves. Can't make ends meet? Marshal your human capital and become an in-demand worker. Learn to code.[30] Neoliberalism asks people to avow that their lives are their responsibility and no one else's. The only proper use of the state is to enforce the market's power on individuals. In neoliberalism, to be responsible is to be forced to live in the world that capitalism has created and that the state insists we can't change. In such a world, it seems the best a person can do is find meaningful work.

Censor shows the flaws in this individual-sized solution. When the press links a gruesome set of murders to *Deranged*, a film that Enid cleared, they begin to hound her. It little matters that, in an echo of the Bulger and Capper murders, the killer never saw *Deranged*. Enid and the press feel that she has failed in her responsibilities to the public, and Enid feels that she has failed in her responsibilities to herself. The film indicates that Enid chose her work as a kind of penance for the abduction of her sister, Nina. She feels a connection between herself and the murderer the press dubs "the amnesiac killer." She too cannot recall what happened the day she and her sister went into the woods. Until now, Enid compensated for her inability to be responsible as a child with an aggressively responsible work ethic as an adult. The amnesiac killer throws her coping mechanism into crisis. She is caught between two demands that only neoliberalism could put at odds, the demand to be responsible for others and to be responsible for oneself. An unfortunate encounter with a film producer, Smart, exacerbates the problem. After the controversy breaks, he stops by the BBFC office at the request of a director, Frederick North, to ask that Enid review his film *Don't Go in the Church*.[31] In the screening room, Enid is stunned to discover the film is based on Nina's disappearance, and its images begin to fill in the blanks in her memory. When the film's heroine chops her sister to bits under the direction of the monstrous Beastman, Enid sees herself attacking Nina. Her terror that the film reveals what her mind has censored shows Enid views repression as a kind of psychological VRA, protecting children from images they shouldn't see. She must have failed to catch *Deranged*, she thinks, because she's "rotten inside," as one harassing caller says. Her inner doubts now overwhelming, Enid casts around for someone or something to blame and lands on the video nasty. It offers her a solution to her sister's abduction that her dissociative amnesia cannot. Frederick North abducted her sister and forced her to make films under the name Alice Lee, she believes. To reunite her family, she must find and save her sister from the horror of making horror. In the film, Enid's search is a psychotic break. From a Marxist perspective, however, Enid's search expresses the social demand to take responsibility for events beyond one's control. While Thatcher might not have believed in society, Enid does. She feels an impersonal social pressure to take responsibility for society's failures, whether her sister's abduction, the violence of the amnesiac killer, or the supposed moral rot created by video nasties. Her parents' woeful looks, her painful meetings with her boss, the harassing phone calls, and the phalanx of journalists waiting outside her office—all these show Enid that society does exist, and it asks of her one thing: Take responsibility for everything.

No wonder she suffers a psychotic break.

It's tempting to read Enid's turn as proof that she censored Nina's murder. A psychoanalytic reading of the film might call Enid's break a return of the repressed; the censored violence she enacted on her sister erupts again at last. However, Enid's traumatic break is more clearly the result of her appropriation by work. We can see this in the film's construction. Visually, Enid's amnesia looks different from her censorship. Her flashbacks appear no different than the rest of the film, indicating their connection to the film's reality. By contrast, her censored perceptions during her desperate search for Alice look radically different. Enid is well aware of the accidental violence she causes after she visits Smart. When she comes to his home to find Alice, Smart tries to rape her. She knocks him back onto a sharp trophy and kills him. All this appears without visual markers of difference or censorship. Only when Enid arrives on the set of North's sequel to *Don't Go in the Church* does the image change. Certain North means to kill Alice, Enid poses as one of the film's actors and winds up in a scene with the Beastman. The film's aspect ratio then shifts to a matted 4:3, the ratio of the VHS tapes that Enid reviews, and its color palette takes on the saturated reds and greens of 1970s Italian horror. They film a scene in which the Beastman encourages Enid to kill her sister. Midway through, Enid snaps. Grabbing a prop ax, she kills the Beastman, and when North intercedes, him too. The image returns to a standard widescreen ratio as Enid comes out of her psychosis and filming stops. While this first shift is internally motivated—capturing the scene in the ratio in which it is filmed—it returns unmotivated after Enid chases a terrified Alice into the woods. Enid pleads that they are long-lost sisters but Alice convinces her that she's wrong. Enid then pulls an inexplicable item from her pocket, a VHS remote, and the image is suddenly crisscrossed with tracking distortion. Refusing to accept what she has done, Enid, in shades

Figure 7. In a censored ending, Enid smiles at the camera, her happy reunited family in the background. *Censor*, directed by Prano Bailey-Bond. Magnolia Pictures, 2021.

Figure 8. Alice breaks through Enid's psychic and visual censorship to scream for help. *Censor*, directed by Prano Bailey-Bond. Magnolia Pictures, 2021.

of Michael Haneke's *Funny Games* (1997), interpolates a new, censored ending.

At this point, the frame returns to its matted aspect ratio and the color palette shifts, this time to the sunny tones of a BBC sitcom. Now there is no doubt that Alice is Enid's sister. The two frolic in the woods, then drive happily to their parents' home. On the car radio, an announcer proclaims: "And what's fascinating is, now these issues have been dealt with properly, the video nasties have been eradicated completely. The crime rate in Britain has actually dropped to zero. It's just like we said, the streets of Britain are safe at last." The happy family reunites and wave to Enid from their garden, the mise-en-scène mimicking that of a family film Enid saw in a video rental store. For the film, this image captures Enid's dream of an untraumatized existence, but we might also say it shows a dream of meaningful work rewards (Figure 7). Enid has at last proven her worth to her family and to society by taking on the difficult but personally rewarding work of censorship.

Of course, this is all fantasy. Enid's censored ending suffers a series of tape stutters. Its sunny tones shift to pallid grey and reveal Alice screaming for help as Enid's parents stand aghast (Figure 8). Lost in her fantasy, Enid is unfazed. She waves at the camera, covered in blood, as the film skitters through video distortion to end on the blue screen of a stopped VHS machine. In the end, the machinery of censorship has absorbed Enid. In a system that demands and eludes personal control, she overcomes her doubts by allowing work to take her over completely. Yet what other options are there when the only solutions available are individual? Meaningful work squares the circle of the demand to be personally responsible and to be responsible for others. It allows someone like Enid to escape the fear that, as one angry caller tells her, "Nothing you ever do will be any good."

Saint Maud: Total Appropriation by Meaningful Work

Doubt drives appropriation in these films, but in none more so than Rose Glass's *Saint Maud*. Like *Censor*, it would be easy enough to read the doubts of the film's central character psychoanalytically. Katie, a nurse, is responsible for a patient's accidental death. In the aftermath, she finds God and marks her religious conversion by changing her name to Maud. Maud isn't a nurse, she's a carer, a position with lower status and worse pay. Her new work is inseparable from her new religious devotion, and the film presents both as forms of sexual sublimation. She tends to Amanda, a forty-nine-year-old dancer and choreographer dying of spinal cancer. Early in their relationship, Amanda asks Maud if she ever hears God. Maud replies that mostly she feels his presence as "warm" and "quivering." If those words imply Maud's relations with God have something in common with Teresa of Avila, her spontaneous orgasm afterward removes any doubt. The film encourages audiences to read Maud's sexualization of God as a displacement of her attraction to Amanda. Maud's work to save Amanda's soul allows her to experience pleasures she is unwilling to solicit or accept from Amanda directly. And it *is* work. Maud not only cares for and proselytizes Amanda, she performs a series of physical mortifications to prove to God her devotion to her work. Still, it's clear that Maud is jealous of Amanda's lover, Carol. She claims Carol is getting in the way of Amanda's salvation. Maud loses this religious-sexual outlet after Amanda makes a joke about her religion in front of her artist-friends and Maud slaps her. Sexually repressed and out of a job, Maud attempts a one-night stand that seems penitential even before it becomes rape. She returns to her bedsit after, only to have another ecstatic religious experience. In an echo of Tarkovsky's *The Mirror*, God raises Maud into the air, then speaks to her in Welsh in a garbled echo of her own voice. At last certain she has been called to save Amanda's soul, Maud sneaks back into her former client's home to find Amanda on her deathbed. Still she rejects Maud's religious advances, and Maud, certain that a demon has possessed Amanda, casts him out with a pair of scissors. Amanda's soul may be saved, but Maud's sexual object is now forever out of reach. Maud then performs one final act of sublimation. She heads to the beach, dowses herself in flammable liquid, and sets herself on fire, a martyr to desire.

    Marxism can help us draw out the links between Maud's religious sexuality and her work. In an interview, Glass explains that she made Maud a nurse because "the closest profession I could think of akin to a saintly figure in a contemporary setting was nurses and medical staff."[32] Characters bandy back and forth the idea that care work is saintly. Late in the film, Maud uses it to glean more information about Amanda from her new carer. She tells the unsuspecting woman, "I honestly have so much respect for anyone in the medical profession . . . I really think it's the most important thing you can do with your life. Almost." Maud can't resist a hedge. Religious work is her real work, or so she thinks. But the carer quickly agrees, and they strike up a conversation. "That's one of the things I love about the job," she says. "You find yourself quickly building these quite meaningful relationships." While *I Blame Society*, *The Power*, and *Censor* show how the demand to find meaningful work naturalizes capital's appropriation of workers' bodies and minds, *Saint Maud* helps us to see what people think meaningful work actually is. It builds relationships.

Yet if *Saint Maud* shows anything, it is that Maud's work hasn't created any relationships at all. Maud is, as Amanda says, "the loneliest girl I have ever seen." The film wants Maud's loneliness to be a psychological problem: her sexual repression kept her from building relationships. Maud's isolation, though, is deeply bound up with her work. Caring involves some medical supervision, but it largely consists of social reproduction work: cooking, cleaning, bathing, as well as moving and socializing with clients. Although Maud works for a private agency that services wealthy clients, in the United Kingdom most carers are employed as private subcontractors for local governments.[33] Prior to the 2010s, carers were accessible through the UK health care system. Following the 2008 financial crisis, however, neoliberal austerity policies privatized a substantial amount of care work. The result was a drop in wages, lower standards for credentialed workers, and an increase in sweated care work.[34] Privatization pushed caring to the bottom of the health care system's status hierarchies. As a job that requires no credentialing and minimal specialized skills, caring became viewed as a job that people take when they can't do anything else. This degradation of care workers' economic position has psychological effects. In her study of the UK care system, sociologist Emma Dowling emphasizes carers' social isolation. Working in the homes of patients, carers have little interaction with coworkers or supervisors; their socialization consists almost entirely of interactions with clients.[35] Although the film would like us to see Maud's loneliness as the result of her disturbed psyche, her situation underscores the real effects of care work's privatization in the UK. The work of caring is intensely lonely.

Maud's search for meaning in her work attempts to overcome this loneliness. What she wants are meaningful relationships in her work and her life, yet she finds them almost nowhere. Her one consequential relationship is with God, and the film makes clear it is a delusion. The film begins immediately after the accident that leads Maud to leave nursing. Traumatized, she sits in a corner with bloody hands, the patient dead across the room. Yet Maud isn't looking at the patient or her hands, but at a roach on the ceiling. The shot reverses to look down at Maud in a state of religious ecstasy. God is a cockroach. Still, Maud remains attached to her cockroach-God. It allows her to make the pain of work a calling and a pleasure. Love your work and you'll orgasm every time

Figure 9. Maud images her martyrdom as an angelic transformation. *Saint Maud*, directed by Rose Glass. A24 Films, 2019.

Figure 10. The final image shows the reality of Maud's sacrifice: burnt flesh, pain, and terror. *Saint Maud*, directed by Rose Glass. A24 Films, 2019.

you clock in! The promise of transcendent connection and pleasure that Maud finds in God reframes pain, both pain in work and pain outside of work, as the precondition for the pleasure and meaning she finds in work. At Amanda's, Maud uses her body to perform her devotion to God, mirroring the title of Amanda's book about dancing, *The Body Is a Stage*. She kneels on corn kernels, burns her hand, and walks on thumbtacks. Yet personal mortification isn't enough. Maud wants meaningful relationships with people and the only path to those relationships runs directly through God and pain. God turns pain into meaning. When he raises her up after her sexual assault, he praises her devotion. Pain and isolation are necessary trials, she learns. She can't have a meaningful relationship with God or anyone else without them.

Maud's attempts to overcome her loneliness reveal what the demand to love your work really means. When Maud immolates herself on the beach, she believes the dedication of her body to God connects her to others. All around her, people fall to their knees, converted at the sight of her devotion. At last, her work has created real meaningful relationships. And Maud isn't just connected to those she has saved. She also believes she has become more fully connected to God. She is now an angel (Figure 9). Yet the film's final moment attacks her fantasies of the rewards brought by meaningful work. Maud's suffering and sacrifice has not raised her in glorious light but left her writhing in fiery agony (Figure 10). No matter how much she loved her work, it did nothing but consume her.

3

NATURE HATES YOU
Psychedelic Eco-horror and Ecological Marxism

Hurricanes, blizzards, firestorms, "wet-bulb" heat waves, derechos, floods, supercell tornadoes—we would be crazy not to think that nature hates us. And why wouldn't it? Over the past two centuries, capitalism has destroyed much of the earth's biosphere, pillaged ecosystems, and pumped massive quantities of greenhouse gases into the atmosphere. In the 1980s, the earth sciences dubbed our time the Anthropocene, a geological era that is distinct from the preceding Holocene as a result of human activity. It took more than twenty years for the term to catch on, but now it's in the title of nearly every book about global warming, including some by Marxists.[1] There's a problem with the Anthropocene, though. It suggests these climate catastrophes are the fault of humanity writ large. It's right there in the name, *Anthropo*-cene. But the problem isn't humanity; it's capitalism. As environmental humanities scholars Christophe Bonneuil and Jean-Baptiste Fressoz note, "we no longer have an undifferentiated 'anthropos,' but rather historical systems of domination that each organize in a distinct fashion flows of matter, energy, commodities, and capitals on a global scale."[2] Marxist environmental historian and geographer Jason W. Moore offers a more suitable name for our era, the Capitalocene. As Moore explains, the Capitalocene isn't defined by undifferentiated human activity but "by relations privileging the endless accumulation of capital."[3]

What's in a name, though? Either way, it seems, we're cooked. The U.S. government's Fifth National Climate Assessment, released in late 2023, declared "current adaptation efforts and investments are insufficient to reduce today's climate-related risks and keep pace with future changes."[4] The problem's scope seems so immense and resistant to human intervention that many in the global North have fallen prey to what Andreas Malm calls "climate fatalism," a way of thinking that finds it "easier . . . to imagine learning to die than learning to fight."[5] Yet even the report's authors note hopefully that we have many possible climate mitigation interventions. They emphasize, "the future is largely in human hands."[6] And here we see what's in a name. As long as we view the climate crisis as the result of simple human activity, we confront a seemingly intractable problem of coordinating individual action. It's no mistake that throughout the global North, people are encouraged to focus on individual actions like recycling and fossil fuel usage, what is often described as a person's "carbon footprint." As Marxist environmental geographer Matthew T. Huber explains, oil companies created the idea of the carbon footprint to minimize discussion of their liability. Huber rightly argues that the environmental problems created by personal consumption begin with what gets produced. "For everything we consume," Huber writes, "there is someone else in the capitalist class who is profiting from our consumption."[7] Feeling guilty about your individual carbon emissions does nothing to change the material conditions that produce those emissions. That's not to say changes in personal consumption won't be necessary to address the climate crises. As we'll see, Marxism has long understood that an eco-socialist future demands changes in production and consumption.[8] But recognizing production's role in carbon emissions shows us where change really needs to start. That's why how we name our era matters. If we want to find a future out of the frying pan, we need to know how we got on the fire.[9]

To say that climate change is humanity's fault, then, is capitalism's deadliest piece of common sense. This is perhaps why popular culture has very little to say about it. For critic and novelist Amitav Ghosh, fiction hasn't engaged with climate change because most of its representational strategies aren't up to the task. For Ghosh, this is a problem about how realist stories are told. Realist tales are tales of everyday life, scaled to human experience in terms of space and time. Global warming's events, however, are outside the everyday and at scales beyond the human, some much larger and others much smaller. According to Ghosh, only speculative genres—science fiction, fantasy, and horror—have managed to engage with it at all. Although Ghosh doesn't discuss film, it offers some of the most striking examples of popular culture about climate. E. Ann

Kaplan describes the emergence of a new speculative film genre about climate change in the 2000s, what she terms "pretrauma climate cinema." For Kaplan, this new genre isn't geared toward representing global warming at varied scales or experiences outside the everyday. Instead, it aims to help audiences grapple with "the uncertainty of human futurity."[10] In Kaplan's account, pretrauma climate cinema offers audiences generic forms to confront losses they know are coming—losses of memory, of history, and of the future itself.

Pretrauma climate cinema, then, reflects Fredric Jameson's memorable claim that "it is easier to imagine the end of the world than to imagine the end of capitalism."[11] For Jameson, this is less a question of climate than of what he sees as a particular era of capitalist production, postmodernity. Postmodernity makes it impossible to imagine the end of capitalism because it has displaced revolutionary political ideas about the future with recycled versions of the past. When a culture can only imagine the future as a repetition of what's already happened, the idea of the future itself withers. "By transforming the past into visual mirages, stereotypes, or texts," Jameson explains, postmodernism "effectively abolishes any practical sense of the future and of the collective project, thereby abandoning the thinking of future change to fantasies of sheer catastrophe and inexplicable cataclysm."[12] That holds true for the science fiction films that Kaplan examines, from the spectacles of mass disaster in Roland Emmerich's big-budget disaster films *The Day after Tomorrow* (2004) and *2012* (2009), to the personal cataclysms of *Take Shelter* (2011) and *The Road* (2009). From a Marxist perspective, then, the feeling of lost futurity that Kaplan locates in pretrauma climate cinema is inextricable from the ways that capitalism itself blocks our ability to imagine other kinds of collective futures.

Earlier waves of eco-horror were less about feelings of the future's loss than about what Ghosh calls "the environmental uncanny."[13] This Freudian return of the ecological repressed consists of two kinds of uncanniness: one reveals humanity's responsibility for the biosphere's degradation, and the other discloses previously unnoticed "nonhuman forces and beings," from greenhouse gases to Earth's manifold forms of life.[14] The environmental uncanny deeply marks 2000s eco-horrors like Larry Fessenden's *The Last Winter* (2006) and M. Night Shyamalan's *The Happening* (2008). Uncanny figures represent climate change violently erupting into everyday life, and force characters and audiences alike to recognize humanity's culpability for climate change, as well as its effects on nonhuman beings. The environmental uncanny remains a persistent feature of cautionary eco-horrors like *Harbinger* (2015) and *Antlers* (2021), where humanity's environmental depredations—fracking and mountaintop-removal mining respectively—unleash vengeful spirits.

However, an emerging subgenre of eco-horror puts the feeling of lost futurity at its center. These films use the environmental uncanny, but they resist the urge to make it a single localizable figure like the wendigo moose of *The Last Winter* or *Antlers*. Their use of a diffuse figure for the environment also differs from *The Happening* in their focus on psychedelic experience. One low-budget horror provides a bridge between these approaches. *Unearth* (2020) tells the story of a cash-strapped farmer who sees no future in farming or his small community. He leases his land to a fracking company, hoping it will provide enough money to get his family out. It doesn't. Instead, the company pollutes his land and unleashes a long-dormant fungus that infects his family and neighbors, filling them with spores and violent hallucinations. In the end, the only survivor is a woman who wanted only to leave her dead town. Instead, the fungus has trapped her on the farm to force her to send its spores into the world along with her meager crops. The psychedelic eco-horrors discussed in this chapter approach climate change by combining this diffuse fungal figure with the feeling of lost futurity. The South African film *Gaia* (2021) and the British *In the Earth* (2021) both show fungal worshippers communicating with nature about the terrors of the Capitalocene through psychedelic experience. In *Gaia*, they ask the fungus to cleanse the earth by destroying humanity, while the worshippers of *In the Earth* try to negotiate their way out of the coming crisis. The American film *She Dies Tomorrow* (2020) resists the lure of the environmental uncanny entirely to focus instead on the feeling of lost futurity. A metaphor for humanity's lost future, the film is about a virus that infects people with the certainty they will die tomorrow, and communicates this coming end through psychedelic epiphanies. As a subgenre, psychedelic eco-horror is held together by its focus on hallucinogenic experience to convey the terrors of climate change and the feeling of lost futurity. To understand what its figures and feelings mean, we need to turn first to ecological Marxism's analysis of capitalism's relation to the biosphere.

Appropriation and Ecological Marxism

Marxism has a term for what capitalism does to nature: *appropriation*. As we've seen, the concept entered contemporary discussions through feminist social reproduction theory. Critics like Claudia von Werlhof, Maria Mies, Veronika Bennholdt-Thomsen, and Silvia Federici used appropriation to rebut claims that capital couldn't exploit women's reproductive labor because it didn't pay them a wage. They argued that women's unpaid reproductive labor revealed something Marxists had long missed: Capitalism relies on the appropriation of labor and resources as much, if not more, than on the exploitation of wage labor. Beginning from the social insistence that women's reproductive labor was innate, they revealed that capitalism relies on constructed ideas of nature and naturalness to take what it likes without recompense. As Werlhof explains, "'Nature' is cheap, even free. It demands no wage for its labor and no price for its products. It has no needs and does not have to be renewed. It is 'forced nature,' subject to forced exploitation."[15] Capitalism made the world and its people into nature and natural beings, they argue, so that it could rob the earth, and kill, enslave, or dominate who- or whatever it classified as nonhuman. In essence, social reproduction theory finds within capitalism the subjugation of nature, genocidal settler colonialism, imperialist extraction of resources, chattel slavery, racialization, patriarchy, and misogyny to show that modernity's violence is inseparable from capitalism.[16] It *is* capitalism.

To ground this understanding of appropriation in Marxist analysis, social reproduction theorists returned to Marx's account of *ursprünglich Akkumulation*, original or primitive accumulation. That's the one section of *Capital* where Marx privileges violence over impersonal market relations. For Marx, original accumulation reveals, as William Clare Roberts explains, "that capitalism has its origins in the opportunistic exploitation of the new forms of freedom created by acts of violence and theft."[17] In other words, original accumulation precedes the development of capitalist production. Nascent capitalists used violence to appropriate the wealth they needed to fund commodity production and to dispossess people from the land so that they would have to sell their labor-power. For many readers of Marx, original accumulation suggested that once commodity production became hegemonic, capitalism no longer relied on violence. That was perhaps urged on by the typical English translation of *ursprünglich Akkumulation* as "primitive" accumulation. Following Immanuel Wallerstein's work on world-systems theory, however, social reproduction theorists refute the idea that original accumulation took place only before capitalist production. Appropriation and dispossession are central features of the capitalist world-system, not violent aberrations displaced by a bloodless system of wage exploitation.[18] The racialization of space, the violence of settler colonialism and imperialism, the use of racialization and gender norms to differentiate the workforce, and the destructive appropriation of a biosphere reduced to the status of resource are as much a part of capitalism as exploitation.

The ecological thought of later Marxists followed the lead of these eco-feminists, though they are often uncited. Marxist geographer David Harvey came to similar conclusions when he grappled with the problem of capital's overaccumulation—that is, when capitalists can't find profitable ways to invest the surpluses they've accumulated. Overaccumulation is a persistent concern for an era in which the wealthy maintain enormous capital reserves. Through his work on uneven development and neoliberalism, Harvey argues that capitalists create new areas of profitable investment by turning to the processes of *ursprünglich Akkumulation*. In *The New Imperialism*, Harvey notes that "all the features of primitive accumulation that Marx mentions have remained powerfully present within capitalism's historical geography."[19] His account of what original accumulation does is a laundry list of activities central to neoliberalism:

> the commodification and privatization of land and the forceful expulsion of peasant populations; the conversion of various forms of property rights (common, collective, state, etc.) into exclusive property rights; the suppression of rights to the commons; the commodification of labor power and the suppression of alternative (indigenous) forms of production and consumption; colonial, neo-colonial, and imperial processes of appropriation of assets (including natural resources); the monetization of exchange and taxation, particularly of land; the slave trade; and usury, the national debt, and ultimately the credit system as a radical means of primitive accumulation.[20]

Harvey rechristens original accumulation's appropriation of labor and resources "accumulation by dispossession," a term we will encounter again when we discuss capitalism's uneven development in the next chapter.[21] Whether original accumulation or accumulation by dispossession, its central function for capitalism is the appropriation of what Jason W. Moore calls "the four cheaps": "unpaid labor-power, food, energy, and raw materials."[22] As Harvey puts it, "What accumulation by dispossession does is to release a set of assets (including labor power) at very low (and in some instances zero) cost. Over-accumulated capital can seize hold of such assets and immediately turn them to profitable use."[23] Taken alongside social reproduction theory, Harvey's insight hammers home a crucial point. Appropriation and dispossession aren't phenomena on capitalism's periphery. The global North preys on the global South's resources, but capital's predations can occur in the North as well. Whenever and wherever capital can no longer find profitable investment, it will leap about the globe in what Neil Smith calls "the 'seesaw' movement of capital,"[24] flitting from place to place in search of labor, food, energy, and raw materials it can steal. What contemporary Marxism shows us, then, is that capitalism reduces the world to a set of resources it can appropriate and recreates this reduction whenever it finds itself short of resources to plunder.

Marx himself has long had a bad reputation as a proponent of industrialization and modernization. However, John Bellamy Foster, Paul Burkett, and Kohei Saito have excavated the ways in which Marx's thought is in fact fundamentally ecological. Recent studies of Marx's late work reframe his critique of political economy as centered around a central purpose: to reveal the dangers that capitalism poses to the continued production and reproduction of life on Earth. In *Capital*, Marx describes how capitalism reorders what he calls *Stoffwechsel*, the "metabolic interaction" between humanity and the biosphere, and introduces a second, social metabolism, that robs the earth of its resources.[25] As Foster first analyzed, Marx drew this insight from the work of German chemist Justus von Liebig on the agricultural depletion of soil nutrients.[26] Liebig's research led Marx to the conclusion that "all progress in capitalistic agriculture is a progress in the art, not only of robbing the laborer, but of robbing the soil; all progress in increasing the fertility of the soil for a given time, is a progress towards ruining the lasting sources of that fertility."[27] The pairing of labor and soil matters. As Paul Burkett notes, it's crucial to the production of surplus value. "The natural basis of surplus value," Burkett explains, "is more than just an initial condition of capitalist production; it is an ongoing determinant of the *amount* of surplus value, hence of the rate of capital accumulation."[28]

Capitalism's robbery of the soil opens what Foster famously termed "a 'rift' in the 'metabolic interaction between man and the earth.'"[29] Liebig's work helped Marx reframe as a metabolic rift the division of the country and the city, the foundational example of uneven development that he and Engels offered in *The German Ideology*. Intensive agriculture in the country transfers soil nutrients to the city, and the waste it produces in the city does not return nutrients to the productive ecological system but to another where it becomes pollution.[30] This is why, in *Capital* 3, Marx decries "colossal wastage in the capitalist economy" with "the excrement produced by 4 1/2 million people [in London]."[31] Such waste is evidence of capitalism's inability to control the metabolic rifts it creates or the destruction it causes. On this point, Marx could not be clearer: "Capitalist production, therefore, only develops techniques and the degree of combination of the social process of production by simultaneously undermining [*untergräbt*] the original sources of all wealth—the soil and the worker."[32]

Drawing on Marx's late work on ecology and primitive communism, Kohei Saito distinguishes three forms of metabolic rifts in Marx's thought: capitalism's disruption of nature's metabolism, its creation of rifts by transporting materials across space, and its use of resources at a far greater pace than nature produces them.[33] We can locate all three in Marx's example of London's excrement problem: the sapping of nutrients by intensive agriculture, the transport of those nutrients from the country to the city where they remain, and the depletion of the soil by planting in cycles that do not allow the cyclical production of more nutrients. To the extent that capitalism recognizes its metabolic rifts, it does so in the name of increased production. Saito identifies three strategies capital uses to shift the effects of its metabolic rifts: technological innovations like chemical fertilizers can redress its disruptions of local ecosystems; uneven development can offload the negative effects of metabolic rifts onto those with less political or economic power (e.g., the urban poor, the global South); and capital can simply try to outrun the effects of its appropriations, stealing resources faster than the effects of its robbery can be felt.[34] No wonder capitalism is always on the hunt for what Jason W. Moore calls "commodity frontiers."[35] It needs a constant supply of untapped resources to appropriate.

This analysis of capitalism's metabolic rifts reveals what eco-feminists first asserted, a deep and abiding link between ecological degradation, white settler colonialism, and imperialism. As we'll discuss more fully in the next chapter, capitalism is always racial capitalism. It not only relies on the extraction of surplus labor in production but on the appropriation of land, labor, energy, and raw materials, often via settler colonialism and imperialism and their attendant racializations of space and spatializations of race. That's certainly clear in the way the extraction economy has made regions of Earth into places where resources can be extracted, and people dehumanized and subjected to the violence of capitalism or of states seeking to preserve capital's power. It's no mistake that racial capital relies on fossil fuels. As Andreas Malm shows, in the nineteenth century, capital went looking for a power source that it could not only appropriate and commodify but use to crush worker power.[36] Over the course of the next two hundred years, what Malm calls fossil capital has brutalized the planet and its workers, swamping us with greenhouse gases and robbing and degrading the systems that would otherwise act as carbon sinks like oceans, forests, and the soil. It has tried to shift the brunt of the climate crisis onto the global South, hoping that technology can mitigate its effects on the wealthiest nations and push the worst off into someone else's future. Ecological Marxism tells us these are false hopes. If we mean to end racial capitalism's destruction of the biosphere, we must check its limitless appetite for unpaid land, labor, energy, and resources.

Marx understood this well. His account of freedom, often quoted but seldom understood, hinges on a renewed vision of humanity's metabolic relations with nature. Freedom in the realm of necessity, Marx explains,

> can consist only in this, that socialized man, the associated producers, govern the human metabolism with nature in a rational way, bringing it under their collective control instead of being dominated by it as blind power; accomplishing it with the least expenditure of energy and

in conditions most worthy and appropriate for their human nature. But this remains a realm of necessity. The true realm of freedom, the development of human powers as an end in itself, begins beyond it, though it can only flourish with this realm of necessity as its basis.[37]

This isn't a plea for Promethean control over nature but for a rational human metabolic relation with nature, one that demands "the least expenditure of energy and in conditions most worthy and appropriate for their human nature." Only an eco-socialism that respects these limits will allow us to discover freedom beyond necessity and the horrors of capitalism's metabolic rifts.

Gaia and *In the Earth*: Fungal Capital

The metabolic rift is crucial for psychedelic eco-horror. It's important, then, to consider why *Gaia* and *In the Earth* both rely on the same type of organism for the environmental uncanny: fungi. Fungi don't open metabolic rifts but close them. Over the last two decades, studies of mycoremediation, the use of fungi to decontaminate polluted environments, have shown fungi's capacity to remove a variety of pollutants, from chemicals and heavy metals to plastics and radiation.[38] Yet these films focus less on fungi's potential for remediation than on the discovery that trees exchange nutrients through underground mycorrhizal networks, a process that some scientists argue is a form of communication.[39] Popular culture has taken this idea up by representing fungi as nature's connective cognitive tissue. One character of *In the Earth* responds to an account of the forest's mycorrhizal mat by saying it "sounds like a brain." The other replies, "Yeah, I suppose it is." *Gaia* and *In the Earth* use these ideas of fungi to represent it as a sort of reparative natural consciousness.

Horror has long seen fungi's powers of appropriation as a source of terror, rather than salvation. Fungi are uncanny because of the way they eat. They aren't plants and don't make their own food through photosynthesis. Like animals, they're heterotrophic: They eat what they don't produce. But they aren't animals either. They're immobile like plants, so they have to eat what comes to them, and they don't have stomachs or other interior organs for digestion, so they digest their food outside their bodies using secreted enzymes and absorb the released nutrients through mycelia, underground webs of hyphae. In the past, horror used fungal appropriation to intimate the horrors of colonization. In "The Fall of the House of Usher," Edgar Allan Poe places a glowing fungus in the foundation of the titular house to suggest the family, house, and land are held together through the fungus's unnatural cohering of life, and in "The Voice in the Night" by William Hope Hodgson, a ravenous fungus colonizes all it touches, including an unfortunate shipwrecked couple.[40] In twenty-first-century weird fiction, fungus became an explicit metaphor for settler colonialism and capitalism's uneven development, from Jeff Vandermeer's *Ambergris* trilogy, where conflicts between humans and fungal creatures capture the genocidal nature of America's settler colonial project, to Silvia Moreno-Garcia's postcolonial *Mexican Gothic*, where a house–turned–mycelium memory network serves as a metaphor of Mexico's long history of exploitation by Western imperial interests.[41]

This horror of appropriation not only gives fungi a metaphorical resonance with capitalism's operations. It also points toward its role in eco-horror's critical representations of capitalism's future. In her work on matsutake mushrooms, anthropologist Anna Lowenhaupt Tsing explores their ability to describe capitalism not as a narrative of progress but one of political, economic, and environmental apocalypse. As Tsing writes, their "willingness to emerge in blasted landscapes allows us to explore the ruin that has become our collective home."[42] That certainly describes their role in *Gaia* and *In the Earth*, and not only because fungi seem like the last power to emerge out of a nature sapped by human interference. Like capitalism, fungi in these films are engaged in a devastating process of appropriation. The saprotrophic, which decomposes what it consumes, mirrors capitalism's unending drive for accumulation; the parasitic, which lives off its hosts, mirrors its vampiric exploitation of living labor; and the mycorrhizal, which creates networks in symbiosis with other plants to exchange nutrients and aid ecological communication, mirrors its status as an unseen world-system. The fungi of these films can be reparative counterpowers because they're endophytic—they appropriate in all these forms—but this also makes them mirrors of capitalism for its appropriation and colonization of life itself.

These eco-horrors draw from two genres: the psychedelic film and the cult film. A loose genre, the psychedelic film is decided not so much by a recognizable set of elements and structures as, in Harry M. Benshoff's words, by "the ongoing discussion and experience of them within a community of drug-using cineastes."[43] Reception and distribution may explain how films as disparate as *2001: A Space Odyssey* (1968), *Alice in Wonderland* (1951), *El Topo* (1970), and *The Wicker Man* (1973) wind up in a single genre. Still, Benshoff notes, psychedelic films share a few formal elements: a lack of narrative (or lack of emphasis on narrative), a focus on visuals potentially enhanced by ingesting psychedelic substances (e.g., abstract or striking uses of color and movement), and, as Benshoff puts it, "the use of the cinematic apparatus to suggest, create, or re-create for the spectator the experience of expanded vision and/or insight."[44] To represent altered states of consciousness, psychedelic eco-horrors rely on psychedelic film's saturated colors and color effects, its visual distortions, strobing lights and afterimages, and time effects, including slow motion, freeze frames, fast cutting, and rapid montage.[45] These experiences emphasize the permeability of the human and nonhuman, connecting characters not only to one another and the web of life but to another genre, the cult film. Barry Keith Grant defines cult films by their need to be "transgressive *and* recuperative, in other words, to reclaim that which they seem to violate."[46] Grant's chief example, Romero's *Night of the Living Dead*, transgresses by satirizing normality—for instance, the dysfunctional nuclear family hiding in the basement—and recuperating otherness—for instance, its uninhibited feasting zombies. Psychedelic eco-horrors rely on a similar dual operation of transgression and recuperation, transgressing the norms of individuality and recuperating the terrors that come from this loss of self as beautiful revelations of the web of life. The resulting films offer a distinctly psychedelic environmental uncanny, one that does not demand audiences simply recognize the existence of nonhuman forces and beings but that they feel their union with them by contemplating fungal beings and mind-bending images. Psychedelic eco-horror means to convey what we might call, from a Marxist perspective, an urge to bridge the metabolic rift by extracting from the terrifying loss of self and of human futurity pleasurable images of a reimagined nature.

No film makes the tension between fungal reparation and appropriation clearer than Jaco Bouwer's *Gaia*. Its title echoes James Lovelock's now-refuted "Gaia hypothesis," the theory that "life on Earth actively keeps the surface conditions always favorable for whatever is the contemporary ensemble of organisms."[47] What would happen, *Gaia* asks, if the Earth realized the best way to maintain surface conditions favorable for life was to eliminate humanity altogether. The film treats this not as a contest between capital and nature but between industrial society and a habitable planet. Its fungus is a diffuse natural consciousness that runs through the South African Tsitsikamma forest and communicates through psychedelic mushrooms that grow at the center of its power, a dead tree that births mushrooms from a vaginal hollow. For its two white Afrikaner worshippers, Barend and his son Stefan, the fungus is wife and mother. It consumed Barend's wife when they first arrived in the forest. Barend preaches a form of Earth-supremacy, denouncing what modernity has done to the Earth. He and his son follow an extreme form of back-to-the-land ideology, living off the land in an abandoned forest cabin and wearing only homespun cloth. He worships the fungus in the hopes it will cleanse the Earth of humanity, and, as he says, "bring an end to the Anthropocene."

Gaia, then, not only solicits capitalism's powers of appropriation; it forces us to confront the connections between capitalism, climate change, and far-right ecologism, aka ecofascism. The far right has long had what Sam Moore and Alex Roberts call "an ambivalence toward capitalism."[48] As they explain,

> it is the source of much that fascism finds appalling, and yet, as the real motor of the domination that fascism affirms, it cannot be entirely rejected. Fascism responds to this ambivalence with a normative racial vitalism: the dominance that capitalism affords is affirmed and naturalized while at the same time its destructiveness towards aspects of nature (and the social relations embedded in nature) is criticized.[49]

This ambivalence allows far-right ecologism to do precisely what Barend does: decry neoliberalism and environmental destruction. Unstated by Barend but running throughout far-right ecology is an important corollary: global warming's catastrophic effects on the global South are the result of "racialized ineptitude."[50] For far-right ecological thought, the solutions to the political-economic impasses of contemporary capitalism are an extolling of nature as fundamentally good and a reassertion of racialized hierarchies. Barend exemplifies elements that Janet Biehl and Peter Staudenmaier enumerate in their definition of ecofascism: "the supremacy of the 'Earth' over people; 'feelings' and intuition at the expense of reason; and a crude sociobiologistic and even Malthusian biologism."[51]

Gaia juxtaposes Barend's endorsement of the Earth's supremacy and crude sociobiologism with a woman of color's endorsement of liberal modernity. As one of two rangers surveying the forest, Gabi seeks refuge in Barend's cabin after she injures her foot in one of his hunting traps. If the film isn't explicit in Barend's white supremacy, his arguments with Gabi about modernity and Earth supremacy split these positions along racialized lines. Barend's fascistic bent is reinforced by the ways the fungus expresses a sort of blood-and-soil ideology. It's relentless in its use of blood to tie characters to the soil. When the three fight off one of its violent mushroom-headed creatures, Gabi winds up coated in spore-tainted blood. The fungus colonizes her dreams before sprouting from her arms. Barend and Stefan ward off its depredations by offering it sacrifices. In return, it gives them mushrooms to cure its infection. Stefan steals one to treat Gabi. We see what would have happened if he hadn't by witnessing what happens to Gabi's boss, Winston. He's been captured and colonized, made into a horrifying yet picturesque fungal bouquet.[52] The film's psychedelic sequences reinforce these images of blood and soil. To convince Gabi that he's right, Barend gives her one of the fungus's psychedelic mushrooms. Her ensuing trip focuses on becoming one with the Earth. Nude, she melts into and out of it, has sex with Stefan, and watches Barend have sex with the Earth itself. At last, she sees Stefan with an arrow through his head, blood dripping out of his mouth and onto the soil below. Barend has the same vision. The fungus, he says, wants him to sacrifice his son. The film reframes this Biblical parallel to the story of Abraham and Isaac as a sacrifice of the future to the present, one that its racialized dynamics suggest is more blood for the soil. Gabi stops Barend from sacrificing Stefan, and Barend himself winds up subject to the fungus's colonization. While *Gaia* briefly gestures toward a pluralist happy state of nature with Gabi and Stefan living together in the woods, the fungus ultimately claims her too, and Stefan then heads out into the world to begin its work remediating the Earth from humanity.

Gaia wants us to view Barend's ecofascist ideas critically, yet the film's aesthetics and gender hierarchies suggest a lingering fascination with fascistic thinking. Early on, Barend insists that infection turns humans into the violent mushroom-headed creatures that roam the forest. However, the two women the fungus infects escape this fate and become instead part of the landscape, first Stefan's mother by the vaginal tree and then Gabi by the forest floor. As ecofeminists know, the alignment of the feminine and the land is one of capitalism's most persistent ideas. Claudia von Werlhof puts it most clearly. In capitalism, Welhof writes, women are "the only people on earth who *always under all circumstances* count as 'nature.'"[53] *Gaia* hammers the point home in its opening and closing sequences. The film begins with a God's-eye drone shot of the forest that reduces the canopy to the texture of lichen. The camera slowly tips over to place the lichen-foliage above and the blue sky below. This inverted image dissolves into a drone shot inside the forest canopy as the camera glides over a riverbed. When the drone approaches a canoe, Gabi looks up and the camera follows her, ending the inversion. The film's closing images reframe this opening inversion to suggest that what we've seen—Gabi's story—inverts nature's true dominion. Only by returning nature to its proper role, the film implies, can the metabolic rift be closed, a salvation available only through the picturesque subjugation of women as landscape. And the film makes this clear through a visual rhyme. When Gabi expires, the overhead shot of her body colonized by fungi dissolves to the opening God's-eye shot of the forest canopy (Figure 11). The film's invasive fungus means to provide an uncanny psychedelic figure able to repair capitalism's metabolic rifts, but its representation of the fungus suggests it succeeds only because it is a more accomplished version of capitalism. The fungus's indifference to the effects of its appropriations pulls whatever gets in its way—the forest, human beings, whatever—into its diffuse impersonal network. *Gaia* may aim to imagine a natural agency able to take on humanity's depredations, but what it produces is a counter-image to capitalism, one that aims to absorb humanity, not free it.

Ben Wheatley's *In the Earth* (2021) offers a useful contrast. In Wheatley's film, the fungal emphasizes humanity's ability to shape its natural and political economic environment. *In the Earth* was released the same year as *Gaia* and by the same company, Neon. It also includes many of the same elements: an uncanny fungus, fungal infection, religious fervor, the racial division of the cast, and foot injuries. However, the fungal worshippers of Wheatley's film aren't back-to-the-landers, but a scientist

Figure 11. An overhead shot of Gabi becoming the forest floor after her colonization by fungus. *Gaia*, directed by Jaco Bouwer. Neon, 2021.

studying mycorrhizal networks, Dr. Wendel, and her deranged ex-husband, Zach. Thinking Wendel is lost in the woods, her friend and colleague Martin goes to find her, guided by a ranger, Alma. Unlike *Gaia*, the real antagonist of *In the Earth* isn't fungal. It's human. To understand this difference, we need to contemplate an important rift in historical experience between these two films. Bouwer wrote and began filming *Gaia* before the Covid-19 pandemic. Wheatley made *In the Earth* during the pandemic and made it part of his story.[54] In an interview, he explained, "It's happening now, and I find it weird that the movies wouldn't acknowledge what's happened."[55] Wheatley's characters mask, test, and decontaminate, and it isn't always clear where filming precautions end and fiction begins (Figure 12). When read from a Marxist perspective, the pandemic reshapes the film's fungal themes. Characters discuss the need to maintain a "sterile" environment to protect humans from the pandemic and the delicate forest ecosystem from human contamination. These characters aren't Martin or Alma, both played by people of color. The language of contamination comes from the film's deranged white researchers–cum–forest-pagans. Fears of contamination drive Wendel and Zach into violence and madness.

Figure 12. Martin gets decontaminated before entering the forest. *In the Earth*, directed by Ben Wheatley. Neon, 2021.

Like *Gaia*, then, *In the Earth* conjures questions of ecofascism, here keyed not to South African culture but to the rise of the far right in Britain. In recent British literature, writers such as M. John Harrison and Sarah Moss have created stories in which fantasies of ancient Britain are inseparable from regressive social and political ideas. Harrison's Lovecraftian fish people in *The Sunken Land Begins to Rise Again* and Moss's tale of an abusive father obsessed with ancient Britons in *Ghost Wall* both offer isolated characters, natural settings, and a descent into irrational violence as characters try to reclaim an imagined lost past.[56] Since its inception in the twentieth century, fascism has relied on claims to a lost origin. Theodor Adorno spent much of his life unraveling this focus. To that end, in *Negative Dialectics*, Adorno deconstructs Karl Kraus's aphorism, "Origin is the goal." Adorno writes, "the goal is not to be recovered in the origin, in the phantasm of a good nature, but rather origin devolves from the goal; it is only from the goal itself that origin is constituted."[57] As we'll see in the next chapter, this search for origin is inseparable from racial capitalism's drive to create pure, homogenous spaces. The demand for a pure origin produces it as an idea, not vice versa.

In the Earth, then, shows us how environmental degradation can activate regressive ideologies as capital strives to maintain its accumulation. One of Cedric Robinson's key insights about racial capitalism is that it uses older ideologies to structure exploitation and social relations.[58]

The turn to British folklore and pagan ritual in the film are one way to get at how racial capitalism adapts to new political and material exigencies. As we see in the film, capitalism, increasingly deranged by climate change, will return to the violent repressions of racism and empire. Wendel has come to the forest to communicate with its mycorrhizal mat. When she discovers its densest region lies directly beneath an ancient Celtic standing stone, she interprets local folklore about a necromancer, Parnag Fegg, as a personification of the mat. While neither Alma nor Martin takes the idea seriously, Wendel does. Desperate to open communications with the mat, she and Zach turn to Celtic human-sacrifice rituals. Perhaps it will talk if they offer up Martin and Alma, the two people of color.

Taken as a whole, then, the cast's racial division, the white characters' demands for a space free from contamination, and Wendel and Zach's adopting of folk religion and human sacrifice suggest another ecofascist story, one about a return to origins. Unsurprisingly, Dr. Wendel is conducting her research for "the Fashdale Institute." This is why, for all its folk horror gestures, *In the Earth* is more circumspect than *Gaia* about the possibility of communication with nonhuman forces and beings. Wendel believes climate change is so pressing that the forest must want to communicate with humanity, if only to protect itself. Because she has translated the name "Parnag Fegg" from the local dialect as *light* and *sound*, she experiments with light and sound equipment to establish communication, triggering strobing lights and feedback loops from the vibrations of the trees. The results are some of the film's most hallucinatory sequences, filled with strobing lights, tracers, and tricks with persistence of vision. Zach's approach is more pagan, relying on trippy images, patternmaking, and offerings (Figure 13). For much of the film, Wendel pretends she doesn't accept Zach's paganism. She tells Martin, "Zach is trying to make meaning where there isn't any. It's a psychological problem with humans. [. . .] Zach seems to think he can communicate with nature through art and worship. It's idolatry." The film seems to agree. Wendel and Zach are represented as deranged and nothing in the film's psychedelia supports ecofascist appeals to feelings and intuitions about nature. While characters are overwhelmed by the mat's spores, they never communicate with the mat itself. At one point, Zach wanders aimless in a hallucinatory daze, asking the forest, "What do you want?

Figure 13. Zach creates images to worship Parnag Fegg, here by posing Martin, Alma, and himself in white robes and covering their eyes with mirrors. *In the Earth*, directed by Ben Wheatley. Neon, 2021.

I'll give you whatever you want. Just tell me." Later in the film, Alma is similarly overcome, but the mat tells her nothing. The experience suggests the mat is indifferent to human existence. It is. She is. At best, they encounter one another. That's it.

When we read this film from a Marxist perspective, these frustrated attempts to communicate with nature help us to see that global warming won't cause capitalism to stop or spin off into reckless incoherence. Wendel's research shows that capitalism hopes climate change will be a mere labor dispute with the Earth. One of her goals in communicating with the mycorrhizal network, she explains, is to increase crop yields. When capital can no longer rob nature, it will try to negotiate with it like a recalcitrant workforce. After all, labor discipline and scientific and technological innovations have reclaimed labor productivity before. However, *In the Earth* adroitly shows that such negotiations won't work. What they will do, however, is encourage murderous fantasies of a purified nature, and as the film shows, people of color will be the first to suffer. Zach systematically tortures Martin, chopping off his toes with an axe, and when Martin escapes to the supposed safety of Wendel's camp, she repeats the torture by cauterizing his wound with a heated iron. Wendel and Zach rationalize their cruelty using the language of care. There's never enough time to get to a hospital, they say. Violence is his only hope. Alma throws this claim back at Zach in the film's conclusion.

Figure 14. Zach toys with a tent spike in his eye while he demands Alma take him to the hospital. *In the Earth*, directed by Ben Wheatley. Neon, 2021.

When he attacks her, she drives a tent spike into his eye. Zach doesn't keel over, though. He futzes with the spike for a moment, then demands Alma take him to the hospital (Figure 14). It's easy to get to! For ecofascists, suffering is for people of color, and the benefits of science and technology for white environmentalists.[59] *In the Earth* refuses this division (Alma drives the spike into his brain). Unlike the reparative fungus of *Gaia*, the forest mycorrhizal mat of *In the Earth* suggests that the biosphere has no representatives to negotiate with. The problems of the Capitalocene won't be solved through racialized hierarchies or an aestheticization of nature, and psychedelic attempts to encourage recognition of ecological solidarity will be no substitute for human action.

She Dies Tomorrow: No Future or Deaccumulation?

Unlike *Gaia* and *In the Earth*, Amy Seimetz's *She Dies Tomorrow* contains no uncanny fungi. Instead, its characters become infected by death's certainty, not in some unknown future but soon. Very, very soon. The film never mentions climate change, but its tale of individuals experiencing the loss of their future clearly aims at the loss of humanity's future. As one character exclaims in the opening sequence, "We had a time, but it's over." Like the films that Kaplan classifies as pretrauma climate cinema, *She Dies Tomorrow* is about the feeling of lost futurity and what will remain after humanity. The film's psychedelia appears when characters confront this loss. Each moves through a variety of emotions—sadness, resignation, euphoria, and panic—but their culminating experience of the end is always psychedelic. In an interview, Seimetz described these sequences as meant

> to mimic whatever I had read [about near-death experiences and] . . . what it would feel like if we could reach this ecstatic state sonically, but then also visually. It's like a bombardment of fear, ecstasy, curiosity, and surrender in a way, both in the sound design and visually speaking.[60]

The saturated colors, visual distortions, and temporal manipulations of these visions link *She Dies Tomorrow* to psychedelic eco-horror but distinguish it from *Gaia* and *In the Earth* in one important respect. None of these visions take place in nature, nor do they aim to repair capitalism's metabolic rifts. They occur in the spaces of twenty-first century capitalism's daily life: polished kitchens, neatly decorated living rooms, and catalog-perfect bedrooms. As characters are overcome by the feeling of the end, these spaces drop away. This turn away from capitalism's developed spaces is clearest with the film's central character, Amy. When she's overcome by death's certainty, her visions literally obscure the interior of her house, leaving only her face in focus as she stares, fascinated, saddened, and ecstatic, into a void of flashing colored lights (Figure 15).

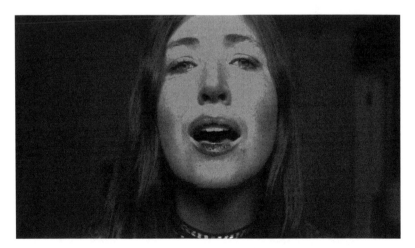

Figure 15. Amy experiences the certainty of death's approach as a psychedelic vision. *She Dies Tomorrow*, directed by Amy Seimetz. Neon, 2020.

For the film, psychedelic imagery means to capture feelings of coming personal and social loss. Indeed, as Amy's vision ends, she is no longer present at all. Instead, the film juxtaposes images of microscopic organic material and the rising sun.

Read from a Marxist perspective, this vision is not only a gesture toward the range in scale of the forces at work in climate change but also an important shift of Amy's attention from the interior spaces of capitalism toward the natural world. That shift in attention comes with a shift in Amy's thinking. She may be infected by death's certainty, but she wants to be useful in death. Early in the film, she lies on the floor of her house, feeling its hardwood panels. Later, she tells a friend, "This used to be alive and now I just walk on it and don't even think twice. But in death it becomes useful, you know?" What would it mean, she wonders, to become useful in death? Her answer seems absurd: to have herself made into a leather jacket. On its own, we might treat this desire as a fantasy of commodification. At last, Amy has been totally appropriated, reduced from person to raw material. Yet when we read her plan in light of other characters' reactions, we see it isn't reducible to commodification. The feeling of lost futurity immobilizes the film's other characters, trapping them in their everyday spaces. Amy's desire to be useful draws her into the natural world. The result contrasts the deathly interior spaces of a doomed humanity with the open spaces of the Earth. While others weep alone in their cars and bedrooms or wait languidly by a pool, Amy heads to the desert to find a leathermaker.

Intertextual reference makes the film's representation of the desert landscape a meaningful ecological statement. Seimetz cast as the leathermaker avant-garde filmmaker James Benning. Likely best known for his California trilogy, *El Valley Centro* (1999), *Los* (2001), and *Sogobi* (2002), Benning crafts films that are part formalist experiment and part social commentary. Each film of the California trilogy consists of thirty-five static shots of the California landscape, each 150 seconds long. The purpose of this formalist conceit isn't to play with film's ability to capture and represent time, à la Michael Snow's *Wavelength* (1967), or its use of light and color, à la Stan Brakhage's *Dog Star Man* (1961–64), but to encourage audiences to reflect critically on the social and political construction of the landscapes around them. In an interview, Benning explained that he included text naming and classifying each shot because

I wanted to code and then cause a rereading of the whole film by naming what you see and exposing ownership. Like, you might not know that this was a cotton-picking machine, and almost all of the land is owned by the large corporations, like railroads, or oil companies, banks, causing a political reading. And so, those titles at the end describe what is seen, who owned the land, and where it was located, what small town it was near. Not only do I want to bring out the politics, but I want the viewer to recall the whole film, to play with memory.[61]

She Dies Tomorrow doesn't rely on Benning's formal constraints—the camera moves, shots vary in length, and no text offers clues as to the ownership or history of the landscape—but the plot, the film's use of landscape, and Benning's presence tell us *She Dies Tomorrow* is about our existential temporal limit. To grapple with the pretraumas of climate change and the loss of human memory and existence, the camera's contemplation of the landscape reflects the limits of a life and of human life as such. In this sense, we might say, *She Dies Tomorrow* means to be a film about the Anthropocene.

Yet a Marxist interpretation can uncover within the film a critical fantasy of the changes we must make in the face of climate change. Here, we must return to Amy's desire to become a leather jacket. This desire isn't a desire to be commodified. A standard-form commodity is useful, but its usefulness is inseparable from its destination, the market. Commodities are made to be exchanged. Their use-value exists to aid exchange, not as an end in itself. Amy's goal is different. She's making the jacket, she tells herself, to keep someone warm. We can find in Amy's jacket fantasy intimations of what nineteenth-century socialist William Morris insisted would be central to a reimagined ecologically viable world: usefulness. In *News from Nowhere*, Morris describes a world where everything is made for use, not the market:

> The wares which we make are made because they are needed: men make for their neighbors' use as if they were making for themselves, not for a vague market of which they know nothing, and over which they have no control: as there is no buying and selling, it would be mere insanity to make goods on the chance of their being wanted; for there is no longer anyone who can be compelled to buy them. So that whatever is made is good, and thoroughly fit for its purpose. Nothing can be made except for genuine use; therefore, no inferior goods are made.[62]

In Morris's reimagined economy, goods are not churned out for an unknowable market but created to answer real needs. This idea of production for use is central to a Marxist reconceptualization of an ecologically sustainable economy. As Paul Burkett explains, production "dictated by use value . . . involves a more human, social, and ecological definition of economic necessity."[63] What's made for use is made to satisfy real needs.

Amy's jacket fantasy, then, offers us a way to understand what ecological Marxists mean when they advocate for what John Bellamy Foster calls "deaccumulation—a transition away from a system geared to the accumulation of capital without end."[64] Sometimes described as degrowth or steady-state economies, deaccumulation would mean, as Foster explains, that

> in a sustainable order, people in the wealthier economies (especially those in the upper income strata) would have to learn to live on "less" in commodity terms in order to lower per capita demands on the environment. At the same time, the satisfaction of genuine human needs and the requirements of ecological sustainability could become the constitutive principles of a new, more communal order aimed at human reciprocity, allowing for qualitative improvement, even plenitude.[65]

Too often people hear "less" in calls for degrowth as a demand for asceticism. But the problem with capitalism is, as Jason Hickel explains, "capitalism produces *too much*, yes, but also *not enough* of the right stuff."[66] Calls for deaccumulation are better understood as calls for, as Foster puts it, "qualitative improvement."[67] It aims for a better, fuller existence. Kate Soper describes this qualitative improvement as alternative hedonism. For Soper, deaccumulation would change practices of production and consumption. These changes would not only allow people to become more ecologically conscious in their daily lives but "more engaged with the pleasures of art, craft, and sociable living."[68] An alternative hedonist society, Soper writes, "would be distinguished by its emphasis on neglected sources of enjoyment and indulgence—more outgoing, more generous and convivial, less narcissistic—and not by the cultivation of inwardness and personal austerity found in the tradition of religious asceticism."[69] From a Marxist perspective, Amy's jacket offers us one way to reimagine our relations with the Earth, one that operates through craft. Craft, as Soper explains, exposes "the estranging impact of modern industry and commerce."[70] With her jacket, Amy hopes to escape the endless cycles of market exchange. By making an object out of herself after death, she cannot be part of any circuit of reciprocity. It's the kind of gift that Georges Bataille might endorse, more sacrifice than exchange.[71]

Some might object that this extolling of craft production isn't Marxist at all but another search for lost origins. It's easy to see how reactionaries could frame artisan production as a return to blood-and-soil peasant life. To avoid these pitfalls, Soper argues that we'll need "dramatic revisionings of [our] affective and emotional responses" to remake ourselves and our relations to things and the world so that "commodities and services and forms of life once perceived as enticingly glamorous come gradually to be seen instead as cumbersome, ugly, and retrograde."[72] We can see Amy's quest to become a jacket as a move toward this aesthetic remaking, an attempt to remake herself beyond the limits of capitalism as a set of aesthetic judgments and a political-economic system, to escape from its exploitation and appropriation for another form of existence with a better metabolic relationship between humanity and the Earth. If *She Dies Tomorrow* conjures this desire, it also doesn't answer it. The film ends with a suspension. Amy asks the leather-maker in vague terms about her plan, and he explains that the body would have to be brought to him at once to remove and cure the skin. In the final scene, Amy sits on some rocks nearby, watching as the sun rises on tomorrow. The camera takes on her perspective to show us a rocky desert hillside. The shot holds for some time, then fades to black, leaving Amy's fate unresolved.

On the surface, the film says little about how communism may be reached. Yet we can find in it what Bini Adamczak tells us: "Before attempting to show that communism might be *feasible*, one has to first present it as *conceivable*. Communism needs to be *imaginable* in order to be *desirable*."[73] From a Marxist perspective, Amy discovers a desire for communism precisely because she confronts the limits the Capitalocene poses for herself as an individual. *She Dies Tomorrow* faces up to the doomed everydayness of capitalism. We can mourn its loss. We can be immobilized by fear. Or we can plan to make something out of its ruins.

4

THE NEIGHBORHOOD HATES YOU
New Black Horror and Uneven Development

The rent is too damn high. When Jimmy McMillan coined this slogan for his 2010 run for New York governor, it seemed like a joke. As the candidate for his single-issue The Rent Is Too Damn High Party, McMillan provided gubernatorial debate audiences with comic relief from the contentious campaign between Andrew Cuomo and Carl Paladino. In the process, McMillan became a minor celebrity. Cable news featured him in clips, *Saturday Night Live* parodied him, and a company offered a doll that repeated his slogan.[1] The media liked McMillan for his eccentricities, from his vocal tics and elaborate moustache to his difficulty paying the rent. For the *New York Times*, rent was strictly a personal problem. They investigated McMillan's rental history under the headline, "How high, exactly, is too damn high for Mr. McMillan?"[2] No one had much interest in the pressures of gentrification on New York City's rental market. A decade later, though, everyone agrees: The rent *is* too damn high. Headline writers can't get enough of the phrase.[3] *Time Out* titled its end-of-year New York City housing-market forecast "Will the Rent Stop Being Too Damn High in 2024?"[4] In January 2023, *Axios* headlined its analysis of the U.S. rental market, "Data Shows the Rent Is (Still) Too Damn High."[5] Just a few months prior, *The Atlantic* had titled its explainer of surging rents, "Why the Rent Inflation Is So Damn High."[6] McMillan's phrase continues to resonate because we're in the midst of a global housing crisis. It's even the subject of a UN report.[7]

We can find beneath the phrase's reception a bit of twenty-first-century common sense: It's not possible to stop rising rents or gentrification, and to say otherwise is to be naïve, misguided, or deranged. Yet as feminist geographer Leslie Kern argues, this "story of inevitability plays too neatly into the hands of those who benefit from gentrification."[8] Capitalism encourages us to view gentrification and rent increases as unstoppable by treating them as the result of natural forces. However, as Kern explains, "casting gentrification as an ecological process . . . works well to foster the idea that the displacement of certain groups is to be expected and that the normal trajectory of urban development is toward increasing concentrations of wealth."[9] What gentrification and rent reveal is that the fundamental political economic question of our time is who gets to be where. As Fredric Jameson memorably quipped, "Today, all politics is about real estate."[10] If the rent is too damn high, it didn't rise of its own accord. It's too damn high because someone wants to force people out or to keep them from getting in, make us competitors for space and resources, and turn neighborhoods into investment vehicles for landlords, banks, and states. When neighborhoods cease to be places where people live, work, and create together, they become spaces defined by value. People live in the capitalist neighborhood on sufferance alone.

From a Marxist perspective, gentrification describes how owners of capital deal with built structures, a particular kind of depreciating asset. Because these assets lose value over time, owners can either invest in improvements to shore up their market valuations or extract as much revenue from their assets as-is. Policy will affect which options they choose, but not as much as what Marxist geographer Neil Smith calls *the rent gap*. In essence, the rent gap is the gap between what a piece of land and its structures take in rent and what it could take in with additional investment. Because the market forces capitalists to maximize their rents, the rent gap drives gentrification. A region becomes ripe for gentrifying speculation, Smith explains, the larger "the disparity between the potential ground rent level and the actual ground rent capitalized under the present land use."[11] While this process is most easily seen in local real estate markets, the rent gap is merely, Smith notes, "the leading edge" of capitalism's larger geographical processes.[12]

To talk about gentrification, then, is to talk about what Marxists call *uneven development*. In Smith's account, uneven development takes two forms. The first is the original accumulation of capital from precapitalist modes of production, the violent processes of primitive accumulation. The second consists of capitalism's use of noncapitalist regions to get out of crises of accumulation, either by appropriating resources or opening new markets.[13] Rosa Luxemburg made this point most forcefully, arguing that European imperialism expressed capitalism's struggle to integrate noncapitalist markets.[14] We've seen both of these forms in our prior discussions of appropriation. Taken together, uneven development helps us to understand something unexpected about how capitalism works. Or rather, how it doesn't.

It's tempting to believe that uneven development's two forms of appropriations create an endlessly expanding capitalism, one that increases its built environment more and more as production expands: more buildings; more infrastructure for transportation and communication; more housing for workers, management, and agents of circulation; more services for those workers; and so on. Yet uneven development doesn't mean that some regions simply develop more slowly than others but always follow the same trajectory. Contrary to some interpretations of Marx, capitalist development doesn't lead invariably to industrialization.[15] As Luxemburg, Smith, and others argue, capitalism purposefully underdevelops regions to make them into peripheries that depend on the developed core, to use the terms of another theorist of uneven development, Immanuel Wallerstein.[16] Uneven development's relations aren't set in stone. What is periphery and what is core can and do change, since capital flees from developed regions whenever accumulation slows. In its wake, it leaves behind the environments it built and the communities that relied on them. In Smith's account, capital flight is the result of regional overdevelopment. As a region's built environment increases, capital sees its rates of profit fall as its operating costs increase: higher rents, higher wages from unionized workers, and higher costs for raw materials. To increase its profits, capital can leave for regions where its inputs have lower costs, or it can cannibalize assets and/or social relations that were previously not commodified. As we saw in the last chapter, David Harvey terms the latter process "accumulation by dispossession."[17] Broadly understood, these strategies describe the deindustrialization of the global North in the 1970s and 1980s as capital abandoned industrial regions and their workers and profited by pushing governments to privatize public assets and services. Of course, regional deindustrialization varies in its specifics. As Gabriel Winant shows in his study of deindustrialized

Pittsburgh, capital did more than flee the costs of unionized workers. It took advantage of changes in policy and governance to leave a region where raw materials had become costly and production plants had been rendered uncompetitive by technological developments.[18] The point, though, is that uneven development describes global capitalism's strategies for regional development as a herky-jerky set of contingent decisions based on material historical conditions and the demands that all capitalists face to accumulate value. These decisions reveal the state's role in uneven development. The state not only monopolizes violence, it sets and maintains property rights and employs agents to protect those rights. There's a reason Mark Neocleous says, "the secret of primitive accumulation might be the secret of police power."[19] As Neocleous explains, the police are the state's violent bureaucrats. They arose historically to do precisely what they still do today: adjudicate in daily life what's private property and what's not, who needs to work and who doesn't, and who can be here and who needs to get lost. The police play an important role in gentrification. They are, as Leslie Kern says, "the shock troops of gentrification," supporting capital's uneven development "by harassing, arresting, and sometimes even killing poor people, disabled people, people with mental illnesses, and people of color in gentrifying neighborhoods."[20]

The state's role in uneven development also shows us that we need to understand capitalism as racial capitalism. Readers in the United States know the term from Cedric Robinson's work, but Robinson drew the term from the South African struggle against apartheid. In 1983, the year that Robinson published *Black Marxism*, Neville Alexander declared at the National Forum in Hammanskraal: "The immediate goal of the national liberation struggle now being waged in South Africa is the destruction of the system of racial capitalism. Apartheid is simply a particular socio-political expression of this system."[21] Like Robinson, Alexander and his audience understood that racial capitalism stratifies its workforce into discrete populations using racialized hierarchies.[22] This stratification of the population is inseparable from stratifications of space. Apartheid controlled where different ethnicities of workers could go. More than that, though, as Alexander explained to his audience, the Afrikaner National Party was practicing racial capitalism when it used ethnicity to create a set of small, seemingly independent nations. These "bogus 'nations,'" Alexander explained, had one purpose: by giving workers racialized nations, they wouldn't come together to demand their rights as South Africans but instead "would agitate for political rights in their own so-called homeland."[23] In short, racial capitalism keeps workers apart by dividing them into ethnicities to squabble over their own limited rights and among one another, rather than aiming their agitations at the real source of their oppression. George Lipsitz describes this use of ethnic and geographical divisions as "the racialization of space and the spatialization of race."[24] Racial capitalism's uneven development is in essence a political-economic battle over space.

We needn't look far to find the horror in these battles. The goal of the racialization of space and the spatialization of race is to eliminate, in Lipsitz's words, "impure populations" and create instead "pure and [racially] homogenous spaces."[25] From the genocide of Indigenous peoples to the many legal and extralegal mechanisms used to create and exclude racialized populations from white spaces, whether Jim or Juan Crow, sundown towns, or redlining, the uneven development of racial capitalism produces racist and genocidal violence. This violence goes hand in hand with the creation of the modern state. For Étienne Balibar, racial capitalism's production of "pure and homogenous spaces" is the heart of nation-making itself. Like whiteness studies scholar David Roediger, Balibar sees race and nation as capitalism's attempts to offer workers what Roediger memorably called, following W. E. B. Du Bois, "the wages of whiteness."[26] For Balibar, this recompense takes the form of membership in an imagined racially homogenous community, the nation-state, rather than a transhistorical idea of whiteness. That doesn't eliminate white chauvinist racism so much as locate it in the nation, nationalism, and the actions of the nation-state's agents. Racial capitalism's uneven development uses the state's monopoly on violence to create and police homogenous spaces, and these imagined spaces are why, as Balibar puts it, "nationalism necessarily takes the form of racism."[27] Racial capitalism's violent exclusion of racialized others creates the very idea of nation and of home. No wonder Alexander focused on the ways racial capitalism divides people and space. To overcome racial capitalism, he exhorted his audience to join together. As we will see, new Black horror offers a similar call to action in its depictions of the horrors of homogeneity.

New Black Horror and the Battle for Genre Space

No subgenre of horror has taken on the terrors of this fight for space more than new Black horror, the cycle of horror films written, directed, and starring Black people.[28] While new Black horror draws freely on horror's narratives and elements to create metaphors for anti-Black racism, its tales, especially in the films that inaugurated the cycle, are about battles for literal and representational space for Black people. New Black horror's conjunction of social critique, metaphor, and meta-commentary on horror as a genre marks it as part of the wider elevated horror cycle of the 2010s and 2020s. We'll look more closely at the aesthetics of elevated horror in chapter 6. For the moment, suffice it to say that, like other elevated horror subgenres, new Black horror builds its appeal to a wider audience using social and genre critiques, this time of anti-Black racism in the world and in the genre's representations of Black people. One cannot talk about new Black horror without engaging with the genre's pernicious representations of Blackness, from its persistent racialization of monsters to its use of Black characters as passive victims. New Black horror knowingly aims to rectify these concerns and often does so by focusing on horror's racial segregation of space. Horror scholar Robin R. Means Coleman locates this genre division of space in the 1980s. "The decade of the 1980s," Coleman writes, "gentrifies and segregates its Whiteness—moving White monsters and prey to the suburbs, places viewed as inaccessible to Blacks."[29] For new Black horror, the genre's use of segregation and gentrification are central themes. The white-coded suburbs in slashers like *Halloween* (1978), *Nightmare on Elm Street* (1984), and *Scream* (1996) become the terrors of white space in Jordan Peele's *Get Out* (2017) and *Us* (2019), Miriam Diallo's *Master* (2022), and Nia DaCosta's *Candyman* (2022), while white-coded summer camps in films like *The Burning* (1981) or *Friday the 13th* (1980) become the terror of being Black in white rural spaces, as in Tim Story's horror-comedy *The Blackening* (2023).

New Black horror has been explicit in its declared intention to make space for Black people in the genre and the world by telling their stories. "I view horror as catharsis through entertainment," Jordan Peele explains. "It's a way to work through your deepest fear and pain—but for Black people that isn't possible, and for many decades *wasn't* possible, without the stories being told in the first place."[30] New Black horror means to undermine the ways that genre fiction can reinforce anti-Black racism. Genres, as Mark Jerng explains, can create "the conditions of racism . . . [by] getting us to embed race into our expectations for how the world operates."[31] New Black horror tells stories about space and place to unpack real experiences of anti-Black racism and to subvert those genre-specific conditions of racism. While these films aren't Marxist in outlook, their focus on the question of *who gets to be where* gives them political and generic stakes that are less obvious in other contemporary horror. For their creators, those stakes allow them to reflect on their fraught position in a culture and a genre predicated on anti-Blackness. This dual focus places new Black horror at the intersection of two kinds of gentrification. Its stories about the racial segregation of space highlight how capitalism's uneven development of the built environment excludes racialized populations, while its use of horror elements to create metaphors for anti-Blackness place it squarely in the elevated horror cycle's attempts to gentrify the genre.[32]

We can see these forces at work in the film that initiated new Black horror as a production cycle, Jordan Peele's *Get Out*. The film's mix of social critique and horror tropes made Peele's $4.5 million film a $255 million global phenomenon and showed studios that socially conscious horror could be profitable.[33] Its success established Peele as one of the twenty-first century's few auteurs and has allowed him to write, direct, and produce a host of projects, including *Us*, *Candyman*, the HBO series *Lovecraft Country* (2020), a relaunched *Twilight Zone*, and an anthology of short stories, *Out There Screaming*.[34] *Get Out* cleared the way for projects by other Black creators, including Diallo's *Master*, Jenna Cato Bass's *Good Madam*, Nikyatu Jusu's *Nanny* (2022), Amazon's streaming series *Them* (2021), Bomani J. Story's *The Angry Black Girl and Her Monster* (2023), and more. Each of these films follows a pattern. First, they rely on irreal figures to create their critiques of anti-Black racism. Second, they refuse older horror's racialized ways of thinking. The creators of new Black horror, then, should be understood as socially conscious Black filmmakers. They understand their attempts to remake a historically anti-Black genre to be fraught. Gentrification and the racialization of space provide them with a complex set of metaphors to explore the contradictions of making and selling narratives about Black pain in a culture industry and political economic system founded upon the exclusion and destruction of Blackness.

Early films in this cycle often seem to have in mind a question that Black studies scholar Frank Wilderson asks of other socially conscious Black filmmaking: Is it possible to tell stories about anti-Blackness using a medium and in an industry and society founded on the oppression, denigration, and exclusion of Black people? Wilderson's answer is a resounding *no*. For Wilderson, the question has little to do with economics or class. It, as he sees it, is an ontological problem. Following the work of Saidiya Hartman, Wilderson argues that Western modernity constructed the human in opposition to an idea of the Black-Slave.[35] Modernity cannot represent Blackness as human because it understands the human only in contrast with the degradation and devaluation of Black life. This Afro-pessimist perspective insists Western modernity is fundamentally anti-Black. What does that mean for socially conscious Black filmmakers? According to Wilderson, no matter their intentions, they can only present dehumanizing representations of Black lives. Their films, he writes in an especially bleak passage,

> make an offering of Black flesh for the psychic accumulation of civil society in a way that not only hides the dimension of gratuitous violence and force necessary to bring about this offering but, like those spectacles of lynching in which a Black penis is cut off and then the victim is not only forced to eat it but must tell his murderers how good it tastes, . . . give civil society the pleasure of seeing Blacks maimed as well as the pleasure of Blacks taking pleasure in this process.[36]

This concern hasn't stopped Black filmmakers from creating, but it has certainly informed the decisions made by the filmmakers of new Black horror. As we will see, its creators take seriously whether representations of anti-Black violence meant to critique anti-Blackness may be recuperated and used to propagate anti-Black racism. For creators, the problem tends to appear as a question of whether to use the genre to witness anti-Black racism or to offer critical imaginary structures to take action against it.

Get Out and *Us*: America's Laboratories of Uneven Development

For Jordan Peele's *Get Out*, the aim is critique. At the core of the film is a battle over space, and its site is the white suburbs. Peele's depiction of this terrifying racially homogenous space draws on two films that represent the suburbs as violently exclusionary, *The Stepford Wives* (1975) and *The People Under the Stairs* (1991). While Peele has discussed the influence of *The Stepford Wives*, his focus on suburbia's whiteness has more in common with *The People Under the Stairs*.[37] Just as the white landlords in Craven's film trap the Black lead in their old dark house, the white parents of Chris's girlfriend trap him in the basement of their suburban manor. In Craven's film and in Peele's, the basement is the space where the film's villains experiment with racist or genocidal violence. In *The People Under the Stairs*, it is where the landlords punish their recalcitrant monstrous children; and in *Get Out*, it is where a cult of white people, the Order of the Coagula, steals Black people's bodies. Where Craven's film attacks exploitative white landlords, Peele's film confronts the anti-Blackness of American culture and society. The Order is a metaphor for white society's belief in the inevitability of Black subjugation. Using hypnosis, it forces its victims to recount their most traumatic experiences—for Chris, the death of his mother—and immobilizes them in their trauma. Trapped, they can only watch as the minds of wealthy white people, implanted by the Coagula's scientists, use their bodies as they see fit. The film's crucial image for this experience is Chris's descent into "the sunken place," the mental space from which he can view his body but not control it (Figure 16). Peele represents this imprisoning of Black consciousness as a form of underwater submersion, a watery image that suggests how the Middle Passage ripped away the identities of African people.[38] Chris's descent into this place of Blackness and nonbeing captures the feeling that suffuses new Black horror, terrified helplessness in the face of seemingly inevitable loss. As we will see, new Black horror is marked by characters immobilized by their confrontation with anti-Blackness. In Peele's film, this feeling is the result of a system built to create and capitalize on Black trauma. Indeed, for Peele, the sunken place is as much about the cooptation of Black art as of Black life. Shortly after the film's release, he wrote on Twitter: "The sunken place means

Figure 16. Chris descends into the watery darkness of the sunken place. *Get Out*, directed by Jordan Peele. Universal, 2017.

we're marginalized. No matter how hard we scream, the system silences us."[39] This is why *Get Out* puts instances of cultural appropriation in its story of bodily appropriation. Chris is a photographer, and the Coagula mean to sell him to a blind art dealer, Jim, who doesn't mince words. "I want your eye, man," he tells Chris. "I want those things you see through."

It is in the film's engagement with art that capitalizes on Black trauma that we can unearth the effects of racial capitalism's uneven development. *Get Out* begins with loving displays of Chris's gentrified neighborhood, moving from its hipster café bakery to his well-appointed apartment of exposed brick and polished metal. On the walls, Chris displays his photographs of Black urban life in disinvested neighborhoods. These photos serve as meta-commentary on the use of Black suffering as art, but they can also help us think about the connection between urban disinvestment, the suburbs, and gentrification in the urban core. As Smith explains, suburbs are part of "a wider pattern of uneven development at the urban scale."[40] Suburban investment is typically bound up with urban disinvestment (though the opposite can also be true) and strategic attempts to drive down prices in the urban core for later reinvestment and gentrification. This movement of investment and disinvestment is inseparable from the racialization of space and spatialization of race. Gentrification's cycles disproportionately affect people of color through devaluation, pollution, and the stigmatizing of areas as crime or drug ridden.[41] Chris's use of disinvested Black life for art reframes the Coagula's seizure of

Black bodies as the seizure of disinvested racialized space. When Jim tells Chris he wants his eye, he wants more than his sense of sight. He wants to become a sort of artistic real estate developer, using Chris's eye to profit off devalued spaces and lives he otherwise wouldn't see. If art and the city are for gentrifying, the suburbs in *Get Out* are for appropriating. Peele models the film's suburb on the ur-laboratory of American racial capitalism, the plantation. The Armitage house is an estate of gardens and gazebos tended by a live-in Black gardener, and its kitchen is overseen by the family's Black cook. If the basement is a mad scientist's lab, the rest of the home is a haunted house, with Grandma in the kitchen in her stolen body and Grandpa in the garden. From a Marxist perspective, we might say that the film's depiction of suburbia as a space of violence follows what Katherine McKittrick calls "plantation logic."[42] The plantation, McKittrick explains, was "key to transforming the lands of no one into the lands of someone, with Black forced labor propelling an economic structure that would underpin town and industry development in the Americas."[43] McKittrick describes three distinct parts of plantation logic:

> it identifies the normalizing mechanics of the plantation, wherein black subjugation and land exploitation go hand in hand and shepherd in certain (present) death; it notices our collective participation in and rhetorical commitment to reproducing this system as though it is natural, inevitable, and a normal way of life; and it imagines the plot-and-plantation as a new analytical ground that puts forth a knowledge system, produced outside the realms of normalcy, thus rejecting the very rules of the system that profits from racial violence, and in this envisions not a purely oppositional narrative but rather a future where a corelated human species perspective is honored.[44]

The horror of *Get Out* is the horror of plantation logic. To enter the white plantation laboratory is to lose yourself to racial capitalism. While *Us* will show us the third, resistant, form of plantation logic, *Get Out* displays the first two. These feelings of inevitability and naturalness are the basis of the sunken place's terrors and the film's evocations of slavery. *Get Out* understands that slavery was not merely a system of coerced labor but, as Robin D. G. Kelley puts it, "a process of elimination: eliminate the culture, identity, and consciousness while preserving the body for labor."[45] The terrified helplessness of new Black horror comes from this threat of elimination, one embedded in the history of real eliminations and presented as inevitable and natural.

The feeling of terrifying inevitability reframes the threat that the police pose in the film. As Stuart Hall argued in the 1980s, the police manage capitalism's contradictions and crises of disinvestment, often disguised as moral panics about crime and Blackness.[46] In the film, a police officer harasses Chris during a traffic stop after Rose hits a deer on their way to her parents. The film presents him as the violent face of anti-Blackness, but he also serves a specific role for racial capitalism. He manages the space that separates the suburbs and the city, literally policing a raced and classed boundary. In the film's original ending, the police reassert this boundary. The film's climax shows Chris fighting his way out of the Armitages' basement. He kills each family member, including his girlfriend Rose, who routinely kidnapped Black people for the Coagula. Victorious, Chris lies in the street covered in blood when police lights appear. In the released cut, the car is a TSA squad car driven by Chris's friend Rod, who drives Chris to safety. In the original cut, however, it is a police car and Chris is arrested. The film ends with Chris in prison, speaking to Rod. While Rod urges him to fight his unjust incarceration, Chris demurs. A final shot frames Chris through the prison bars to underscore the irony of the film's title. You can't get out of white supremacy and anti-Blackness, the film insists. Marxism helps us to find something more here. The film's use of the police to evoke terrified helplessness reveals racial capitalism's relentless cycles of predatory investment and disinvestment. The police do more than enforce racial capitalism's hierarchies and divisions of space. By arresting Chris, they have made him into territory for exploitation. As Ruth Wilson Gilmore explains, "criminalization transforms individuals into tiny territories primed for extractive activity to unfold."[47] In the film's original cut, then, Chris isn't just pushed out of the white suburbs and his gentrified urban neighborhood. He becomes himself another territory for racial capitalism to appropriate. The released edit may sidestep this explicit form of territorial extraction, but it offers Chris no protection from uneven development's threats of displacement and appropriation. In racial capitalism's laboratories, there's no telling when the rent gap will come for you.

Peele's next film, *Us* (2019), returns to the mad scientist's lab with its tale of a host of doppelgangers, the Tethered, who escape their underground labs in search of revenge. At first, *Us* seems a different kind of film, a home-invasion horror. As a subgenre, home-invasion films are often marked by distressing scenes of graphic violence, most notably in European films like Michael Haneke's *Funny Games* (1997, 2007) and New French Extreme films like *Them (Ils)* (2006), *Inside (À L'Interieur)* (2007), and *Martyrs* (2008). *Us* avoids home invasion's violent extremes while drawing on its menace and tension. Like other home invasion films, its terrors are those of helplessness. Some of its most striking imagery is drawn from the New French Extreme and its Hollywood pastiche, *The Strangers* (2008), from the way the invaders stand motionless in the distance to the masks they wear during the assault and the scissors they use to attack their victims.[48] What *Us* makes explicit is that home-invasion stories are about who gets to be where. In *Us*, that *where* is Santa Cruz, California, a gentrified tourist and university town just over the mountains from Silicon Valley. The Wilsons, a Black family come to the area to stay in their summer home, a small one-story ranch inherited from Adelaide Wilson's mother. The Wilsons's place is hidden down a rural street, on the water but not the beach. It's all walls, narrow corridors, and 1970s furniture. It's not clear whether their house is in one of Santa Cruz's suburbs or an outlying town like Aptos or Capitola, but *Us* wants audiences to know their place isn't as fancy as their white friends', the Tylers. The Tylers have an ultramodern two-story beach house in Santa Cruz proper, and its open-plan first floor with huge glass windows makes the house, the beach, and the city into one massive recreational space for their enjoyment. The Wilsons would like Santa Cruz to be their place—it's where Adelaide grew up!—and believe wealth would fix their differently raced and classed experiences of this gentrified space.

The invasion of the Tethered suggests wealth isn't the solution. It certainly doesn't help the Tylers, whom the Tethered dispatch without difficulty. The Wilsons are made of sterner stuff, especially Adelaide. Although the first confrontation with the Tethered leaves her immobilized like the rest of her family, Adelaide quickly overcomes her fear and acts. Adelaide's agency seems a response to horror's long history of making the Black woman, in the words of Kinitra D. Brooks, "a mistreated tool . . . to further the more careful and considerate construction of other characters."[49] Adelaide is nobody's tool. She fights off the Tethered time and time again, saves her children, and in the end leads them to safety. Yet the conclusion shows what Adelaide's activity was really all about: getting stuff. The film's twist ending reveals she already knew about the Tethered. In fact, she is one. The film's opening sequence appears to show Adelaide as a child when she encounters her Tethered double, Red. The conclusion reveals it was *Red* who encountered the Tethered Adelaide. Adelaide dragged her aboveground double into the underground lab, chained her there, and escaped. The person truly immobilized in terror was Red, unable to speak from a throat injury and bound to her double's bed. The film's earlier comments on wealth and class, then, are part of a larger critique of middle-class striving. Adelaide is the film's ambivalent portrait of class-climbing Blackness. She may not have what the Tylers have, but she understands what it takes to get ahead: You can't get what you want without oppressing someone else.

From a Marxist perspective, Red and her uprising of the Tethered offer another way. Red leads the Tethered's resistance movement because she knows what she has lost and what she never had. At first, Red isn't interested in controlling space at all. She wants to share it with everyone. "You could have taken me with you," she tells Adelaide. It is Adelaide who refuses to share. In this sense, *Us* uses home invasion to dramatize an uprising of people united by their oppression, what Frantz Fanon called "the wretched of the earth."[50] The violence of the Tethered is inseparable from the violence that Fanon believed necessary for decolonization. No surprise, then, that the Tethered are the result of a similar experiment in social control. The good lives of those above ground, Adelaide is told, were to be the result of the oppressions of their doppelgangers below. The Tethered were created as a vast underclass to be held in terrified helplessness, an embodiment of class oppression. If all this conjures the history of slavery, colonialism, the Jim Crow South, and South African apartheid, it should. Much like those regimes, this experiment in social control was also abandoned without dismantling the structures of oppression that it created. The Tethered were left to live in untended but no less operational structures of domination. Red realizes what all revolutionaries do: If they can overcome their feelings of helplessness, they are free to choose another kind of life. She leads them out of the lab to sever their oppressive connections to those above ground. Their matching red jumpsuits, big golden scissors, and joining of hands to recreate the 1980s charity stunt Hands Across America are expressions of solidarity. The Tethered assert their right to space—the right to live above ground—by recognizing themselves as an oppressed class and joining together to remove their literal overlords. Their refusal of personal subjugation begins with the realization that the inevitable is anything but, if you recognize your shared interests.

While a Marxist interpretation draws out this line of resistance, *Us* is ambivalent about Red. Adelaide kills her, but this doesn't stop the Tethered's uprising. The film's final sequence shows the Wilsons driving away. A drone shot lifts above their car to reveal a vast line of the Tethered holding hands. Smoke on the horizon and helicopters circling overhead make their triumph appear apocalyptic, turning the Tethered's evocation of solidarity into one more instance of terrified helplessness. The entire world now seems to confront an impossible situation. Still, Marxism helps us to see in this image a fractured, utopic vision of class consciousness. After all, what did Red do but start a revolution to reclaim her community from the gentrifiers who forced her out.

Master and *Good Madam*: The Haunted House and Gentrification

Horror has long had a narrative ready-made for these battles over space: the haunted house. Its structuring questions are ones well suited for arguments about gentrification: Who was here first? Who has to leave? Who has the right to stay? Battles over the built environment run through haunted house films. In Lewis Allen's *The Uninvited* (1944) and Stuart Rosenberg's *The Amityville Horror* (1979), bargain-hunters vie with ghosts to hold onto beautiful houses they bought on the cheap. In Robert Wise's *The Haunting* (1963) and John Hough's *The Legend of Hell House* (1973), psychics try to force ghosts off luxury properties. Tobe Hooper's *Poltergeist* (1982) makes this an explicit question of real estate development as ghosts force out the residents of a suburban development built atop a razed cemetery. We might say the haunted house plot provides popular culture with a narrative able to capture an underrepresented fact of life in capitalism: people get evicted from their homes. In haunted house tales, inhabitants are kicked out, killed, or forced to come to an agreement with those who are already there, whether the living join the dead in an endless ghost party (e.g., *The Shining* [1980], the first season of *American Horror Story* [2011], and *The Haunting of Hill House* [2018]), or the living and the dead reach a gentrifying détente (e.g., *Beetlejuice* [1988], the UK and U.S. versions of the television series, *Ghosts* [UK, 2019–23; US 2021–]). New Zealand horror-comedy series *Wellington Paranormal* (2018–22) uses this idea to satirize white settler colonialism. A Māori police chief gets the white ghosts haunting his station to leave by showing them a deed to the land. "As is the pakeha way," he explains to a ghost named Mr. Whiteman, "to own land, you need a piece of paper." Whiteman examines the deed, grudgingly admits his mistake, and returns to the grave.

We see a similar use of the haunted house narrative in new Black horror. In Mariame Diallo's *Master* (2022) and Jenna Cato Bass's *Good Madam (Mlungu Wam)* (2021), the haunted house provides Black filmmakers with an expedient genre form for their critiques of white, settler colonial, and anti-Black spaces. *Master* and *Good Madam* share a number of traits. Both use the haunted house to show that the racist violence of the past haunts the present, both follow a trio of women to track the effects of this violence across generations, and both sets of women want to reclaim these haunted spaces from whiteness. These similarities highlight the films' quite distinct responses to the question that we approached at the start of the chapter: Should new Black horror use genre to bear witness to racism's oppressions or to offer critical imaginary structures for action?

Master takes the side of witnessing. In its tale of three women at an elite college modeled on Diallo's alma mater, Yale, action seems impossible. The experiences of Gail, the institution's first Black housemaster, Jasmine, a Black first-year student in Gail's house, and Liv, a Black studies professor, weave together different forms of anti-Blackness that pervade the institution. As house master, Gail finds evidence of the institution's racist past, from a tiny servant's quarters full of bells to keep Black servants on call, to an old mammy figurine stuffed in the back of a kitchen cabinet. While Gail has climbed the ranks, Liv finds her white colleagues using their institutional power to keep her from earning tenure. Jasmine has the worst of it, though. The university thoughtlessly places her in a room where another Black student committed suicide decades earlier. The university's upper-class white students use that history to subject her to a barrage of racist bullying. They play up the story of a long-dead witch whose ghost reputedly persecuted the student. Whether the witch is real or not, she provides a metaphor for the institution's oppressions, and drives Jasmine further and further into herself until she attempts suicide. When Gail visits her in the hospital, she wants to dissuade Jasmine from leaving the university. There's no escape from the horrors of white America, she says. And she should know. Her colleagues spout microaggression after microaggression. Still, Gail insists, an Ivy League education will give Jasmine power. "You can't get away from [white supremacy]," she says. "It'll follow you. Believe me. I know." Gail's talk is effective, but not how she hoped. She's convinced Jasmine there's no way out, and the girl returns to her room and completes suicide.

Master's most horrific scenes appear after Jasmine's death, and that's because only Gail seems to care. At a party, she tells other faculty that she'll be haunted forever by her inability to protect Jasmine. If they don't understand, that's because they're all happy to live in the university's haunted milieu, including Liv. The university granted her tenure as part of their publicity-focused push of diversity, equity, and inclusion initiatives to tamp down the bad publicity from Jasmine's death. Gail discovers Liv is more than an opportunist, though. She's also a fraud. In a plot twist based on the case of Rachel Dolezal, an instructor in Africana studies at Eastern Washington University who pretended to be a Black woman, Gail finds that Liv has spent years masquerading as Black. Liv's betrayal is the film's culminating indictment of American higher education. Jasmine's enrollment, Gail's job, and Liv's scholarship are allowed to exist at a fundamentally racist institution, the film insists, because they don't threaten it. Their existence gives it a patina of diversity, while the structure and culture of the institution make it clear it's not a space for Black people. Gail thought she could remake this space by taking control of one of the university's houses. By the film's end, though, she realizes she may have become a house master, but she will never be the house's master. The ghosts of the past own the institution. She can do nothing but walk away, and she does. To where isn't clear, since, as Gail told Jasmine, you can't walk away from white supremacy.

The South African film *Good Madam* (in Xhosa, *Mlungu Wam*) refuses to treat this sort of exodus as an option. As an allegory for post-apartheid South Africa, *Good Madam* knows the difference between abandoning an Ivy League institution and a country. In the film, Tsidi and her daughter Winnie lose their home after Tsidi's grandmother dies and her uncle asserts his patriarchal right to divide family assets, giving Tsidi's house to a cousin. Homeless, she and her daughter move in with Tsidi's mother, Mavis, who lives and works on a suburban Cape Town estate. Tsidi has never liked staying with Mavis in the servants' quarters of her longtime employer, known only as Madam. They must be quiet, stay in Mavis's rooms or the kitchen, and not touch Madam's things, especially her collection of Africana. It doesn't matter that Madam is comatose. She's still in charge, even if she isn't all there. Tsidi wants to leave but has nowhere to go. Mavis is no less trapped. If Madam's children learn their mother is comatose, they'll put her in a nursing home and Mavis will be out on the street. It doesn't help matters that Tsidi thinks something is wrong with Madam's house. She has strange dreams there and the grounds seem to be haunted by ghosts that she's convinced want to take Winnie.

Good Madam, then, has in its sights how white landlords continue to control South African land and resources whether they are conscious or not. White power haunts the nation. Like the women of *Master*, Mavis, Tsidi, and Winnie are trapped in a house built and haunted by anti-Blackness. The film's international promotion positioned the film in relation to U.S. new Black horror for this reason. Its poster, an image of Tsidi's terrified face with a white hand over her mouth, bears a striking resemblance to the poster for *Get Out*, which features Chris's tear-streaked face as he enters the sunken place. From a Marxist perspective, the difference between *Good Madam* and *Master* is that *Good Madam* treats anti-Blackness as an aspect of racial capitalism, while *Master* does not. We see this in its exploration of the built environment. Madam's neighborhood captures the violent uneven development of white settler colonialism. Even if no one directly asks Tsidi and Winnie for employment passes, the subdivision's physical layout and the house's midcentury architecture speak as plainly of the apartheid era as Mavis's uniform. Madam's control over physical space creates their structural exclusion. And we can see this in the film's representation of the division of racial capitalism's working classes by the interests of white capitalists. Madam, Tsidi discovers, is a sorcerer. She enslaves her employees' ghosts with the help of Tsidi's half-brother, Stuart. Madam paid for Stuart's education and adopted him, and he sees himself as her child more than Mavis's. Stuart represents in particularly gruesome form those South Africans willing to maintain the power of white landlords. As Madam's assistant in her magical work, Stuart is tasked with making Tsidi, Mavis, and Winnie her servants for all eternity, and he begins his task by putting Tsidi into a state of terrified stupefaction. What saves her is Mavis's recognition in Tsidi of her own resignation to the indignities of work. Together, they kill Stuart and render Madam powerless. The three women then reclaim the house and shift the magically neutered Madam into the servants' quarters. An occasional call suffices to convince her children in Australia that, as Mavis says, "everything is under control here on the other side." *Good Madam* helps us to see, then, how new Black horror's feeling of terrified helplessness can do more than evoke the horrors of witnessing what has happened. It can goad those witnessing into action.

Candyman: Remaking Genre, Reclaiming Space

While *Master* and *Good Madam* use the haunted house as a metaphor to allegorize conflicts over racial capitalism's construction of space, Nia DaCosta's *Candyman* (2021), cowritten with Jordan Peele and Win Rosenfeld, draws the links between the haunted house, racism, and gentrification in big bold lines. For some viewers, this overt commentary was too much. On NPR's popular podcast *The Pop Culture Happy Hour*, producer Mark Rivers complained the film's dialogue about gentrification was "more like a Ted talk than a horror film."[51] The other hosts agreed. Gentrification was a ruse obscuring what the film was really about, Black trauma and storytelling. A Marxist reading of the film, however, shows that gentrification isn't simply the vehicle in a metaphor whose tenor is anti-Blackness. When we pay attention to racial capitalism's uneven development of the built environment, we see that gentrification is the relation that gives the metaphor its sense, what rhetoricians call a metaphor's ground. The film's discussions of anti-Blackness and art can't be separated from its talk of gentrification. They all depend on racial capitalism's stratifications of the population, the built environment, and the genre itself. Like *Get Out*, *Candyman* uses gentrification to think about the problem of telling stories of Black trauma within a system that profits off anti-Blackness. This concern is built into the plot. Its central character, Anthony, is an artist making his name through art about Black trauma. And Black trauma shapes the film's relation to horror as a genre.[52] Terror here is found not only in the central character's immobilization by anti-Blackness but in the demand that he make something salable out of anti-Blackness. For this reason, *Candyman* is clearer in its engagement with gentrification and in its need to gentrify its source material. As a relaunch of the popular 1990s series, DaCosta's film presents itself as an intellectual reworking of the series' problematic premise. Its primary intertext is Bernard Rose's *Candyman* (1992), the first of the series. Rose's film captures many of the representational problems typical of horror films featuring Black actors but written, directed, and/or produced by non-Black people, what Robin R. Means Coleman calls "Blacks in horror films."[53] As Coleman details, Blacks-in-horror films like *Candyman* or *The People Under the Stairs* offered Black audiences screen representation but always with a levy of anti-Blackness. The 1992 film means to comment on anti-Black racism and violence with Candyman's origin story, but these origins, coming from a story by Clive Barker, a white Briton, and in a film directed by another white Briton, are heavily freighted. Candyman is the ghost of a Black artist, Daniel Robitaille, lynched by a white mob after the discovery of his relationship with a white woman. The specifics of Robitaille's lynching become Candyman's calling card. Before the mob killed him, they replaced his hand with a hook, covered him in honey, and set bees on him. Candyman pays back this violence with his own, killing his victims with his hook and announcing his presence with bees. Candyman isn't an avenger of anti-Black racism, though. Rose's film struggles to suggest Candyman is somehow oppositional but presents him as a disgust-inducing monster who preys on Black people, kills or contaminates whatever he touches, and is obsessed with white women. As Coleman puts it, "the film strays from the monster-with-a-heart-of-gold theme by playing on fears of the big Black boogeyman coming in and taking away a White woman."[54]

DaCosta's *Candyman* needs to talk about the built environment directly because infrastructure plays a critical role in Rose's film. Its central character isn't Candyman but Helen, a white anthropology student writing a dissertation about urban legends. When she learns there's a legend about a Black hook-handed killer who appears when you stare in a mirror and repeat his name five times, she heads across town to the tale's source, Chicago's public housing project Cabrini–Green Homes. In Rose's film, Cabrini–Green is a racialized version of the dangerous cities of nineteen-century Gothics like *The Mysteries of Paris* (Eugène Sue, 1842–43) and *The Mysteries of London* (George W. M. Reynolds, 1845). The filth, degradation, and violence of the mysterious city become inextricable from Blackness, and the Black characters who live in this abject space are presented as violent gang members or hapless victims. If Cabrini–Green is the space of abjection and abnormality, then the white gentrified city is the film's space of normality. This is, of course, where Helen lives, and her apartment is a mirror image of the apartments in Cabrini–Green. She explains to her friend Bernadette that her building is a reclaimed former project remade into luxury lofts, and they can see Cabrini from Helen's window, a distorted reflection of her world kept at a comfortable distance by the new freeway. Helen's movement between these mirrored racialized spaces of gentrification and disinvestment is central to the film's attempts to thematize so-called urban renewal. The use of mirroring here is important. Rose's film wants viewers to think about the demands of recognition and the potential violence of that recognition as inextricable from the construction of the built environment. It's no mistake that the film begins with a bird's-eye establishing shot of Chicago's infrastructure and returns to this architectural gaze throughout to establish different locales (Figure 17). The camera's steady glide over highways, buildings, and plazas visualizes the divisions of urban planning just as the mirrors that Candyman appears in visualize the division of space. The urban legend collapses these divisions, whether that's Candyman emerging from mirror space into a room or Helen entering Candyman's lair through a hole behind a bathroom mirror.

Rose's film wants this movement between mirrored spaces to be a plea to reclaim disinvested racialized urban spaces. The problem is that what interests Rose isn't the violence of racial capitalism or uneven development, but rather the violence that disinvestment leaves in its wake.

Figure 17. An aerial shot of Chicago's freeways maps the 1992 film's interest in urban space. *Candyman*, directed by Bernard Rose. Columbia Tristar, 1992.

This shift in focus is part and parcel with what Karen E. Fields and Barbara J. Fields describe as the "sleight of hand" that "transforms *racism*, something an aggressor does, into *race*, something the target *is*."[55] No wonder, then, that Rose's film centers Helen as a white savior. She sacrifices herself for the good of the Black community. This begins by allowing Candyman to contaminate her sexually. In Rose's film, Candyman's sexual interest appears in scenes redolent of the anti-Blackness that Fanon described as "terror mixed with sexual revulsion."[56] Candyman reaches a gore-encrusted hook up Helen's skirt, kisses her with a bee-filled mouth, and experiences orgasmic pleasure when covering her in spurts of blood. Helen accepts this degradation to save the residents of Cabrini–Green. When Candyman takes her to his lair beneath a garbage bonfire, believing she will sacrifice herself to join him forever, Helen stops him and saves the infant he had kidnapped. She returns the child to their mother's arms, then expires from her burns. This sacrifice of a white woman, Rose's film suggests, might be able to reclaim the Black community from the terrors of disinvestment—or would, if contact with disinvested spaces didn't contaminate. Helen hasn't saved them at all. She's simply become another Candyman. The film's final scare sees Helen return to slaughter her husband in their apartment. Helen, Coleman argues, "can do what Candyman would not: terrorize those on the other side of the tracks."⁵⁷ A Marxist reading of Rose's film suggests something far more dour. Candyman isn't a figure that avenges racist violence or the violence of disinvestment so much as an avatar for the violence of disinvestment itself. His contaminating touch highlights the social corrosiveness of disinvestment and its racialization of the people most affected by it. Yet the film's decision to link race and disinvestment's erosion of social connection insinuates that disinvestment contaminates everything that falls under its racialized touch. The result suggests nothing can be done to stop racial capitalism's uneven development. At best, one can express dismay and concern at its existence, preferably from afar. As Aviva Briefel and Sianne Ngai explain, "Candyman is less a film about the implications of being haunted than about the superior privilege of transforming oneself into the haunter, now from the standpoint of liberal empathy."⁵⁸ Helen can't stop disinvestment, but what she can do is bring its violence to white, gentrified spaces.

So DaCosta's *Candyman* has a lot of work to do to reclaim the Candyman story. Like other relaunched pieces of cinematic intellectual property, *Candyman* rewrites its precursor text, in this case creating a story that makes the humanity of Black people its central concern. Its principal character, Anthony, a Black artist, is drawn to parallel Helen. Like Helen, Anthony lives in a luxury loft that was once part of Cabrini–Green. Like Helen, he lives with his partner, art gallery co-owner Brianna. Like Helen and her professor husband, Anthony and Brianna are well-off intellectuals for whom the urban legend of Candyman is an anthropological oddity, a tale told by Brianna's real estate–broker brother. And like Helen, Anthony wants to use the story to forward his career. His latest work, a painting of a Black chest with a noose and a tattoo of the racial epithet, leaves Brianna's partner, Clive, cold. He wants something new. "Dig into that history of yours, dude," he cajoles. Casting about for an idea, Anthony haltingly pitches something about gentrification: "I'm . . . I'm thinking about doing something about the projects. And about how, uh, white supremacy . . . how it creates these spaces of rampant neglect for communities of color, in particular Black communities." Now Clive is interested. "Yeah, yeah. Like where you're from," he suggests, looking for a way to yoke art, politics, and biography into a saleable package. "Yeah," Anthony replies, "Bronzeville." Suddenly Clive isn't so impressed. "Eh, the South Side is kind of played," he says dismissively. "Uh, or Cabrini–Green?" Anthony offers, remembering Candyman. Yeah, Clive says, *that* would work. And so, like Helen, Anthony heads to Cabrini–Green for a story to exploit.

Anthony's decision thematizes a central aesthetic concern for new Black horror: What does it mean to commodify Black trauma? *Candyman* understands itself as part of elevated horror's attempts to gentrify the genre and uses Anthony and the Candyman legend to consider why it's necessary to make horror about Black trauma. Its answer is the first thing that Anthony sees in Cabrini–Green: the shock troops of gentrification, the police. As he hides from a patrol car, an older resident, William, approaches. The police were never around when people needed help, he says, but now that developers want the land, they never leave.

From a Marxist perspective, the horror that *Candyman* highlights is the horror of the ways in which the police manage racial capitalism's uneven development, what Ruth Wilson Gilmore and Craig Gilmore call racial capitalism's "organized abandonment" of communities of color.[59] As they explain, in disinvested communities, the police are often the only institution the neoliberal state maintains. Using arrest, incarceration, or death, the police bottleneck racialized populations into disinvested areas or force them out when investors want areas cleared for development. In DaCosta's *Candyman*, horror doesn't come from the violence left in disinvestment's wake, but from the force that the state deploys against racialized populations to support gentrification. Instead of mirroring luxury lofts across town, the apartments in Cabrini–Green are

Figure 18. Anthony faces the gentrified Chicago skyline while standing amid Cabrini–Green. *Candyman*, directed by Nia DaCosta. Universal, 2021.

architecturally unique, the last vestige of a Black working-class neighborhood that capital now wants to reclaim. No wonder one of the film's most striking images is of Anthony in the midst of the projects, facing new construction on the horizon (Figure 18).

If *Candyman* doesn't dwell on class differences, it does make clear that BIPOC people are only welcome in gentrified spaces if they have the right amount of financial and cultural capital. For Brianna and Anthony, these gentrified spaces seem like their spaces, until they're not. For DaCosta and Peele, this is a question of anti-Blackness. As a theme, gentrification allows the film to examine how policing creates spaces defined as not-Black and unleashes violence to maintain these spaces. This Afropessimist perspective has much in common with Wilderson's position. Class doesn't matter if what makes one vulnerable to violence is the mere fact of being Black.[60] Marxists insist that class does matter. Stuart Hall famously described race as a "modality of class," which isn't to reduce race to class but to understand the two as entwined in how people live classed existences.[61] Adolph Reed approaches the question differently, responding to this Afropessimist argument by focusing not on how people live but on how they are identified. In the twenty-first century United States, Reed explains, "race is a visible shorthand for class."[62] We can use these distinctions to consider how the upper-middle-class artist Anthony gets the Candyman story from the working-class William. He tells Anthony he knew Candyman as Sherman Fields, a mentally handicapped man who used to give candy to children until police blamed him for a string of poisonings. In a negative reflection of the series' bee imagery, the police beat him to death in a "swarm." But Sherman is only the most recent Candyman. Candyman has been other victims of anti-Black violence, reaching all the way back to Daniel Robitaille. William understands Candyman as a swarm that counters the violence of white supremacy. His lived experience of race as class makes this resistance necessary, and he kidnaps Anthony to make him into a new Candyman to protect lower-middle-class and working-class Black people.

For Anthony, though, class has nothing to do with it. For him, Candyman is a collective legend, a piece of oppositional folk art to memorialize and manage the injustices of anti-Blackness. Like the filmmakers, Anthony repurposes the Candyman story to comment on gentrification's violence. His piece "Say My Name" is a bathroom mirror that opens onto a hidden space filled with figural paintings depicting Sherman's story. As its Black Lives Matter–inspired name indicates, "Say My Name" doesn't give viewers metaphors for anti-Black violence. It simply represents it. In this sense, Anthony's art doubles new Black horror, representing anti-Black violence with only the barest of window dressing. The art world responds with critiques that could just as readily be lobbed at DaCosta or Peele. Brianna worries it isn't intellectual enough and doesn't "leave much room for viewer interpretation moving from the symbolism of the violence to the actual depiction of it." An art critic sniffs at its "didactic kneejerk cliches about the ambient violence of the gentrification cycle." She then unleashes on Anthony the commonsense view of gentrification. Its real agents, she says, are "your kind." "Artists," she explains, "are the real pioneers of that cycle. Artists descend upon disenfranchised neighborhoods, divining cheap rent so that they can dick around in their studios without the crushing burden of a day job." The parallels here are purposeful and disconnected from class: Is the representation of anti-Black racism and violence meaningful, or is it another way to profit from anti-Blackness, perhaps even to create spectacles that anti-Blackness may recuperate?

It's no mistake, then, that the film has Candyman aim his violence at white people exploiting the commodification of Black trauma, beginning with Clive. He doesn't like "Say My Name" but exhibits it anyway. His murder gives Anthony's work notoriety, and the once derisive critic now showers Anthony with praise. Her connection to the event has given her career a boost too, and Candyman also kills this white profiteer. Now Anthony is no longer welcome in the white art world. He's a suspect. It doesn't matter that there's no real connection between him and the murders. He's been identified as the sort of person who shouldn't be in these (white) spaces. After Candyman's next victims, a group of middle-class white teenagers who imitate what they saw at the exhibit, it's clear that Candyman's choice of prey not only refuses horror's cliched use of Black people as victims. It also indicates that Candyman wants to ensure his story can't be gentrified. No wonder his violence eventually lands on Anthony. Anthony's attempted artistic appropriation of Candyman becomes Candyman's appropriation of Anthony. Or rather reappropriation. Anthony, we discover, was the baby Helen saved from the bonfire. So, like Helen, he too is destined to become Candyman.

His transformation begins with a bee sting on his first visit to Cabrini–Green. The sting necrotizes, and by the film's final reel, Anthony looks like he never escaped the fire. From a Marxist perspective, we might say Anthony's transformation is the result not of contagion but of his fraught position, caught between a story that refuses to be sold and the demand to produce art commodities. Candyman's resistance to gentrification and the pressure Anthony feels to gentrify his story immobilizes Anthony, trapped between the social pressure of anti-Blackness and the economic pressure of artistic production. The only solution is one neither Anthony nor Brianna want: to become Candyman.

The film's conclusion debates the meaning of this transformation. The working class–coded William fights with the proper bourgeois Brianna over Anthony's body and the act of storytelling. After kidnapping Anthony, William cuts off his hand and sets him up to be killed by the police. As the new Candyman, Anthony will direct his violence outward. "This time he'll be killing their fathers, their babies, their sisters," William vows. Brianna is disgusted by William's abuse of Anthony and the literalness of his tale. Like Anthony's art, it leaves no room for interpretation. Still, William is undeterred. He's rewriting the legend to suit his needs. As he replaces Anthony's hand with a hook, he deadpans: "You can really make the story your own, but some of the specifics should be somewhat consistent" (Figure 19). Brianna manages to overpower William, but her success isn't a victory for intellectual art about anti-Blackness. The police still arrive and act just as William expected: They

Figure 19. William gives Anthony a hook as part of his attempt to keep the Candyman legend alive. *Candyman,* directed by Nia DaCosta. Universal, 2021.

shoot and kill an injured and unarmed Anthony. The film takes this as proof of Afro-pessimism's analysis of anti-Black violence. Anthony was shot because he was Black. Yet we see more than anti-Black violence in this scene. The police rely on race and space as visible shorthand for class. Being Black and in Cabrini–Green becomes evidence to them of Anthony and Brianna's classed and raced vulnerability to state violence. This isn't a question of Blackness or class. It's Blackness and the *perception* of class.

The film's final scene makes the case for new Black horror and, from a Marxist perspective, the need to imagine critical forms of resistance to racial capitalism. After Anthony's execution, the police put Brianna in the back of a squad car. An officer threatens her to support their version of Anthony's murder. She agrees, but only if they let her see herself in the mirror. In her terrified and helpless reflection, Brianna recognizes why William's adaptation of the Candyman story matters and, by extension, why new Black horror matters. Literal and figurative representations of anti-Blackness can offer forms of resistance for people living under racial capitalism's oppressions. The feelings of terrified helplessness they can conjure aim to incite resistance. Say his name, as Black Lives Matter activists urge. And Brianna does. Five times. Candyman appears, dispatches the officers on the scene, and frees Brianna before retreating down the alley where Anthony first saw the police roll through Cabrini–Green. Brianna follows him to find he is no longer Anthony but Daniel Robitaille. "Tell everyone," he says, as police lights surround them and the film ends.

Candyman wants its viewers to tell everyone the story that new Black horror tells, the story of anti-Blackness. From this perspective, Candyman is a form of vengeance unleashed against anti-Blackness. Yet the film tells more than that. Its persistent focus on gentrification as a metaphor of anti-Blackness means that Candyman unleashes his vengeance against racial capitalism's uneven development. *Candyman*, we might say, is a story about abolition. As Ruth Wilson Gilmore writes, "the undoing of bondage—abolition—is quite literally to change places; to destroy the geography of slavery by mixing their labor with the external world to change the world and thereby themselves—as it were, habitation as nature—even if geometrically speaking they hadn't moved far at all."[63] In genre terms, *Candyman*, like many of the films in this chapter, aims to remake genre space. Their narratives use the realities of racial capitalism and its racialization of space to create irreal narratives of spaces reclaimed in and outside the genre. Tell everyone we're here, Candyman says. We can read this assertion of presence and commitment as one that means to remake the space of racial capitalism itself, even if, as Gilmore says, no one has moved far at all. Read from the perspective of racial capitalism, *Candyman* changes how we might understand the terror of new Black horror. Its horrors come from racial capitalism's seeming inevitability, but its tales underscore what Marxist analysis shows, that racial capitalism's uneven development is not an unchanging, natural process but the result of policy, decision making, and action. Knowing that, we might just find a way out after all.

5

COMMODITIES HATE YOU
Mass-Culture Horror and Commodity Forms

It can seem like Marxism believes that capitalism commodifies everything it touches, but this idea doesn't come from Marx so much as Hungarian philosopher Georg Lukács. Writing in 1922, Lukács argued that a social world completely reorganized by commodity exchange would alter human consciousness itself. The process of commodification, Lukács contended, seeps into cognition, a process that he called *Verdinglichung*, usually translated as *reification*. While Lukács claimed Marx used the term in his discussion of the commodity form, Gillian Rose shows that Lukács borrowed it from German sociologist Georg Simmel.[1] Like Simmel, Lukács was less concerned with alienation's economic effects than its social ones. For Lukács, industrial capitalism's factory-bound, rationalized labor encouraged rationalized and calculating thought. Instead of being afforded the unity of thought and activity that Lukács ascribed to workers in precapitalist societies, workers in capitalism were reduced to passive objects. Capitalism rendered them "contemplative," in Lukács's language.[2] As a result, workers find that all their relations—to objects, to other people, to themselves, and to society—become in capitalism non-relations, experiences of "isolation and fragmentation," or, more properly, relations between objects, not subjects.[3] To overcome this alienation, Lukács maintained, workers would have to recognize their proper "standpoint" as a class in and for itself.[4] This Hegelian process of recognition would allow the proletariat to throw off its reified consciousness, assume the mantle of world-historical subject, and reclaim capitalism's social totality for its own use.

Lukács's account of how the commodity form came to dominate social reality was particularly important for mid-twentieth-century Western Marxists. With the 1932 German-language publication of Marx's

Economic and Philosophical Manuscripts of 1844, and French and English translations following soon after, alienation became a central term for Marxist thought. The young Marx's Hegelian discussion of alienation gave theorists a new way to talk about capitalism's effects on social relations. While some looked back to Hegel for greater insight into the function of alienation, many adopted Lukács's often expressly Hegelian reworking of Marx's thought in *History and Class Consciousness*.[5] Indeed, while Lukács's discussion of reification isn't as explicitly Hegelian as his earlier work, *The Theory of the Novel*, Lukács himself would later critique his analysis as "an attempt to out-Hegel Hegel."[6] Western Marxism drew on Lukács's theory of reification and Hegel's discussion of alienation to produce such influential mid-century works as Herbert Marcuse's *One-Dimensional Man*, Guy Debord's *Society of the Spectacle*, and Fredric Jameson's *The Political Unconscious*.[7] For Marcuse, capitalist alienation kept people from differentiating between appearance and reality. According to Marcuse, alienation reduces the world to one dimension of commodities, leaving people unable to understand themselves beyond their commodified experience, let alone to do the work necessary to transform themselves. Debord also focused on the psycho-social alienation of the commodity form, arguing that the commodity turns members of capitalist society into passive contemplators of their own instrumentalization. Jameson draws on Lukács's account of recognition to salvage culture produced under capitalism. By revealing submerged utopian impulses in culture's seemingly negative abstractions, critics can draw readers into a revolutionary process of recognition. Capitalism's social totality may be riddled with abstraction and alienation, as Jameson shows, but critical analysis of its texts can remake capitalism's otherwise passive contemplations of reified consciousness into the basis for radical action.

When horror satirizes popular culture, we see a similar focus on passive spectatorship. In these films, popular culture is always mass culture—that is, culture mass-produced for the masses—and its terrors are the threat that mass culture will reduce us to mindless spectators. Mass-culture horror expresses a form of common sense in capitalism about what commodities are and do. If that common sense sounds a bit like Lukács, Marcuse, and Debord, it should. These films reflect the popularization of countercultural critiques of mass society undoubtedly influenced by their work, though not reducible to it. In *The Conquest of Cool*,

Thomas Frank neatly describes this countercultural perspective as one that insisted "the failings of capitalism were not so much exploitation and deprivation as they were materialism, wastefulness, and soul-deadening conformity."[8] This perspective defines two mass-culture horrors from the dawn of the neoliberal era, George Romero's zombies-at-the-mall *Dawn of the Dead* (1978) and Philip Kaufman's remake of the 1950s classic *Invasion of the Body Snatchers* (1978). Both took aim at consumerism and conformity, and show mass culture turning its consumers into mindless zombies and pod people. In the 1980s, horror made mass culture's mindless passivity into the stuff of disgust. With its tale of an alien goo that people love to eat even when it's eating them, Larry Cohen's *The Stuff* (1985) lacquered horror's feelings of revulsion to a satire of advertising and consumerism. John Carpenter's *They Live!* (1988) similarly makes advertising the basis of its horror after a man discovers a cheap pair of sunglasses that reveals the revolting commands of alien overlords in the endless come-ons of the society of the spectacle. In these films, recognition is what matters. It's not only the highest form of insight, but hard won. As Slavoj Žižek points out, seeing through ideology is tough: it takes the hero of *They Live!* six minutes of fighting to convince someone else to put on the glasses.[9] For these films, the real challenge of mass culture is being able to see through it.

No wonder, then, that mass-culture horror of the 1970s and 1980s aren't just horror films but cult films. In chapter 3, we discussed the cult film as defined by a need to be "transgressive *and* recuperative," in the words of horror scholar Barry Keith Grant.[10] Here, I want to focus on the affect of the cult film, the feeling of being inside and outside what the film subjects to critique. In cult films, "viewers laugh at the normal, [and] tame the Other," Grant explains, "but nowhere see themselves."[11] The pleasure of watching a cult film is the pleasure of knowing who the real mindless viewer is, someone who isn't watching cult movies. We should understand mass-culture horror as a subgenre of cult film for this reason. It's made for audiences who take pleasure in not being consumers of mass culture, or, at least, who don't consume mass culture without contesting at some level what Stuart Hall calls "the dominant cultural order."[12] We can see this clearly in mass-culture horror in the '70s and '80s where consumerism's passivity is a problem for the films' characters, not their audiences. Lamberti Bava makes this idea the conceit of *Demons*

(Dèmoni) (1985), a gross-out satire of conservative fears that horror films destroy their viewers' minds. Where films like *Videodrome* and *Ringu* extend the horror of spectatorship to their audiences, *Demons* aims instead for the cult film's pleasures of being inside and outside at once in its mass-culture critique.[13] In *Demons*, when a horror movie turns its audience into flesh-eating demons the film doesn't try to wring terror from its audience that they might suffer the same fate. As we will see, twenty-first-century mass-culture horror continues to rely on countercultural critiques of mass culture and the cult film's affect of being inside and outside the subject of critique. Marxist analysis can help us find in these films' view of commodification the real horrors of the commodity form in capitalism. It doesn't turn workers into passive consumers. It urges them on in the work of their own destruction.

We'll get a better sense of what this means if we look at Rob Savage's found-footage film *Host* (2020). Shot and edited to look like a free forty-five-minute Zoom call, *Host* seems to exemplify mass-culture horror's terror of passive contemplation. Capturing a period when Zoom calls were novel, *Host* features a group of friends gathered online during the first UK-mandated pandemic lockdown.[14] The call's host, Haley, reveals she's got a special activity for this social call: a séance with a real medium. It quickly goes wrong when they summon a demon that murders them one by one. The story can seem the logical end to the commodity's deadly push toward contemplation: the Zoom demon turns the callers into passive spectators of their own deaths. A subtle shift in the way the footage of this found-footage horror is found, however, makes these victims anything but passive. Starting with early found-footage films like *The Blair Witch Project* (1998), the genre relies on two conceits: Characters film themselves during the story's events, and viewers watch what happened based on what they left behind. Found-footage films can't happen unless everything has already happened and left behind a stack of video cassettes, hard drives, or flash cards. However, the viewers of *Host* aren't supposed to be watching the playback of events in the past. Like the film's characters, they're simply part of the call. The film begins when the call begins and ends when it ends. The footage really isn't found at all.[15] It presents itself as consumed while it is being made. Like Vanessa and Joseph Winter's *Deadstream* (2022), *Host* is part of a new subgenre, streaming found-footage film. Where *Deadstream* presents itself as a videostream that anyone can consume, though, *Host* is just for the call's participants. No one is passively watching themselves. They're actively producing and consuming these images simultaneously.

Host lets us describe something that Marx emphasizes in his account of the commodity: It takes work to make commodities and to realize their value in exchange. This is why Marx places the commodity form at the heart of his theory of value. It captures the flux and reflux of abstract and concrete labor as workers sell their labor-power for money and exchange it for other commodities to keep themselves alive. That means we aren't simply dominated by the commodity form as a conceptual abstraction, passively reduced to contemplating some alien image of our real activity. We're also *actively* dominated by it. Our activity continually creates it. Reification theory misses the point by emphasizing the commodity's reduction of workers, people, and objects to passivity. Alfred Sohn-Rethel called the commodity capitalism's "real abstraction" for a reason.[16] As an abstraction, the commodity is the result of people's real "spatio-temporal activity."[17] It is what keeps that activity going. It's a persistent demand to act.

And Marx would agree. In his discussion of the commodity form, Marx describes commodities as "the material bearers of . . . exchange value."[18] In German, the word for "material bearer," *Träger*, denotes a living entity that carries something and a material thing that serves as the substructure for something else. In other words, it's an action *and* a form. While we're used to thinking of Marx's account of the commodity as one about form—it is the commodity form, after all—his goal is to explain the context in which commodity owners act, or what Michael Heinrich calls "the form determinants of the commodity."[19] The commodity form matters because it makes people (and the biosphere, as we saw in chapter 3) into what Marx calls in German *Charaktermaske*, or mask wearers. As political philosopher Luca Basso explains, Marx wants to show us that capitalism does more than reduce people to legal persons who recognize one another as property owners in a purely legal relation. It also requires people to "take the role of 'economic masks,' 'personifications' of economic dynamics."[20] To be a mask wearer is to be "reduced to a bearer of labor-power," Basso explains, "which has a value like all the other commodities."[21] People *are* caught up in the process of commodification, but they aren't simply reduced to objects by it. It forces them to take on legal and economic roles in the world of capital so that they can act. For this reason, the mask provides a useful model for understanding the commodity form. It's an empty form produced by human activity that its wearers use to terrorize and dominate. And that describes the demon in *Host*. Unlike demons in other films, which usually have names and histories, the demon in *Host* is nothing more than an empty form. Early in the séance, one of the callers, Jemma, fakes a supernatural presence because she's bored. The medium is horrified when Jemma reveals what she's done. She created a kind of story mask, the medium explains, for any entity to put on or take off.[22]

The demon mask of *Host*, then, helps us to understand what Marx means when he describes commodity fetishism as "spectral objectivity" [*gepenstige Gegenständlichkeit*].[23] For Marx, value is a demonic thing because it guides our actions even though we can't see it. The terror of commodity fetishism isn't that it's an illusion that obscures the reality of socially produced value. Contrary to some readings of Marx, we haven't mistaken a social relation for a thing or thought that material things carry around value on their own. Those interpretations come from eighteenth- and nineteenth-century usages of "fetishism" to describe misrecognized social relationships, as William Pietz shows.[24] That's not the case with Marx. His account of commodity fetishism describes real activity. As Basso puts it, "the fetish phenomenon has to do with how reality manifests itself."[25] What commodity fetishism describes is the conjunction of form and action that makes capitalism go: the exchange of goods and services for money. It's capitalism's real and necessary process for socializing private labor. Capitalism can't exist without the activity that the commodity form's spectral objectivity creates. It doesn't matter whether we see through it as an abstraction or recognize labor as social. What matters is what we *do*.

Are we active, then, or is the form? Well, it's not really an either/or question. We can see what that means via *Host*. The callers create an empty form that comes back to haunt them, and it leaps from object to object and attacking them with whatever is ready to hand. We might better understand the violence of this empty form if we look at Marx's description of the commodity as an uncanny object. In *Capital*, he describes a table that "not only stands with its feet on the ground, but, in relation to all other commodities, . . . stands on its head, and evolves out of its wooden brain grotesque ideas, far more wonderful than if it were to begin dancing of its own free will."[26] What the table's brain evolves are the grotesqueries of value, tentacles that allow it to communicate with other commodities as abstractions rather than material wealth. Those relations are what haunt us in capitalism, forcing our activity into particular channels. That doesn't make us capitalism's passive spectators. Our activity is the crucial component of capitalism's destructive reduction of us to mere bearers of value. The callers *want* to be on the Zoom call, and they go out of their way to capture what they see for others and for themselves. Not only does the film not exist without their camerawork, it is the means of their destruction. The film's conclusion underscores this point. After the demon has killed multiple callers, Jemma runs to Haley's in a futile attempt to save her. Together, the two become the active filmmakers and spectators of their own end. As Jemma surveys Haley's darkened apartment with her cellphone, Haley uses her tablet to shoot flash photographs. Together, they capture nothing but images of empty space until the moment the demon leaps out and kills them.

Like most found footage, screens die in *Host* when their filmmakers die. *Host*, however, does not end with a cut to black. After Haley and Jemma's deaths, the Zoom interface appears. The film's final image shows an unknown force bringing up a list of the call's participants, but this isn't part of the fiction. These are the start of the film's credits. After scrolling through the names of the writers and actors, the application closes and more credits roll. We can read this as more than a clever collapse of text into paratext. By the film's end, the demon has become the call's host—in Zoom parlance, the person who controls the call—ready to find more people willing to take on the work of their own destruction, all ironically embedded in a display of the work of filmmaking. That continued demonic search for workers matters. Capitalism aspires to activity without *you*, but it's never managed it. Once you're gone, value, that aimless demonic urge, must find another bearer. Commodification hates us not because it turns us into mindless objects but because it can't work without us.

Horror and the Four Commodity Forms of Integral Capitalism

Twenty-first-century mass-culture horror, then, can help us to see commodification is more than mass production. We have to get outside the factory to understand commodities and the commodity form. It's a form that allows other people to appropriate your labor. When Alfred Sohn-Rethel calls the commodity form capitalism's real abstraction, he wants us to see how its separation of use from exchange naturalizes capitalism's appropriation of use-value across many different forms. The real abstraction not only separates use from exchange in physical commodities but also in capitalist thought and society. Intellectual labor develops abstractions, Sohn-Rethel argues, to rationalize its appropriation of the products of manual labor and of the natural world.[27] The commodity is central to capitalism because it is a highly malleable form for the appropriation of value.

No one has demonstrated commodification's malleability in the twenty-first century better than Luc Boltanski and Arnaud Esquerre. In *Enrichment*, Boltanski and Esquerre describe four distinct types of commodities in contemporary postindustrial capitalism, what they term "integral capitalism."[28] For Boltanski and Esquerre, integral capitalism sidesteps some of the problems that we find in other attempts to describe neoliberal or postindustrial capitalism. At the end of the twentieth century, theorists were flummoxed by what they took to be the end of industrial capitalism as what they called a *mode of production*, a term from Marx that is so vague that people tend to use it interchangeably with the form of labor's exploitation (e.g., slavery, serfdom, wage labor, etc.). Jarius Banaji shows that arguments about the modes of production that ran through the 1980s were predicated on a simple confusion of two distinct terms. Instead of taking the mode of production as an epoch of production, as Marx describes it, critics took it to mean specific forms of the exploitation of labor—e.g., enslaved labor, slave labor, corvée labor, and so on. This misunderstanding led critics to describe any number of things as modes of production rather than analyzing the specifics of a given conjuncture. Through the 1970s and 1980s, the idea that the mode of production was simply the form of exploitation was widely accepted even as (or perhaps because) it became clear that contemporary or postmodern capitalism wasn't based on a single form of exploitation. Some Marxists argued that colonialism and postmodern capitalism revealed a new situation that consisted of a variety of modes of production—meaning forms of labor exploitation—and this necessitated new forms of analysis.[29] Banaji rightly argues that this turn to the supposed pluralization of modes of production was a mistake. Marxist thought is better served by analyzing the articulation of capitalism's different forms of production, labor exploitation, and relations of production in a given historical conjuncture, rather than casting around for new modes of production. With integral capitalism, Boltanski and Esquerre offer us an example of such an analysis. They don't define integral capitalism using one hegemonic form of labor exploitation but a set of tendencies that "pushes accumulation by extending the cosmos of commodities."[30] Beyond the mass-produced commodity we know from Marx, what Boltanski and Esquerre call "the standard form,"[31] integral capitalism offers three others: *the collection form*, or goods sold due to a narrative that suggests they will increase in value; *the trend form*, or mass-produced goods given an additional aura of value by connection to brand names, celebrity, and so on; and *the asset form*, or goods bought as stores of value and readily resold.[32] Each of these commodity forms creates new masks for workers to wear. As we'll see, twenty-first-century horror captures this newly expansive world of commodity forms in its uncanny objects, phantasms, and deranged instances of performance art. With each commodity form, horror helps us to see how capitalism entwines form and action to make us active participants in its violence, turning us against one another and ourselves.

In Fabric: The Standard Form

For Boltanski and Esquerre, the standard form is the commodity that everyone knows, a mass-produced object. They add one important distinction: the standard form commodity is a mass-produced object *sold for its use-value alone*. To see this form in action, let's consider Peter Strickland's British horror *In Fabric* (2018). Released by A24 Films and produced by Ben Wheatley, Strickland's film was positioned as part of the 2010s elevated horror cycle. Unlike other arthouse horrors, Strickland's film has less to do with the arthouse aesthetics we'll discuss in chapter 6 than 1960s Italian horror. His earlier film, *Berberian Sound Studio* (2012), was a direct homage to the atmospherics of Italian horror and *giallo*, and *In Fabric* consciously evokes the look of Mario Bava's fashion horrors, *Blood and Black Lace (6 donne per l'assassino)* (1964) and *Hatchet for Honeymoon (Il rosso segno della follia)* (1970). Set in the 1980s during the post-Christmas sale season, *In Fabric* is another of horror's consumer satires. A coven-run department store sells a cursed dress that destroys its wearers, first Sheila, a bank clerk, then Reg, a washing-machine repairman, and Babs, his fiancée.

The film's use of catalog, television, and personal advertisements suggests its ostensible theme is consumer desire run rampant. The coven even imbues their goods with occult power through the ritualized masturbation of a store mannequin and their male leader. Yet these desires are at best banal. The cursed dress is interested enough in sex that it drags itself to wherever people are at it, but it doesn't send its wearers into sexual ecstasies or destroy them in the throes of passion. Its victims die in mundane accidents: a car crash, a misfiring gas heater, a department store fire. What makes *In Fabric* a film about the standard form commodity is the weakness of consumer desire. To its victims, the dress is just one more mass-produced good. When Sheila comes to the coven's store, she is looking for *a* dress, not *this* dress. It fulfills a purpose. She needs something to wear on a date, and the sales-witch convinces her to buy it even though she doesn't care for it. When she later tries to return it, the head of the coven insists the dress is interesting and unique, but no one else sees it that way. Reg only puts it on after he spills beer on his shirt during his stag night and his future father-in-law goads him into it. He bought it secondhand to humiliate Reg; any dress would have done. Babs puts it on for a similar reason: she's doing laundry. When she finds something better at the department store, she drops it on the floor and doesn't think about it again. The coven may want the dress to capture consumers' desires, but for its victims, it's just a use-value, a dress.

We can see in the film's conclusion that even what makes the dress unique, its curse, makes it nothing more than a standard form commodity. In the final scene, we discover that the dress doesn't just kill its wearers. It presses them into service after death. After frenzied consumers destroy the department store, one of the witches descends through the store's lower levels, revealing in separate locked rooms each of the dress's

Figure 20. Sheila reproduces the cursed dress that killed her. *In Fabric*, directed by Peter Strickland. A24 Films, 2018.

victims. They have been brought back to life to produce identical versions of the dress that killed them. Boltanski and Esquerre note that this use of a prototype is specific to the standard form: "the standard mode of manufacturing entails reproducing a *prototype* by producing a potentially unlimited number of *specimens*."[33] The dress was unique in the only way that matters to the standard form commodity, as a prototype for mass production (Figure 20). We might say that *In Fabric* traces the destructive path of the standard form commodity from prototype to specimen.

In Fabric, then, lets us describe something essential about the standard form commodity, something that Marx understood well. In capitalism, consumption and production are inextricable. We must consume to survive, and the commodification of the means of subsistence means we must work to be able to consume. While Strickland's film focuses its critique on consumerism's wasteful desires, Marxist analysis helps us see the problem isn't one of desire. In capitalism, the first action that binds us to the commodity form is the act of living. Our most basic needs drag us into the basement and chain us to our workstations.

Slaxx: The Trend Form

The trend form commodity might seem like a minor variant of the standard form. It's a mass-produced good meant to be used and discarded. The difference is how quickly the trend form commodity becomes trash. Standard form commodities get thrown away when they no longer serve their purpose. Trend form commodities become trash when they're no longer trendy. While they have use-value, they aren't sold for it. They're sold for their narratives. The dress of *In Fabric* is a standard form commodity because it wasn't sold as part of a larger narrative that people wanted to join. It was just a dress. By contrast, narratives drive the sale of trend form commodities, and these narratives must be created, fostered, and sold. Makers of trend form commodities often employ "trendsetters," Boltanski and Esquerre explain, to "'feel' an emerging trend" and "put it into a form that is compatible with the organization and financial possibilities of the firms that employ them."[34] If that sounds like a description of fast fashion, it should. The trend form wouldn't surprise Walter Benjamin. For Benjamin, fashion was the model for commodification itself. In *The Arcades Project*, he argued that fashion taught capitalism how to give "sex appeal" to "the inorganic" commodity.[35] For Benjamin, reification was essentially a sexual enlivening of the inorganic. (We might say that the witches of *In Fabric* wanted to give their dress a narrative but couldn't manage it.) By imbuing objects with desire, capitalism created what Benjamin called the phantasmagoria of the commodity fetish, a world of images and objects to be desired. Benjamin's account of the social types produced by this phantasmagoria can help us to better understand the difference between the trend form and the collection form. For Benjamin, the flaneur produces "phantasmagorias of the market." His constantly roving eye surveys capitalism's ever-changing public displays of the day's fashions and imbues them with desire. By contrast, the private collector accumulates objects slowly through the result of careful examination and deliberation, producing "phantasmagorias of the interior."[36]

While Theodor Adorno dismissed Benjamin's use of these allegorical figures to describe commodification, Boltanski and Esquerre's account of the trend and collection forms suggest that Benjamin was onto something. For Boltanski and Esquerre, the trend and collection forms commodify narratives of authenticity. The collection form uses narratives of authenticity that tend toward the unique—luxury commodities closely connected to history, most especially the historically existent bodies of their creators, famous possessors, and so on. A painting can be a collection form commodity because its connection to the painter's body, its physical uniqueness, and its historical existence over time give it value, what Benjamin called "aura."[37] If the collection form is a work of art, the trend form is the work of art in the age of mechanical reproduction. It consists of goods and services that let the masses get close to something *like* the authentic: a knock-off dress modeled on a luxury brand, a pair of inexpensive shoes that look like a more expensive brand, a celebrity-branded mass-produced product, and so on. Because it is like the authentic but not authentic, the trend form is haunted by sudden catastrophic depreciation. As Boltanski and Esquerre explain, the trend form "has to gamble on the quest for distinction and on the process of imitation."[38] That gamble means the trend form "generates enormous quantities of trash, even more than the standard form does."[39] Why? Trends are ephemeral and can end at a moment's notice. Its producers are essentially speculators. Like risk-takers in any market, they want their trends to last just long enough that they aren't left holding the bag. And if the capitalists making and selling trend form commodities are in a risky position, that goes double for the people they employ. As Boltanski and Esquerre note, trend form workers are "condemned to short term and precarious employment."[40] With the trend form, everyone is a moment away from being discarded.

Disposability is at the core of *Slaxx* (2020), directed by Elza Kephart. Like *In Fabric*, *Slaxx* satirizes consumption using a cursed object. Instead of a dress, *Slaxx* has a pair of killer jeans, and they're on the loose in the flagship store of a fictional clothing company, Canadian Cotton Clothiers (CCC). On the surface, *Slaxx* gives a Marxist spin to the subgenre of cursed objects, though it has more in common with *Death Bed: The Bed That Eats* (1977) than *Christine* (1983). Its dead-alive jeans are the uncanny commodity form par excellence. They don't simply talk among themselves like Marx's table; they dance and write notes in blood. The film wants audiences to see these pants as an irreal figure for how capitalism grinds its workers into abstract labor's meat jelly. It's no mistake that they feed vampirically on the blood of the store's workers.

When we read the film through the trend form commodity, though, we see the horror of *Slaxx* lies not in the commodity's violence, which is largely silly, but in the way the store's workers act to make themselves part of the company's narrative about ethical consumption. The film's satirical target is the self-righteousness of so-called mission-driven companies—that is, firms that use social justice mission statements to build their brands. CCC's store is festooned with empty incitements like "Make a Better Tomorrow Today" and "Now Is Now," juxtaposed with more recognizable appeals to ethical consumption like "Sweatshop Free. Organic. GMO-Free. Fair Trade." These claims are part of how CCC uses its mission to create a trend narrative, linking social justice with fast fashion so consumers can narrate their consumption as ethical. To buy CCC clothes isn't to identify just with its fashion sense but with its ethos. For the film's main character, the good-natured liberal Libby, this is CCC's appeal. Newly hired to work an overnight shift launching the latest line, Libby wants to work at CCC for its mission and its employee discount. And she's going to need that discount. To work the floor, CCC workers must wear the company's latest season, and "seasons" change monthly. Still, Libby's attraction to the mission is why she wants to be part of what the store manager, Craig, calls the "CCC family."

Slaxx helps us to describe the activity that undergirds the trend form commodity. The victims of *In Fabric* were inveigled into work by the alienation of their basic needs. The victims of *Slaxx* seek out their oppression. Libby wants to work at CCC because she's already a customer, and so do the store's other employees. They may view the company's mission more cynically, but, like Libby, they work at CCC by choice, not necessity. *Slaxx* shows the destructiveness of this choice with the introduction of its killer pants. One clerk can't wait until the next morning to buy a pair of CCC's new jeans, so she puts on a pair in the employee bathroom where a drop of menstrual blood brings them to life. It's no mistake that this first victim is also the most sexualized. When the pants chew her in half, she's eaten up by the object of her desire. In this sense, *Slaxx* is about what the commodity does to consumers: They don't consume the clothes, the clothes consume them. The trend form, however, also helps us to think about these characters as workers. Marxism has often treated retail work as nonproductive, if not unproductive.

In *Capital*, Marx lumps retail clerks into his category "agents of circulation."[41] Capitalism needs circulation agents—the value in a commodity can't be realized unless it circulates and is sold—but Marx maintains that circulation agents can't add value to a commodity the way that workers do in the production process. For Marx, retail clerks, like warehouse workers, truck drivers, and other circulation agents, "must be paid by way of production agents."[42] In other words, circulation agents are paid out of the surplus-value that capitalism extracts from workers in the production process. That isn't to say circulation agents don't matter. They're important for speeding up turnover, and this allows capital to realize the value bound up in commodities quickly and reinvest in production. But for Marx, that's it. Circulation agents help capital to circulate, not accumulate. The trend form forces us to revise this account. It needs trendsetters to give its commodities value, and retail worker-consumers like Libby help employers showcase these trends. They are at the front line of narrative promotion. Companies select employees who can look the part and present the proper affect. It may be difficult to quantify how much surplus value trend-form workers add to the commodities they sell, but the trend form can't exist without their labor.

It's useful to see, then, that *Slaxx* connects the company's murderous exploitation of workers in retail to its exploitation of workers in production. When Craig discovers someone is killing his crew, he happily covers up their deaths to ensure the new line will launch. After all, trend form commodities don't hold value for long; one setback and the entire line could become trash. The killer pants origin shows that CCC is as wildly indifferent to the lives of its workers in production as it is to those of its circulation agents. CCC's lack of safety precautions in its cotton fields killed a thirteen-year-old Indian girl. She's back for revenge. And when the rest of the inventory comes to life at the film's end, it's clear she's not alone. The trend form reframes the pants' violence as something more than the revenge of exploited labor in the global South on deluded consumers in the global North. These different forms of exploitation are linked by the demands of fast fashion's mass-production cycles. The pressures of the trend form encourage the CCC to view its production and circulation workers as disposable. If the film suggests that the circulation agents who promote the trend form's narratives aren't as resistant to their exploitation as workers in

Figure 21. Libby tries to keep consumers away from an army of killer pants. *Slaxx*, directed by Elza Kephart. The Horror Collective, 2020.

production, we might understand this as part of the trend form narrative. They don't believe they're being exploited. In their minds, they're acting on their desires.

Slaxx can show us, then, how the trend form relies on workers' and consumers' active desire to become part of somebody else's narrative. While our necessary consumption draws us into domination by the commodified use-values of the standard form commodity, our desires for social display and connection draw us into domination by the trend form. For the film's first third, Libby helps Craig hide the bodies of other clerks because she wants to be part of the CCC family. Only when she realizes CCC's trend narrative is fiction—nothing is organic, fair trade, or ethically sourced—does she try to save herself and the customers outside. She even reaches a sort of cooperative agreement with an army of possessed pants. Still, Libby can't convince the rabid consumers outside not to run into the jean's deadly embrace (Figure 21). Caught up in the store's "Monday Madness," customers knock open the doors, desperate to consume the products that will consume them. As the violence of production meets the violence of consumption, Libby, the trend form worker, is stuck in the middle and trampled to death. We can find in *Slaxx* not only what the trend form has to offer capitalism, but also a new way to intensify its exploitation of labor through narrative. We can also see what this new form of exploitation means for workers: You'll kill yourself to be part of someone else's story.

Personal Shopper: The Collection Form

The collection form relies on something most people don't expect of commodities: authenticity. The narratives that support the trend form matter even more to the collection form. Here, narratives tightly link goods or services to a person, place, company, production run, or whatever. The tighter the link, the higher the commodity's "memorial force," in Boltanski and Esquerre's words, and the higher its potential price on the market.[43] In essence, the collection form commodifies history itself. This isn't to say that commodified histories are naively present in collection form commodities. Hayden White famously argued that people create history's narratives using the detritus of the past, selecting and emplotting events, people, and objects into stories defined by genre and ideology.[44] Producers of collection form commodities are no less engaged in narrative work. They understand that the histories they sell need to be shaped to give value to otherwise unremarkable goods or services. Narratives imbue collection form commodities with authenticity by integrating them into larger historical narratives. Sometimes, these narratives may be of notable craftsmanship or precious materials. This is why luxury goods might seem synonymous with collection form commodities. They aren't. The collection form commodity is any commodity that gains value through its claims to historical uniqueness, including tourist activities based on a region's political, social, or economic history; commodities marketed or protected by law as traditional; first editions of books; limited editions of toys; inclusive sets of mass-produced goods; and so on. It's anything sold based on claims of historical authenticity.

Creating history takes work, and it isn't the same kind of work as the work of trendsetters. Like Benjamin's flâneurs, trendsetters must see and be seen to keep their trend narratives going. Collection form narratives are private and the narrative work that sustains them is often camouflaged as brute historical fact, especially when one confronts commodity-objects. A Stradivarius violin or a Klein guitar is collectible for its rarity, craft, and function as an instrument, which makes it easy to overlook the centrality of narrative labor to these commodities. Narrative labor, though, is what gives collection form commodities their value. It is the work of creating authenticity. It documents production and ownership, connects and documents objects in relation to famous bodies, and places objects alongside other objects to increase their value through context. Such work might seem like more unproductive circulation work. After all, objects exist in time whether someone documents them or not. Yet one need only glance at popular antique appraisal shows to see the importance of this ghostly labor. A narrative of authenticity can turn a piece of junk into a collection form commodity.

We can find this ghostly labor in Oliver Assayas's arthouse Gothic *Personal Shopper* (2016). Assayas's film tells the tale of a woman searching for her authentic self while being pulled between invisible forces. Written for actor Kristen Stewart, then grappling with her fame from the *Twilight* films, *Personal Shopper* follows Maureen, a young woman caught between two images of herself that she cannot control. One comes from her dead twin brother, Lewis, whom she spends most of the film trying to contact through various forms of spiritualism. The other comes from her employer, Kyra, an actor. The film's tripling of personal image, spiritual work, and paid work reflects the influence of Guy Debord. In an interview, Assayas explained Debord's effects on his attempts to weave together art and politics. Reading Debord taught him, he explains, that "the issue of politics—meaning politics in art—is a way of understanding the subtext of society. It's about having real life characters having to deal with those invisible forces and being determined by them."[45] That's certainly the case with *Personal Shopper* and its metacommentary on Stewart's experience of fame. Maureen is torn between two invisible forces that wish to reduce her to a state of Debordian contemplation, another victim of the society of the spectacle. We see this most clearly when the dead Lewis begins to text Maureen. Although she's spent years trying to contact him, she can't tell if this is really Lewis. She's encountered other spirits, but never her brother and never via text. That's Kyra's preferred mode of communication. Still, she replies. Eventually, Lewis convinces her to sneak into Kyra's apartment and put on the clothes she chose for her. Maureen stands before Kyra's many mirrors, entranced and repulsed by the image of herself as someone else. Later, she will take a picture of herself for Lewis in another of Kyra's outfits (Figure 22).

The film's Debordian critique aims to help Maureen/Stewart overcome her false identification with external images before they destroy

Commodities Hate You | 141

Figure 22. Maureen takes a photo of herself in one of her employer's outfits. *Personal Shopper*, directed by Oliver Assayas. IFC Films, 2016.

her. Because *Personal Shopper* is a commentary on celebrity, what matters is Maureen's recognition of herself, not the image she creates in expensive clothes. Those images are a trap, as the film's murder plot reveals. Maureen discovers Kyra murdered, and Lewis then discloses that he's in fact Kyra's boyfriend, Ingo. The photos he solicited were tricks to incriminate her. He lures Maureen to a hotel room, ostensibly to blackmail her but more likely with the hope that her bad heart condition will kill her and leave him in the clear. She's saved by what seems like the intervention of her ghost-brother. When she enters the room, the door behind her opens and the image fades to black. The next sequence follows a disembodied camera as it floats out of the room, down the hall, and out of the hotel, Maureen nowhere to be seen. When it cuts back to the hotel, Ingo walks out alone and into the waiting arms of the police. Yet this isn't the triumph of her brother's image over her employer's. It's the unveiling of Maureen's sense of self. Throughout, the film shows the presence of spirits. Glasses vibrate and break, emanations appear, and so on. The conclusion reveals these weren't ghosts but emanations from Maureen herself. Once again, Maureen is speaking with what she believes to be a ghost. When she asks if it is her brother, she gets no response. But when she asks, "Or is it just me?" she receives a pounding *yes*, and the film ends. This conclusion seems based on a split between nineteenth-century occultists. Spiritualists thought mediums could contact the dead, while Theosophists insisted spiritual activity was the result of the medium's own mental powers.[46] From an occult perspective, Maureen is a Theosophist medium who has been under spiritualism's delusions. Or more simply, she's been doing it all herself. What flees the hotel, then, isn't a ghost but the apparatus that doubles Maureen's image of herself. To save herself, she has to dismiss the camera she's carrying around within her head.

A Marxist reading of commodity forms can help us to locate something else in *Personal Shopper*: the labor that goes into the collection form. Like the retail clerks of *Slaxx*, Maureen's job as a personal shopper seems like circulation work. After all, she literally circulates luxury goods from designers to Kyra and back again. However, in shuttling these goods to and fro, Maureen also imbues them with history by connecting them with a celebrity body. After all, designers lend celebrities clothes to increase the value of their work and perhaps to stir up enough interest to produce a trend form commodity. Maureen's work is part of this circuit and valorizes the clothes she borrows for Kyra by giving them a narrative of authenticity. Of course, Maureen doesn't see her work this way. To her, this work is meaningless. It fills up time while she tries to contact her brother. Even here, though, we find something meaningful. The collection form needs workers and consumers not to recognize the work that goes into creating narratives of authenticity. Why? Maureen doesn't merely select, sort, and transport clothes. She's Kyra's body double. In this sense, her work undermines whatever story of authenticity the joining of designer brands and celebrity bodies means to evoke. Kyra's clothes aren't really Kyra's. They're made for her, but it is Maureen who shows up for measurements and fittings, Maureen who delivers them to Kyra, and Maureen who returns them to the designers after Kyra wears them. If there's a story of authenticity, it's the story of Maureen's work.

From this perspective, *Personal Shopper* lets us see how the work of creating narratives of authenticity is kept obscure, lest it insert distance and inauthenticity into the narratives that give these objects value. Little wonder that Maureen is entranced by the ghostly. She is a medium for value. When she takes photos of herself in her boss's clothes, she creates more than alienated images of herself. She captures the absent presence of her labor. These twenty-first-century spirit images offer a glimpse of the labor in the collection form commodity.

Murder Party: The Asset Form

Each of the commodity forms relies on our activity for its destructive appropriation of value. They give us masks to put on and we do, but our actions make commodification work. What mass-culture horror underscores is that we're never entirely at ease in these masks. We're always inside and outside the demands of a form, even when we do whatever it takes to satisfy it. We see that conflicted experience in Jeremy Saulnier's debut, *Murder Party* (2007). The film begins with Chris, a middle-aged loner, discovering an invitation to a Halloween "murder party." To prepare, he makes a knight costume out of cardboard boxes and bakes a loaf of pumpkin bread from the remains of his smashed-up jack-o-lantern. When he gets to the party, though, he finds it isn't a murder-themed party. It's a party to murder whomever was dumb enough to show up. Wealthy art dealer Alexander has promised each member of an art collective a sizable chunk of money from a grant he administers if they kill someone and document it in their art. When Chris arrives, they tie him up but can't decide what to do. No one has the stomach to kill him, not even when one of the artists dies of an allergic reaction to Chris's pumpkin bread. They pass around drugs to delay and defer, and a stoned Alexander unwittingly admits he's a conman. He's never sold art or administered a grant. His plan was simple: Collect art from unknown artists, kill them, and profit off their now valuable art.

What Alexander wanted to do was to create what Boltanski and Esquerre call asset form commodities. He's miscalculated, though. The asset form isn't speculative. It stores value in durable, easily resold objects. As Boltanski and Esquerre explain, "we must stress here that an object, as an asset, does not produce revenue."[47] Asset form commodities might produce revenue when they are sold, but their function for capital has nothing to do with profit or the creation of more value. People churn other commodity forms for profit. Asset form commodities are for storing value. For Boltanski and Esquerre, the high-end art market exemplifies the asset form. These pieces are assets because they are durable, limited in number, highly sought after, readily authenticated, and, most importantly, their value remains stable over time. The owners of asset form commodities must be able to treat them as "a virtual reserve currency."[48] If they need cash, these pieces must be easy to sell at value. The problem with Alexander's plan is that the artists he's invited aren't famous enough to create asset form commodities on their own. He hopes the murder party will be enough to do it. The crime would produce a limited number of pieces, imbue each with a narrative of authenticity, and make them highly sought after, at least in theory. The problem is that their valuation can't be known until they enter the market. The durability of their value is even less certain.

Murder Party does, however, help us to locate the work that goes into making asset form commodities. Take a look at the film's artists. They know their art may not be fully commodified, but they also know art production should aim for the asset form. Their goal is to create rarefied objects for collectors to hold as assets. They aren't eager to die, but they understand death can be key to making a piece of art into an asset. The joke is that these artists are willing to make sacrifices for art, just not their own. Their planning and sniping, however, show they've already sacrificed something: their humanity. While they call themselves a collective, they hate one another and themselves, and mock each other's art out of jealousy and self-loathing. *Murder Party* satirizes the world of high art to show how much life gets sacrificed to ideas about art and authenticity. It's this murderous commitment to authenticity and the violent expulsion of the work behind it that matters to our understanding of the asset form. The one artist recognized by the rest as talented is Bill, and Bill is the collective's most homicidal member. When he discovers Alexander's scheme, he goes on a rampage. "Fuck this whole scene," he says, "everyone dies!" Bill recognizes there's no place for people in the asset form, only dead value. Everyone must die so value can live!

In this sense, the violence in *Murder Party* is part and parcel of what sociologist Andrew Ross calls sacrificial labor. In his study of workers in the culture industries, Ross describes sacrificial labor as "governed by the principle of the cultural discount, by which artists and other arts workers accept non-monetary rewards—the gratification of producing art—as compensation for their work, thereby discounting the cash price of their labor."[49] People might shorthand this as *paying your dues*, but what it means in practice is that employers can extort labor from workers as the price of employment in their desired industry. For workers to do the work they want, they're expected to accept hyperexploitation.

Figure 23. When Bill slaughters an entire performance art troop, this sign hangs ironically on the back wall. *Murder Party*, directed by Jeremy Saulnier. Magnet, 2007.

And that is what we find in *Murder Party*. The asset form calls for workers to make the ultimate sacrifice, themselves.

If the asset form is commodification at its most abstract and extreme, it is also a form that offers us a glimpse of a path out. Commodification is all about our activity. The problem isn't that we have to act. Alienation is part of human existence and has been long before capitalism's hegemony. The problem with capitalism is that we aren't in control of our activity. The commodity forms are. We put on their masks to make value and move it along, and we get dragged in its wake. We could, however, imagine a different world where we valued production by making conscious choices based on what is at hand and what is needed. We could make what is necessary rewarding and share work's burdens by taking it for what it is, work, without needing to hide or eliminate the fact that it is the result of work. We catch a glimpse of this other world in Chris. As a character, he's a stand-in for the film's creators, a group of friends who made the film on a shoestring budget. Like them, Chris is a bricoleur, making do with what he has. His smashed pumpkin becomes pumpkin bread and his old boxes a costume. He defeats Bill with a chainsaw he sees falling past an open window. It's telling, then, that when he gets home, he turns to genre fare to unwind. The film's last shot is of

Chris starting a horror movie on his VCR. We might take the fight between Chris and Bill as a sort of confrontation between genre texts and high art. There's even a piece of metacommentary hanging on the back wall, spattered with blood, a sign reading "Art?" (Figure 23). Chris manages to escape the scene of Bill's massacre because people treat it as a piece of performance art, something to be looked at passively. This scene of violence is the scene of high art, of passive spectatorship, of the asset form. It achieves what capitalism dreams of doing, reducing people to passive viewers. We might contrast this with the way the film views genre fare. Genre doesn't care if its elements or structures repeat, its imagery is copied, or its characters are clichéd. These are all masks, true, but we take them on and put them off as we need. One might argue that makes genre texts into standard or even trend form commodities, but I want to suggest something else. *Murder Party* helps us to see what it means to make use of what's at hand to make something new. Its elements aren't abstract, nor do they operate via some spectral objectivity that forces the text to fit a Procrustean genre bed. They're the subject of choice, selection, and shaping. They serve a purpose for the moment, and then they can be disassembled and made into something else. It is this making do with what's at hand that matters, a making do that isn't guided by unknown forces but by active choice. If we mean to wrest our activity back from the forced activity of the commodity forms, we will have to make conscious decisions about our actions, from what we make and how we make it, to who those productions serve and why. Without that, commodity forms will continue to force us to work toward our own annihilation.

6

THE FAMILY HATES YOU
Elevated Horror and Family Abolition

For Marxists, revolution means the expropriation of the capitalist class. Marx locates revolution's possibility in capitalism's internal development. Its centralization and accumulation of wealth foretells, Marx explains, that "what is . . . to be expropriated is not the self-employed worker, but the capitalist who exploits a large number of workers."[1] In the twentieth century, the Soviets took up Marx's vision of Communism as "the centralization of the means of production and the socialization of labor."[2] Wielding the power of the state, they expropriated the capitalist class and centralized production to create a uniquely Communist command economy. While the Soviet Union endured for seventy years, the Soviets found it difficult to juggle competing political and economic demands, and lacked the tools to coordinate supply and demand adequately.[3] Since the collapse of the Soviet Union and its command economy, Marxists have focused less on state centralization than on decommodification— that is, the removal of goods and services from the market, either through intensive regulation *or* direct provision by the state.

Yet Marx's work also includes another kind of revolution. In *The Communist Manifesto*, he and Engels call for the "abolition of the family."[4] In the early days of the Soviet Union, Alexandria Kollontai agitated for family abolition and succeeded in organizing creches and communal kitchens before revanchist patriarchal policies resumed under Stalin.[5] Twenty-first-century materialist feminists like Sophie Lewis, M. E. O'Brien, and Kathi Weeks have brought family abolition back to the forefront of Marxism's revolutionary demands, and for good reason. The family is the form that capitalism uses to appropriate the care and reproductive work of pregnant people and caregivers, and to reduce those who receive care to the status of dependent properties. Capitalism has shaped the family to meet the demands of white, heterosexual, cisgendered, and wealthy people, and to ignore the needs of working-class people, including people of color and LGBTQIA+ and gender-fluid people. The family is inseparable from the normative ideals of settler colonialism in its use of racial hierarchies and gender and sexuality norms to differentiate and oppress. Capitalism's disparate forms of violence hold the family together. As M. E. O'Brien explains, "the external terror of the state, settler colonialism, and fascist violence all help consolidate the normative family based on whiteness and property," while "the normative family form, obscured from view, is a private domain of control and subjugation."[6] If calls to abolish the family respond to this violence, they can produce a no less violent reaction. It little matters that such calls date back to Plato in *The Republic*, and preceded Marx and Engels in the nineteenth century in work by socialists like Charles Fourier and Robert Owen.[7] In 1848, Marx and Engels noted that "even the most radical flare up at this infamous proposal."[8] The proposition remains no less inflammatory nearly 175 years later. Sophie Lewis ventriloquizes the scandalized reactions of her twenty-first-century readers: "Abolish the family? You might as well abolish gravity or abolish God. So! The left is trying to take grandma away, now, and confiscate kids, and this is supposed to be progressive? What the fuck!?"[9]

If people resist calls for family abolition, that's because capitalism encourages us to think of the family as a place of refuge. The ideal of the family, as O'Brien explains, "embodies stability—for individuals, for a neighborhood, for a nation."[10] It doesn't matter that families can be abusive or that reactionaries use it as a normative ideal to validate their attacks on trans and queer people. Since capitalism has made the family seem like the only place where people are allowed to give and receive care, it's no wonder that people flare up at calls for its abolition. As Lewis declares: "It's existentially petrifying to imagine relinquishing the organized poverty we have in favor of an abundance we have never known and have yet to organize."[11] Yet family abolition means to expand care, not destroy it. It attacks the idea that the family is or should be the only set of caring relations available to us. This restrictive notion of care grows out of what feminists call separate spheres ideology. The separate spheres divide the world into a masculine public sphere of work and a feminine private sphere of domesticity, encouraging people to see the home as independent from the market. For men, it became a place of retreat from the cutthroat world of business, while for women, it was constructed as a place of safety from the market and its sexualized whims. Of course, this is all bunk. The idea of the "family exists only among the bourgeoisie," as Marx and Engels noted.[12] The family was not then, and has never been, outside the market. In *Capital*, Marx uses governmental reports to show that every member of nineteenth-century working-class families had to work, and that women and children were often more likely to be employed than men because they could be paid less and were easier to control or abuse. The bourgeois family was no less under the market's thrall. Its separate-spheres ideal was the result of eighteenth-century capitalism's increasing division of labor. During this time, historian Nancy Cott observes, male wage labor moved "toward calculated time-disciplined work habits," while women's unpaid domestic labor "retained the irregularity, the responsiveness to immediate and natural demands, and the intermixture with social occasion common to preindustrial occupations."[13] The family's separate sphere wasn't the result of some natural predilection for domesticity. It was the result of capitalism's division of labor into forms that were easily rationalized and subject to time-discipline and those that weren't. The separate spheres and their gender norms are addendums to this division, not its basis.

If this separation retains its hold today, that's because social reproduction work remains resistant to time-disciplined work habits. The family remains the one place where we can give and receive care freely because we still live in a system that needs to separate labor into forms it can easily exploit based on labor time, and those it needs to appropriate because it extends over wide swathes of lived time. Family structures are a result of how capitalism organizes work—where it occurs, who gets paid, and how much. This isn't limited to the bourgeois familial ideal. To take the most horrific example, capitalism's different regimes of enslaved labor reshaped the families of the enslaved and their descendants.[14] Simply put, capitalism shapes family structures to *its* needs, not ours. No wonder, then, that when people try to subvert the family's norms, capital calls on the power of the state to reestablish them through policy or violence. As O'Brien explains, "the family, the market, and the state collectively enable the reproduction of capitalist society."[15] The state may offer individuals minor policy rewards like tax incentives or social welfare benefits, but its primary role in family formation is, as O'Brien notes, "violence—such as through the use of mass incarceration, state murder, border enforcement, or public policies that increase mortality risk [such as the criminalization of abortion, sex work, and gay sex]."[16] Family abolition aims to remove the pervasive violence that capitalism uses to enforce the family as the sole location where care may be given and received.

Capital insists on the violent repression of attempts to subvert the family because, as Marx and Engels explain, the family is private property's origin and guarantee. Unfortunately, they rooted their analysis in nineteenth-century anthropology's studies of communal societies, which often bear more resemblance to just-so-stories than historical fact. Still, from this questionable ground, Marx and Engels articulated the family's role in private property. Their argument focused on the rise of patriarchy and its effects on the way societies transmit wealth. Communal societies, they argue, passed wealth through lines of maternal descent, allowing it to remain with the mother's clan. When men decided to seize this common wealth, they created systems of paternal descent that reduced women to child bearers and children to possessions—the patriarchal family. By allowing men to dispossess women of their bodily autonomy and to reduce women, children, and the elderly to dependents, the patriarchal family provides capitalism with a model for domination. In *The Origin of the Family, Private Property, and the State*, Engels traces its effects in law by examining the origin of the word *family*. In Latin, Engels explains, *familia* means "the total number of slaves belonging to one man," the paterfamilias, or patriarch.[17] Under Roman law, everyone in a household was subject to the patriarch's absolute control, from servants and the enslaved to wives and children. The right of usufruct gave the patriarch absolute power over his household: the rights to their bodies, the right to the fruits of their labor, and the right to destroy them, too.[18] Whether this is historically correct is beside the point. What Engels is doing is using extant historical analysis to argue that there are deep and abiding links between the terrors of the family and the terrors of private property, and there are. As we will see, it's the social form that capitalism uses to shape our most intimate relationships. The family terrifies because capitalism terrifies.

My Heart Can't Beat Unless You Tell It To and *The Witch*: Framed by the Family

The family's terrors have long been central to horror and the Gothic. It is no mistake that modern horror scholarship begins with an array of concepts focused on reproduction and femininity, from Barbara Creed's monstrous-feminine and Julia Kristeva's abjection to Carol Clover's final girl. For good or ill, women's oppression remains perhaps horror's central theme. As Erin Harrington shows, this oppression includes the reduction of femininity into something monstrous, what she calls "gynaehorror."[19] In chapter 7, we'll discuss elevated horror's use of metaphors to capture women's often elided or suppressed emotional experiences. Many of these films reshape horror's use of the monstrous feminine into more direct social critique, using feminist film theory and the woman's film to talk back to the history of women's oppression and their representation in horror. In this chapter, I focus on the family's role in elevated horror and what it can show us about the oppressions of the capitalist family. In the process, I also describe elevated horror and an emerging subgenre, the elevated family horror.

If this subgenre has gone largely unremarked, it is because fans and critics tend to define elevated horror by its aesthetics rather than its narrative elements. It's easy to see why. Films like Jennifer Kent's *The Babadook* (2014), Robert Eggers's *The Witch* (2015), Oz Perkins's *The Blackcoat's Daughter* (2015), Liam Gavin's *A Dark Song* (2016), Ali Abbasi's *Shelley* (2016), Ari Aster's *Hereditary* (2017) and *Midsommar* (2019), Adam MacDonald's *Pyewacket* (2017), Severin Fiala and Veronika Franz's *Goodnight Mommy* (2015) and *The Lodge* (2019), Jonathan Cuartas's *My Heart Can't Beat Unless You Tell It To* (2020), Alice Lowe's *Prevenge* (2016), Ruth Paxton's *A Banquet* (2021), Valdimar Jóhannsson's *Lamb* (2022), Alex Garland's *Men* (2022), Lucy Gaymer and Sian Robbins-Grace's *The Baby* (2022), Hanna Bergholm's *Hatching* (2022), and Michelle Garza Cevera's *Huesera: The Bone Woman* (2022) share an arthouse aesthetic that means to widen horror's audiences.[20] Horror has gone through earlier cycles of attempted gentrification. In his analysis of attempts to expand the genre's audience in the 1980s, horror scholar Richard Nowell offers a description of genre gentrification that also nicely describes the rhetorical purpose informing elevated horror's aesthetics. To elevate the genre, filmmakers use "markers of prestige or distinction which a targeted public is likely to recognize with little effort" and "objects and ideas that unequivocally invoke cultural and economic capital."[21] As we will see in the next chapter, the use of horror elements as metaphors is one important aspect of elevated horror's play for cultural capital. Its arthouse aesthetics are another. What makes elevated horror films "elevated," as David Church explains, is their "tone," which "can register through a film's apparent generic or formal/stylistic distance from established norms."[22] Church rightly identifies elevated, or in his term *posthorror*, as the most recent cycle of art horror, a subgenre that reaches back to Georges Franjou's *Eyes without a Face (Les yeux sans visage)* (1960) and Nicholas Roeg's *Don't Look Now* (1973). Elevated horror has a shared aesthetic that Church describes as "vulnerable stillness."[23] "Stylistically," Church writes, these "films evince minimalism over maximalism, largely eschewing jump-scares, frenetic editing and/or handheld cinematography in favor of cold and distanced shot framing, longer than average shot durations, slow camera movements, and stately narrative pacing."[24] Elevated horror's cinematography emphasizes natural light and shows a preference for painterly visual tones; the camera holds characters at a distance, with long shots to indicate a character's powerlessness by reducing her to a speck in an indifferent landscape. Elevated horror also tends to use music sparingly. Soundtracks emphasize ambient diegetic sound, often producing studied forms of silence, and when music is used, it is often harsh, dissonant, and abstract, reflecting the influence of avant-garde classical music like that used by Stanley Kubrick in *The Shining* (1980). In these films, discordant sounds appear alongside images meant to shock and disgust: a severed head (*Hereditary*), a dismembered child (*The Witch*), a demonic mouth in the back of a child's head (*A Banquet*), and so on. The result imbues an otherwise meditative mise-en-scène with unseen threat. While arthouse aesthetics make elevated horror a recognizable if capacious genre, it is also one readily subdivided by narrative elements and structures. In chapter 7, we'll see the importance of metaphor and allegory for the construction of a subgenre of therapeutic horror. Here we will trace the role of the family.

In many respects, elevated family horror is a continuation of the themes found in earlier cycles of family horror. Tony Williams described 1980s family horror as revealing the family's oppressions and a social urge to escape the family's violence.[25] That remains true of elevated family horror. Indeed, the centrality of the family to contemporary horror has led Johanna Isaacson to argue that horror "help[s] us understand that the *exploitation of social reproduction* makes the capitalist system possible."[26] That's exactly right. For Isaacson, horror reveals the "monstrosity" of the choices that capitalism offers women and gives us forms of refusal that can serve as models.[27] I want to focus on an important difference between elevated family horror and prior cycles. In earlier cycles, the family terrifies because someone can't perform their familial role. Films like *Psycho* (1960), *The Bad Seed* (1956), *Carrie* (1976), and *The Shining* are cautionary tales of bad children, bad mothers, and bad fathers. In elevated family horror, the family's terrors come not from the failures of individual family members to fulfill their roles but from the family's patriarchal and heterosexual norms. Two recent queer horrors underscore this point, Lucy Gaymer and Sian Robbins-Grace's horror-comedy series *The Baby* (2022) and Michelle Garza Cevera's *Huesera: The Bone Woman* (2022). The horror of the family in these films is the horror of compulsory heterosexuality. In *The Baby*, the titular demonic child parasitically attaches itself to women, demands they act the part of its mother, and kills them when they fall short. For Gaymer and Robbins-Grace, the baby enforces the family's norms. In flashbacks, we see how its first mother was alienated from her lesbian lover and kept under house arrest by her husband. When she escapes, she abandons the infant and walks forlorn into the sea. The series' critique of the family is explicit: You will be drowned by the family's norms, which are as vast and inescapable as the ocean. *Huesera* places this alienation in a contemporary context. Valeria's husband pressures her into having a child, and she quickly loses her sense of self as the child's nursery replaces her workshop. Once born, the child consumes her every waking hour. Desperate to escape, Valeria finds herself haunted by a threatening spirit, the bone woman. Only when she rejects the family's strictures and reunites with her former female lover do the spirit's threats cease.

Elevated horror's critiques of the family's norms are inextricable from its aesthetics. Their use of minimalism and aesthetic distance translates into visual experiences of the control imposed by the family as a normative ideal. The resulting experiences of dread and indifference reveal the family's terrors to be *structural*. No film makes that as clear as Jonathan

Cuartas's *My Heart Can't Beat Unless You Tell It To*. The tale of three siblings desperate to keep their family together after their parents' death, *My Heart* includes one irreal element: the youngest sibling is a sickly vampire who cannot feed himself. The two older siblings murder people on society's margins to keep him fed. They hate it. Not only does this violence disgust them, it's also why they can't have any friends or relationships. The family may be a safe space to give and receive care, but the film indicates that it's also a trap. One scene in particular highlights how elevated horror's aesthetics translates the family's structural oppression into visual form. The older brother brings home an unhoused man to kill, but the man fights back. As they grapple in the kitchen, his sister rushes in and together they overpower the man, draining his blood into the sink. It is a strange, conflicted scene. The cinematography captures it in a near-static medium shot. Its distance and duration force viewers to witness these events from afar, unable to intervene (Figure 24). This medium shot is broken only by a countershot close-up of the horrified vampire brother in the doorway, as immobilized by this horrifying scene as the audience.

Figure 24. When one brother kills to feed his weak vampiric sibling, the film traps viewers in this static medium shot. *My Heart Can't Beat Unless You Tell It To,* directed by Jonathan Cuartas. Dark Sky Films, 2020.

Cuartas's use of visual distance and duration is typical of the aesthetic representation of violence in elevated family horror. *My Heart* opens with a shocking murder captured in a similar long static shot. The brother picked up another man and took him back to the house. When they get out of his truck, the camera doesn't follow them. Instead, it pulls behind the truck, doubly framing the yard through its front and rear windshields. From this distance, we watch as the brother rushes up with a bat and beats the man to death. Distance is a crucial strategy for elevated family horror's representation of the ways in which characters are trapped by the norms they enact. In this sense, elevated family horror has much in common with literary naturalism. The coldness and distance of its aesthetics recall the impassivity of Émile Zola's and Thomas Hardy's narrators, and the fates of its characters are equally naturalistic. The implacable forces of an indifferent universe doom characters to an unchangeable fate.

One of the key differences between elevated family horror and other forms of elevated horror, like therapeutic horror, is its studied distance from metaphor. Compare Robert Eggers's *The Witch* (2015) to Jennifer Kent's *The Babadook*. Unlike Kent's film, Eggers's has no interest in allegory or metaphor. Its avowed commitment is to *realism*. In interviews and commentaries, Eggers describes his film as a careful recreation of seventeenth-century New England life.[28] It includes the supernatural because it represents a world where people believe in witches. There's a hitch in Eggers's reasoning, though. *The Witch* doesn't represent a world in which people *believe* witches exist but a world in which witches *do* exist. In an interview, Eggers tried to sidestep this problem by calling the film a "folktale."[29] The result is, as Aviva Briefel argues, a folktale naturalism that allows audiences to feel a particular worldview, "merging historical drama with the 'body genre' of horror."[30] While the film isn't metaphor or allegory, it does have an underlying purpose, to critique the patriarchal family's oppressive norms. The film's father, William, is at once in control of the family and responsible for its plight. In its opening scene, William, his wife Katherine, and his five children, are cast out of his seventeenth-century settlement by the village elders because William refuses to yield on any of his religious beliefs. We might take his refusal as an insistence on his right to absolute dominion, and it is this insistence that drives his family into an unpeopled wilderness.

When the witch appears, she is an inverted reflection of William's patriarchal power. Over the course of the film, she will claim each of his family members, beginning with the theft of their unbaptized infant, and there's nothing he can do to stop her.

William's adolescent daughter Thomasin provides the other pole of this critique. After the infant's loss, her mother falls into a depression, and Thomasin must care for the household. As her responsibilities increase, so too do the witch's depredations. William and Katherine, unable to locate the witch, turn their ire on their daughter. If the witch is the patriarch's double, as Amanda Howell and Lucy Baker say, Thomasin is the witch's.[31] Her emerging sexuality is part of this doubling, as the film shows when her brother Caleb, who William has begun to train in head-of-household tasks, begins to ogle her. When witchcraft claims him too, on his deathbed Caleb accuses her of being in league with the witch. The film's climax sees Thomasin fighting off both her parents. She survives, but alone in the wilderness, she has no choice but to become a witch. She approaches the supposedly bewitched family goat and makes a deal. The devil asks if she wants to "live deliciously" with the other witches in the forest, and she does, floating into the air, nude, with the other occultists. No wonder some took *The Witch* for a story of women's empowerment. At least, Anya Taylor-Joy, the actor who played Thomasin, did. In a 2016 Q&A at the Brooklyn Academy of Music, Taylor-Joy explained that Thomasin's deal with the devil "was the first choice she really got to make."[32] Critics didn't disagree, though they took the film more broadly for a critique of the patriarchal family and the ways it limits young women's choices.[33]

A Marxist reading can help us draw out something more than a critique of patriarchy: the family's role in capitalist accumulation. As materialist feminists have shown, capitalism used accusations of witchcraft as part of a multifaceted biopolitical strategy to appropriate land, labor, and resources. Silvia Federici and Maria Mies both argue that in Europe, accusations of witchcraft were used to strip women of property rights, forcing them into unpaid domestic work and sexual servitude.[34] Accusations of witchcraft were important and underrecognized tactics in what Marx calls capitalism's processes of original or primitive accumulation.[35] As Federici shows, outside of Europe, accusations of witchcraft were used by settler colonialism's genocidal appropriation of native lands. In the new world, Federici explains, witch hunting was not only "*a deliberate strategy used by the authorities to instill terror,* destroy collective resistance, silence entire communities, and turn their members against each other. *It was also a strategy of enclosure* which, depending on the context, could be the enclosure of land, bodies, or social relations."[36] We can find this dual strategy embedded in the aesthetics of *The Witch.* The camera presents the land outside the plantation as European colonists saw it, an empty and dangerous wilderness. Europeans rationalized their seizure of land in the Americas through the doctrine of *terra nullius.* By insisting the lands of the Americas were neither cultivated nor improved, colonists could declare Native Americans to be squatters, rather than members of civilizations with recognizable rights.[37] This genocidal nonsense obscures the fact that New England, the film's setting, had long been densely settled and remained so throughout the seventeenth century. The land wasn't wild but carefully cultivated for food production, and at least one European observer at the time noted Native American forest management: "Though the country be wild and overgrown with woods, yet the trees stand not thick but a man may well ride a horse amongst them."[38] If settlers thought the land was depopulated, this was the result of sequential plagues that hit the Wampanoag and Narragansett peoples just before their arrival in Plymouth. It was still populated, though. The film's aesthetics operate as a kind of visual *terra nullius.* Its empty shots of the landscape evoke how the settlers felt living in this seeming wilderness. Long shots reduce them to specks in a vast and indifferent world. It also empties the world of other inhabitants, presenting it as ready for enclosure by the white settler colonial family, even if not this particular family.

In *The Witch,* opposition to the settler colonial family must be European. Except at the margins, Eggers's realist film refuses to recognize the settler colonial family's actual opposition, Native Americans. Thomasin briefly glimpses two Native men as the family rides out of the plantation and into the wilderness. The film needs them to appear within civilization, if not themselves civilized, to justify its settler colonial view. This repressed opposition erupts in the film's conclusion when the devil claims Thomasin's body. When she accepts his deal, Thomasin flees to the woods in a sort of mythical retelling of the real women and men who abandoned settler life across the Americas to be adopted by Native tribes.[39] And the devil's overturning of hierarchies recalls seventeen-century accounts of Native American societies as less bound by hierarchies of power and gender than the status-conscious and property-focused patriarchies of Europe.[40] From a Marxist perspective, if not the film's, this refusal of the family can be a glimpse of the refusal of settler colonialism and its capital accumulation.

Hereditary: Choice and the Cult of the Family

With its use of an irreal figure to double and reverse the patriarch's power, *The Witch* reveals elevated family horror's central narrative strategy. The subgenre, however, prefers cults to witches. Like the witch, the cult asserts the patriarch's right to use and abuse his household but with a figure for collectivity. From the Paimon worshippers harassing the family in Ari Aster's *Hereditary* (2017), the pit-worshipping patriarchy of Chad Crawford Kinkle's *Jug Face* (2013), and the New Age grief cult of Karyn Kusama's *The Invitation* (2015), to the pagan death cult after a hitman in Ben Wheatley's *Kill List* (2011), the cloaked Cthulhu worshippers who corner a grieving couple in Jeremy Gillespie and Steven Kostanski's *The Void* (2016), and the nihilist Buddhists chasing a bereaved parent in David Prior's *The Empty Man* (2020), cults in elevated horror use their collective power to destroy patriarchs and their families. Sometimes they dupe men into doing it themselves. In *Kill List*, a cult manipulates the hitman protagonist into murdering his own family. After he defeats a strange beast in ritualized combat, his moment of triumph disintegrates when he discovers who was in the beast's costume. In other films, cults unveil how the father's supposed power masks his lack of knowledge. In *The Lodge*, a father-psychologist refuses to recognize his children's animosity toward his new fiancé, a young woman he has rescued after an abusive childhood in a cult. As they torment her, she becomes increasingly haunted by her past, yet her fiancé pays no attention to what's happening. While he claims responsibility for deprogramming her, he ignores the ways their romantic relationship echoes the cult's abusive crossing of personal boundaries. No surprise, then, that when the children's abuse causes her to suffer a psychotic break, she kills him, not the children.

In elevated family horror, cults show that what makes the family's norms so destructive is that people choose to follow them. Consider *Jug*

Face. Sustin, the film's patriarch leads a rural cult that worships a demon in a pit. The pit demands sacrifice, and communicates its choices to the cult's potter, who creates portraits of the chosen victims on jugs. Sustin's daughter Ada throws this system into crisis when the pit chooses her. She just hides the jug. Sustin knows the pit wants someone, but now he doesn't know who. And he needs to. When the pit doesn't get who it wants, it starts killing cult members until it's satisfied, so Sustin keeps looking. Is it his neighbor? His son? By the time he discovers the pit wants Ada, he's already sacrificed much of the cult. Still, into the pit she goes. What choice does he have? "The pit wants what it wants," he says.

Marxism can help us to reframe the role of choice in these films. While the eighteenth century's gendered division of labor in the middle classes gave us the ideal of the bourgeois family, the twentieth century's legalization of birth control and abortion altered how this division worked. The expansion of bodily autonomy, the joint result of feminist organizing and elite fears of overpopulation, coincided with the global North's deindustrialization. Lower demand for labor made the expansion of bodily autonomy politically attractive, especially in the United States, where the state has long targeted BIPOC people for sterilization. This isn't to say that capitalism's lessened demands for labor simply translated into legalized birth control and abortion. For political elites, birth control promised to lower the costs of social benefits, bringing down Scrooge's "surplus population." Arguments by conservatives against social benefits lessened the headwinds faced by advocates for bodily autonomy.[41] In the United States, the legalization of birth control and abortion occurred almost simultaneously with the collapse of union power and the disappearance of the family wage. This isn't to say that bodily autonomy came at the price of the family wage but rather that it afforded households a way to escape the collapse of workers' earnings.[42] In the global North of the 1970s, this was the dual result of inflation and unemployment. In 1972, Italian Marxist feminist Mariarosa Dalla Costa noted that "those of us who have gone out of our homes to work because we had to or for extras or for economic independence have warned the rest: inflation has riveted us to this bloody typing pool or to this assembly line, and in that there is no salvation."[43] Dalla Costa rightly expected that capitalism would adjust its norms to suit exploitation, and it did. Over the next fifty years, capitalism across the global North happily allowed more people who could bear children to enter the workforce while wages stagnated and the family wage disappeared. Without the material support that allowed one person to stay home and engage in unpaid social reproduction work, working people, mostly women, found themselves forced to perform what Arlie Hochschild calls "the second shift," eight hours of unpaid domestic labor on top of a day's work.[44] Capital continues to accumulate value, but now in ways that resemble earlier regimes of accumulation. Like nineteenth-century workers, twenty-first century ones endure their daily round of exploitation, then return home for another of appropriation.

No wonder birth rates across the postindustrial North have collapsed. According to abortion rights activist-scholar Jenny Brown, pregnant people "are staging a production slowdown, a baby boycott, in response to bad conditions."[45] And why wouldn't they, especially in a country like the United States, where capital refuses to bear the costs of social reproduction, whether parental leave, childcare, health care, or higher education. It makes sense to refuse reproductive labor under these conditions. And even in countries that provide seemingly generous levels of social welfare, it is less than clear that such compensation adequately covers the real costs of social reproduction work. Choice provides capital with ideological cover for this lack of compensation. It reshapes the refusal of reproductive work into a more malleable form of common sense that reinforces the family's power as a normative ideal. From capitalism's perspective, the falling birth rate isn't a refusal to work under bad conditions but the result of rational economic choice. U.S. readers may be used to *choice* as a cognate for bodily autonomy, but, as Brown spells out, the word hides a set of corrosive economic assumptions. "Choice," Brown explains, "makes it seem that parents are indulging a personal whim by having children rather than making a valuable contribution to the ongoing existence of society."[46] In effect, choice turns reproductive labor into idle consumption. Instead of bodily autonomy, the focus becomes the different forms that value can take. *Can I afford the rent? Can I afford a car? Can I afford a baby?* Angela McRobbie links this shift to neoliberal capitalism's attempts to integrate women into the workforce. Neoliberal feminism can look past the drudgery of housework and child rearing, McRobbie asserts, because it has framed them as problems of personal responsibility. "The ideological force of choice has a de-socializing and de-politicizing function," McRobbie points out.[47] Choice divides people into the deserving and undeserving based on economic status: *Given your income, is having a child the right choice?* What choice does, then, is to make community and solidarity unthinkable. *Your choice* is just another way of saying *your problem*.

Cults in elevated family horror can be read as an attack on this piece of common sense. In these films, the family's protection isn't the result of good choices but of forces beyond the characters' control. The family isn't a space of protection but vulnerability. We can find this critique in Ari Aster's *Hereditary*. A variant of the demon-baby plot found in *Rosemary's Baby* (1968), *The Omen* (1976), and any number of imitators, *Hereditary* follows a coven trying to incarnate a demon. Like *Rosemary's Baby*, it narrates these events from the unwitting family's perspective. The chief difference is that Aster allows the plot to unfold like a melodrama. The story follows Annie, a miniature artist, after the death of Ellen, her strange and secretive mother. Their complicated relationship was marked by mental illness and abuse, and Annie's childhood left her uncertain about parenthood. She had her son Peter only after she and Ellen were estranged. However, the two reconciled after the birth of her daughter, Charlie, and Ellen lived with them until her death. The film's first act follows Annie trying unsuccessfully to mediate her grief through art. She's behind schedule on her latest show of dioramas that depict traumatic events in her family life. To make time for her work and to keep Charlie from feeling alone after her grandmother's death, Annie forces Peter to take his younger sister with him to a party. There, she has an allergic reaction to nuts and a stoned Peter must drive her to the hospital. When Charlie sticks her head out of the car window, desperate for air in her anaphylactic shock, a telephone pole decapitates her. Stunned, Peter drives home and goes to bed, leaving his sister's headless body in the backseat of the car for his mother to discover in the morning. Grief unravels Annie. She blames Peter for getting stoned and herself for sending Charlie with him and even more for having children at all. Peter is trapped in his own grief and shame, and Stephen, Annie's husband and Peter's father, cannot reconcile the two, let alone process his own grief. At this point, *Hereditary* would seem little more than a family melodrama were it not for a gruesome jump cut to Charlie's severed head swarming with ants.

By the final act, though, it's clear *Hereditary* is as much horror as melodrama, and the source of its horror is choice. Ellen, the story reveals, led a coven and orchestrated each of the film's events from beyond the grave. Her goal was to move the demon Paimon from Charlie's body to Peter's. While Annie and Peter may blame themselves for their choices, they had no more control over their lives than the figures in Annie's dioramas. The cult manipulated Annie to appropriate her reproductive labor, rendering the bodies of her children fungible commodities, Charlie for Peter, and Peter for Charlie. The cult chose to murder Stephen. The cult chose to possess then kill Annie. The cult chose to turn Peter into Paimon. What the cult shows us, then, is that the family isn't the result of individual choice but of collective forces hellbent on exploitation and appropriation. The more that people labor to maintain its norms, the more they strengthen their own domination. We can see this lack of agency in the film's use of distance. The opening and closing shots visually reduce the family to manipulable dolls in a world the cult controls. The film opens with a long tracking shot through Annie's studio of dioramas, ending as the camera stops on her model of the family home and slowly zooms in on Peter's room. Once the room is fully in frame, Stephen enters to wake Peter for school. Initially, this trick shot seems without purpose, but it is the film's first indicator that its characters are trapped in a world controlled by somebody else. Their inability to see how the cult has shaped their lives reaches its visual apex when a possessed Annie creeps along the walls and ceiling of the same room as an unsuspecting Peter. No one in the family ever realizes they're just figures for the cult to manipulate, their heads interchangeable, their bodies easily dragged wherever the cult pleases. In the film's final shot, Peter, now possessed by Paimon, is surrounded by the cult in the family tree house. The camera cuts away from an interior shot to a wide shot of the treehouse interior in cross section (Figure 25). The family is and has never been anything more than dolls to be posed as the cult sees fit.

Annie's art, then, is key to the film's critique of the family. Joanna Isaacson rightly sees Annie's destruction of her miniatures as an attempt to destroy the limitations the family has placed on her.[48] Yet we can also see in it a doubling of the cult's power. Her miniatures intuit the cult's manipulations of the family, and suggest the cult isn't a substitute for the

Figure 25. The cult reduces the family to mere figurines in a dollhouse. *Hereditary*, directed by Ari Aster. A24 Films, 2017.

family so much as a collective that refuses its norms. True, the cult figures the destructiveness of the family. Yet it also suggests other forms of collective belonging outside the family. After all, Ellen has found belonging in her coven. We might read in a different light Annie's shock after she discovers a coven member in her mother's photo album. For Annie, the horror isn't about what's in the pictures. These photos aren't of blood sacrifices, strange rites, or ritual orgies, just of older women having a nice time. The film suggests it's because she realizes the cult's manipulation. But isn't it also that she and her mother found comfort and care from people outside the family? *Hereditary* may imbue this alternate form of collective belonging with danger, yet we can find in it a glimpse of the sort of collective belonging and care that feminists have long imagined outside the family and its norms, from Shulamith Firestone's artificial wombs to Marge Piercy's radical lesbian utopias.[49] Dismantling the family could extricate women from the drudgery of the family, as Alexandra Kollontai suggested, with a national "network of social kitchens and canteens";[50] or as Angela Davis imagined, with a world of industrialized housework where "teams of trained and well-paid workers . . . could swiftly and efficiently accomplish what the present-day housewife does so arduously and primitively."[51] In *Hereditary*, we see ever so briefly the possibility of other forms of collective belonging and care.

Shelley: Full Surrogacy Now

This is not to take the cult as a model for care or collective belonging. We're better served by turning to the work of Audrey Lorde. In her essays on parenthood, Lorde reimagines mothering as a relation not based in patriarchy's command over bodies or capitalism's notions of property rights. "What mothers teach," Lorde maintains, is "love and survival—that is, self-definition and letting go."[52] Lorde describes this practice of acceptance and autonomy as learning to "mother ourselves."[53] Mothering is, as Alexis Pauline Gumbs explains in her analysis of Lorde, "a queer thing."[54] Lorde's notion of mothering aims to replace the capitalist patriarchal family's assertions of property rights over the bodies of others with relations of care that treat everyone as ends in themselves. Instead of the family's binary coupledom and what Kathi Weeks calls its "model of bio-genetic kinship,"[55] Lorde's mothering would offer people a variety of relations and practices of "commoning," to use Sophie Lewis's word.[56] It would create a world in which we recognize and act, as Lewis says, as "the makers of one another."[57] Lewis underscores that mothering isn't a biological relation. It is a chosen way of relating to one another. Lewis prefers a term that separates this care entirely from biology, *surrogacy*. For Lewis, family abolition would mean a world of what she calls "real" or "full surrogacy"—that is, a world in which we all recognize ourselves as surrogates for one another.[58]

Of course, as Lewis explains, full surrogacy stands in contrast with surrogacy as it currently exists. Instead of relations of care that value the autonomy and singularity of each person, capitalist surrogacy reduces surrogates to abstract labor-power. A surrogate's body is necessary to the production process, but it doesn't matter *which* body. As philosopher Kathryn Russell explains, surrogacy through in vitro fertilization makes "childbearing labor . . . materially equivalent."[59] Lewis terms this form of abstract labor "gestational labor-power."[60] Like other forms of capitalist labor-power, it is defined by being massified, anonymized, and de-skilled. Unlike other forms of abstract labor, however, surrogates don't produce commodities. Even in proletarianized surrogacy clinics, surrogates don't produce children to sell on the open market. They are contracted in advance to create children for specific clients using provided reproductive raw materials. Money is exchanged for children, but what capitalism has done is subsume the labor of child-making, not commodify the children themselves. The process of exchange in surrogacy, though, does reveal how tightly entwined capitalism and the family are. For children to be traded like any other commodity on the market, they must appear shorn of the labor that produced them. What the economic process of exchange does, then, is serve to naturalize the family's model of biogenetic kinship. Capitalism means to keep abstract reproductive laborpower locked in the hidden abode of production. The family is its most reliable jailer.

We see this most directly in Ali Abbasi's Danish surrogacy horror *Shelley* (2016). Its poster makes clear that the film is about the terrors of capitalism's subsumption of reproductive work. A pastiche of Polanski's *Rosemary's Baby*, it features a 1960s-era pram over the image of a pregnant person. Where Polanski's film placed the pram over a transparency of Rosemary's face, however, Abbasi's places it over a depersonalized silhouette. The resulting image captures reproductive labor's reduction to gestational labor-power, a reduction that erases its existence for the seemingly natural institution of the family. And the family in *Shelley* is inextricable from nature. The film begins with the Norwegian Kasper driving his new Romanian maid, Elena, to the home he shares in the countryside with his Danish wife, Louise. The two have hired Elena to help Louise recover from a miscarriage and hysterectomy. Kasper explains that they are vegetarians, live off their organic garden, and don't have electricity or running water. Yet, as Elena discovers, they aren't back-to-the-land hippies so much as New Age Nordic yuppies. Kasper commutes to a job in the city while Louise tends the garden, swims in the lake, and spends time with her spiritual guru. In this isolation, Elena quickly becomes less of an employee than a member of the family. During the day, she and Louise do housework together, and in the evenings, they eat, play games, and talk into the night. Elena reveals that she came to the West to earn enough money to buy an apartment for herself and her five-year-old son, and left with her mother in Romania. It will take her three years. When Louise proposes that Elena act as their surrogate, it seems an expression of friendship and support. If Elena will help them have a child, they will help her return to hers early, paying her for three years of work in one. And when she agrees, it is as much out of friendship as economic necessity. They have become, it seems, a group of people working toward their common good.

The horror of *Shelley* is how capitalism and the family can deform these urges toward commoning. The film's scenes of terror have nothing to do with demonic children or medical procedures and everything to do with Elena's work. Although no longer their servant, Elena remains isolated in their home and subject to their constant supervision. At first, this seems an expression of care. Louise and Elena are friends. So what if Louise monitors her for cigarette smoke or insists she not eat white flour or refined sugar? Louise's monitoring becomes more menacing as Elena's gestational labor becomes more debilitating. Like Rosemary, Elena's pregnancy drains her lifeforce. Kasper and Louise take her to the doctor, but he allays their concerns. The baby is developing perfectly, and Elena's suffering is beside the point, though not for Elena. She wants to quit. They won't let her. When she beats her belly and screams, they sedate her. Over her drugged body, Kasper suggests they let her return to Romania. Louise refuses. They may never get the baby if she leaves. Their only choice, she asserts calmly, is to keep Elena there.

More than any other elevated family horror, then, *Shelley* shows how capitalism uses the family to control women's bodies in the service of private property. In the name of tradition and morality, it restricts abortion, forces pregnancies and births, and extracts care work. Louise and Kasper defend their decision to keep Elena under house arrest for her own good and to protect their new family, but these appeals to morality and tradition serve only to protect their investment in the cost of the procedure and Elena's labor, and in their biological property, the fetus. Labor, of course, resists such oppression. When Elena finds one of Louise's misplaced knitting needles, she attempts an abortion. She dies, but the child lives. When Louise and Kasper return home jubilant with their newborn daughter Shelley, they erase any evidence of Elena's labor and they sink back into their nature- and wellness-centered lives. Elena is not so much forgotten; it is as if she never existed.

Louise and Kasper's devaluation, then erasure, of Elena's existence underscores capitalism's reliance on racial, ethnic, and cultural divisions to devalue, dominate, and discipline working peoples.[61] As a presumed biological entity, the family serves an important role in these divisions. The Nordic Louise and Kasper treat Elena as a friend, then a prisoner, and then nothing, because they can use her racialization to change their relation as they need. In the end, they can simply insist that she could never be part of their family, not really. Their treatment of her suggests they resented her ability to have children from the beginning. *This poor Romanian woman can have a child and we wealthy northern Europeans can't?* It doesn't matter to them that their decision to hold Elena against her will kills her. To them, it seems right and fitting to sacrifice Elena for their reproduction.

Yet they find Elena's work can't be easily erased. It will always confront them in Shelley. While Elena's difficult pregnancy implies Shelley may be a demonic figure, a Marxist reading would insist that Shelley's demonic nature represents her parents' exploitation and erasure of Elena. Indeed, the film avoids the standard demon-baby explanations. There are no occult rituals or deals with the devil. If Shelley is demonic, it is because, as Hegel would put it, she is the objectification of the family.[62] Her evil is the result of Louise and Kasper's insistence on a child who would be their genetic property. They could have adopted, but they chose to purchase the goods and services required to make a child who would be theirs. It is this conjunction of choice of and desire for private property that drives their subsequent exploitation, appropriation, and destructive racialization of reproductive labor.

While Louise and Kasper are responsible for the decisions they make, the horror of the family is that they too are caught in its normative grip. After Shelley's birth, Kasper can't sleep. The child emits strange noises. Elena and Louise's guru took these sounds as evidence of some eldritch evil. For Kasper, they are the tell-tale heart of Elena's mistreatment. Louise, however, is unfazed. There's nothing wrong with *her* child. Still, she is haunted by the idea that she doesn't have any real claim to property in her daughter. In a nightmare, she imagines Kasper reaching into her vagina and the empty space where her uterus had been. Like other elevated family horrors, *Shelley* relies on distance in this sequence of body horror. The camera focuses on Louise in a medium shot, holding viewers at a distance, albeit with a brief close-up of Kasper's hand as it deforms her abdomen. From a Marxist perspective, we should understand Louise's nightmare as a reminder that her family isn't possible without the destructive exploitation of reproductive labor. The invisible hand of the market is a real, visible hand that reaches into Elena's body to take what it wants. When she awakes, she explodes with rage at being forced to recall her actions and her dependence. She discovers that Kasper isn't in bed but outside, distraught and in the car with Shelley. In a fury, she crushes his skull in the car door, then carries Shelley inside. The film concludes with Louise staring out the nursery window as Shelley sleeps. In a corner of the room behind her looms Elena's ghost. Louise turns toward her for a moment, yet remains unable or unwilling to see or acknowledge her. Instead, she returns to staring blankly forward. *Shelley* lets us see that the capitalist family doesn't need the binary couple or the patriarch so much as *property*. In capitalism, the family is, and will always be, haunted by the labor and laborers on which it depends.

Prevenge: Reject the Bourgeois Family

Alice Lowe's *Prevenge* (2016) has the exclusion and devaluing of reproductive labor in its sights. Written and directed by Lowe, the film features her in the starring role, eight-months-pregnant. Its plot follows Ruth, alone, distressed, and enormously pregnant, as her demonic fetus forces her to murder the members of a climbing party that killed her partner. At first, the story seems a parody of sociocultural claims about pregnancy's effects on the brain.[63] Ruth's OB/GYN provides metacommentary throughout, at one point telling her: "You have absolutely no control of your mind or body anymore. This one does! She's got all the control now . . . Baby knows what to do, baby will tell you what to do." Ruth replies tonelessly, "I think she already does." In this sense, Amy C. Chambers is right to claim that *Prevenge* "challenges the traditional approach to gynaehorror" by making visible "lived experience that is biologically unavailable to male directors."[64]

Yet Lowe's comments to *The Independent* suggest that *Prevenge* is about more than pregnancy as a lived biological experience. In an interview, Lowe explained that she made the film after recognizing pregnancy's effects on her career. She was "terrified" of being out of work, she told the interviewer.[65] "As a freelancer, having a baby," Lowe explained, "you feel like you will never work again. There is no support network really."[66] Lowe described the British film industry as indifferent to the needs of parents and indicated a lack of labor solidarity among British actors. "As soon as you said I'm on strike in the UK, there would be 20 other actors saying, 'I'll do it,'" Lowe declares. "You just don't trust it, there is, sort of, this fear."[67] Lowe's remarks bring out what Marxist analysis of the film also indicates: *Prevenge* is about the horrors of pregnancy in a society where workers lack protections, solidarity doesn't exist, and reproductive work sits on the lowest rung of the social hierarchy. Ruth's revenge, and the comedy that Lowe extracts from it, comes from the exclusion and mistreatment of pregnant people in a world of precarious work and self-interested workers. Her murders defend reproductive work from the depredations of a hostile world. For her victims, pregnancy is an affront, whether to the male gaze or the job market. When she approaches one of the climbing party, an overweight, balding DJ well into his forties, he loudly explains he doesn't want to be tied down with kids. Still, he takes Ruth back to his place, declaring, "I love fat birds. You're a little bit more open minded, so you don't mind what people do to you." His selfishness can't overcome the palpable disgust he feels when the fetus kicks, and Ruth's revenge is to cut off his genitals. After all, he can't be bothered with social reproduction's actual demands, only his own sexual needs. Similarly, when she applies for a job from another member of the climbing party, the woman can't stop herself from telling Ruth "no" before the interview has even begun. Ruth wouldn't be unpacked before she was out on maternity leave, she says. From her perspective, reproductive work just gets in the way of business. She offers Ruth "a word of advice: get out of your system the motherhood thing. Sort out your own business before you interfere in other people's." Ruth tells her "I will," then slits her throat in another bit of social commentary on business's cutthroat world.

The violence of *Prevenge* may sound less like elevated horror than slapstick horror-comedy, but the film's aesthetics have less in common with the broad humor of *Hell Baby* (2013) than Lowe's collaboration with Ben Wheatley, the black comedy *Sight Seers* (2012). Its mise-en-scène reflects the sort of realism found in contemporary UK cinema, while its cinematography emphasizes Ruth's isolation and loneliness, presenting her almost uniformly alone in a one-shot. While Ruth's victims are execrable people, the film represents her vengeance as *de trop*, and avoids musical intensifiers or other dramatic indicators that would lighten the mood. *Prevenge* wants audiences to keep their distance from Ruth even as it documents pregnancy's social degradations. Still, there can be no doubt that the social degradation of reproductive work drives Ruth's violence. Although she believes the fetus is urging her on, Ruth is driven by her anger at how little anyone values care. She tries to demonstrate her commitment to care by not hurting those who need or support it. When the DJ's elderly mother, suffering from dementia, appears after Ruth has murdered her son, Ruth doesn't kill her too. She tucks her in. When the fetus later forces her to kill a caring man because he was a witness, Ruth expresses a surprising level of frustration. "Kids these days are really spoilt," she mutters to herself. "It's like, 'mummy, I want a PlayStation! Mummy, I want you to kill that man!'" Ruth's need to protect reproductive work shapes the film's climax. She saved for last Tom, the climbing party's leader. Dressed as death, she tracks him to a Halloween party (Figure 26). But she relents when she finds him tending to his pregnant partner. "I can't put her in the same position," she says. The fetus disagrees. "Kill him or I kill you!" it demands and bursts its placenta in anger. When Ruth comes at him with a knife, the climbing leader does what no one else has the entire film: He recognizes her. Tom knows she must be upset. During the climb, he explains, her partner slipped. As leader, he had to make a life-or-death decision for seven people. When you see it like that, really, he had to cut the cord. In the next scene, Ruth's OB/GYN echoes these words after Ruth has been rushed to the hospital for an emergency cesarean. "When it's life or death," she tells Ruth, "we have to make that cut."

After the baby's been delivered, something has indeed been cut—Ruth's fantasy of the demonic fetus. "I've done some really terrible

Figure 26. Ruth prepares for her final victim. *Prevenge*, directed by Alice Lowe. RLJE, 2016.

things," she tells her OB/GYN. "I've got it all wrong... I thought I was doing it for her, but I was doing it for myself, and I've only just realized that because she's not talking to me anymore." With this abandonment of the supernatural, *Prevenge* seems headed for a saccharine denouement. At the party, Tom revealed that his final conversation with Ruth's partner was about his decision to leave her. Ruth's sudden penitence suggests this is the truth her violence tried to repress. When she leaves the hospital and her child, she goes to the scene of her partner's death, apparently now ready to mourn the reality and the fantasy of the man who has died. After lighting candles around his photo, she wanders toward the cliff face and imagines her partner standing there. As she approaches, his figure resolves into that of Tom, the climbing leader. He too is revisiting the site of the tragedy. He looks sadly at her, then is surprised as she charges him, and the film cuts to black.

This abrupt ending is more than a piece of genre play with the final scare. It destroys any contrition audiences might attribute to Ruth and tells us something about social reproduction work. Initially, the conclusion seems to aim for Ruth's psychological recuperation. From a Marxist perspective, though, her final turn reveals that the problem Ruth recognized at the hospital wasn't that she'd done terrible things for no reason but that she'd done terrible things for the wrong reason. She wasn't revenging the fetus's loss of a father but her own abjection as a reproductive worker. Her violence rejects society's degradation of reproductive work and its insistence that the family's binary partnership alone provides adequate care. In the end, Ruth attacks the normative ideal of the family itself, from its refusal to pay for reproductive work and its devaluation of care to its assertion that the child is a piece of property and its demand that care come through partnership alone. *Prevenge* shows us that the problems of the capitalist family can be boiled down to Tom's utilitarian calculus. In capitalism, some people must suffer so others can live. Someone has to be poor. Someone has to be uncared for. Someone has to die. This isn't a just or equitable process, and the family naturalizes these inequities, papering over how capitalism determines who gets care and who doesn't. No father? Bad family. No mother? Bad family. Didn't get ahead in life? Bad family. The idea that everyone's needs could be satisfied, that people could live together and support one another collectively, is off the table. All that's on offer is the family table, and Ruth sees what that means. The family helps capital appropriate our reproductive labor, but it can't hide the fact that we're all one bad footing away from getting cut loose. Marxism lets us see in elevated family horror that you don't need to be in command of the entire social structure to be a monster. You just need to be one step above with a knife.

7

FEELINGS HATE YOU
Therapeutic Horror and Emotion Work

Everyone knows capitalism is depressing, but perhaps no one knew it better than Mark Fisher. For Fisher, depression is twenty-first-century capitalism's defining affect. What makes capitalism depressing isn't just that it dominates our lives through value. It's that it insists it's here to stay. As we saw in chapter 2, capitalism's defenders maintain that it is the only practical economic system, no matter the destruction it wreaks. Fisher dubs this piece of common sense "capitalist realism."[1] You encounter it whenever someone tells you there's no alternative to the way things are, or that it's unrealistic to believe you can have it any better than you already do. Capitalist realism offers, Fisher says, "the deflationary perspective of a depressive who believes that any positive state, any hope, is a dangerous illusion."[2] Capitalist realism isn't just depressing because it insists there's no way out. It's depressing because of its bootstrap ideology, what Fisher elsewhere calls "magical voluntarism."[3] Magical voluntarism refuses to recognize the structural forces and contradictions that affect our lives. Instead, it maintains that our successes and our failures are our responsibility and ours alone. Depression seems to support to this conceit. As Fisher explains, depression is "the internalized expression of actual social forces, some of which have a vested interest in denying any connection between depression and politics."[4] Depression is political, Fisher contends, because it attacks our ability to imagine and strive for a better future. As he explains in an interview, "Depression involves a self-fulfilling prophecy: one's conviction that one is worthless, useless, good for nothing, feeds into an inability to act, which in turn reinforces those feelings."[5] The only way out of capitalist realism's depression, Fisher argues, is to expand the realm of the possible. "Direct action," he writes, "while of course crucial, will never be sufficient; we

173

also need to act *indirectly*, by generating new narratives, figures and conceptual frames."[6]

It might seem unlikely to find those new narratives in horror. Its roots in the Gothic would suggest horror is a depressive's genre. After all, depression runs like a red thread through the Gothic, from graveyard poetry and Horace Walpole's and Ann Radcliffe's melancholic heroes and heroines to the pervasive use of suicide to represent characters' struggles with social isolation and mental illness.[7] However, American horror in the twentieth century avoided melancholia in its early run of Gothic adaptations. *Dracula* (1931), *Frankenstein* (1931), and *Dr. Jekyll and Mr. Hyde* (1931) emphasized the Gothic's spectacular and grotesque qualities rather than its melancholic ones. Yet in the 1940s we can glimpse the emergence of a new narrative built in response to depression. Mark Robson's *The Seventh Victim* (1943) begins as Mary's search for her lost sister Jacqueline, but ends as the story of Jacqueline's depression. Harry Benshoff attributes the film's interest in depression to its barely hidden subtext of same-sex relationships. In the film, Benshoff notes, cult members' same-sex relationships "depict complex erotic relationships that ultimately defy the traditional narrative demands of a happy Hollywood ending."[8] Robson's film uses Jacqueline's depression to reveal the oppressions of a homophobic social order. She joins a Satanic cult to escape those oppressions, and when she threatens to reveal the existence of this other world of relationships, the cult uses her depression to drive her to suicide. Jacqueline's depression and death provide viewers with a narrative that exemplifies the ways that social exclusion can lead to despair and death.

However, depression's crucial role in *The Seventh Victim* is a mere prelude to its centrality in twenty-first-century horror. Its increased thematic importance has much to do with horror's supposed therapeutic value. As we discussed in the introduction, fans and critics alike extol the genre's therapeutic benefits, from S. A. Bradley's personal reflections on the ways that horror helped him "[cope] with trauma and tragedy"[9] to Mathias Clasen's evolutionary psychological argument that horror provides audiences with emotional resilience.[10] Horror-as-therapy offers audiences a Freudian *fort-da* game with their fight-or-flight responses. Just as in Freud, the game's goal is, as he puts it, "instinctual renunciation."[11] It allows viewers to recuperate even the most transgressive and disturbing films as meaningful reworkings of their affective lives. This drive to make horror a therapeutic tool helps us to locate in horror the piece of common sense that most affects our inner lives: *You've got to control your feelings.* As we'll see, emotion work and emotional management are key parts of twenty-first-century capitalism's work discipline. The idea that horror helps people manage their feelings reflects these widespread political and economic demands that workers regulate their emotions for the benefit of their employers.

Horror captures this demand to manage your feelings in its newfound reliance on a particular narrative structure, tales that make overcoming trauma the necessary precondition to self-improvement, or what Eva Illouz calls "therapeutic narratives."[12] Therapeutic narratives were crucial to the 2010s cycle of elevated horror, and led to the creation of a new subgenre, therapeutic horror. As we saw in the last chapter, elevated horror tends to be understood more as a question of aesthetics than of narrative elements and structures. In his account of this cycle, though, David Church rightly links it to Richard Armstrong's concept of the "mourning film"—that is, films that use modernist formal experimentation to visualize grief and often put women at the center of their narratives.[13] It is perhaps no surprise, then, that Danish filmmaker Lars von Trier's *Antichrist* (2006) and *Melancholia* (2011) were important precursors to this cycle of elevated therapeutic horror. Both offer now-standard features of the subgenre: modernist arthouse aesthetics, representations of depression and grief, and irreal elements that serve as metaphors for these feelings. While von Trier's films were sold to audiences as arthouse productions, his influence marks this cycle of horror through his connection to Jennifer Kent. The Australian director responsible for the film that began this cycle of therapeutic horror, *The Babadook* (2014), Kent began her career as an actor. When she decided she wanted to direct, she contacted von Trier and asked to work with him. Surprisingly, he agreed. Kent called her experience working on *Dogville* (2003), "my film school."[14] Like von Trier's films, *The Babadook*, Kent's first feature, wasn't initially marketed as a horror film; only when it was picked up for international release did the distributor retool its marketing to sell the film as horror for an arthouse audience.[15]

The crux of this promotional shift was the film's use of its titular monster as a metaphor for the depression and grief of Amelia, a distraught single mother. What the film gave audiences was a recuperated intellectual horror, one that focused on dread, not disgust. The monster's appearance has more to do with early and avant-garde film than anything dreamed up by Tom Savini. The film makes the Babadook's terrors inseparable from its metaphorical work. The Babadook frightens because Amelia's depression frightens. The film's intellectualized reframing of horror appealed to critics and audiences alike, earning near-universal acclaim and more than three times the film's $2 million budget. *The Babadook* heralded the launch of the elevated horror that we've seen throughout this book.[16] In the years that followed, horror saw a veritable deluge, not only of elevated horror films but of horror films that made use of this therapeutic framework. The same year that *The Babadook* was released also saw the release of Severin Fiala and Veronika Franz's unnerving portrait of family dynamics in the Austrian film, *Goodnight Mommy* (2014). Unlike Kent's film, *Goodnight Mommy* holds its metaphor in reserve until the very end. The story follows two boys who torment and assault a woman they are convinced is not their mother. Only in the final sequence does the audience learn that they don't recognize her because she was disfigured in an auto accident, and that this accident killed one of the boys. The dead boy's violent haunting serves as a metaphor of the viciousness of suppressed grief. The film cannot resist a final therapeutic turn, though. When the child sets the house ablaze, mother and child finally recognize their trauma. They can't escape it in life, but the final image shows them reunited and happy after death.

At its simplest, then, therapeutic horror is about the need to manage your bad feelings before they consume you. This emotion work drives a host of European elevated horrors, including Liam Gavin's Irish/Welsh film *A Dark Song* (2016), Natalie Erika James's Australian *Relic* (2020), Kate Dolan's Irish *You Are Not My Mother* (2021), and Alex Garland's British *Men* (2022). U.S. filmmakers also adopted the therapeutic narrative in Karyn Kusama's *The Invitation* (2015), Ari Aster's *Midsommar* (2019), Keith Thomas's *The Vigil* (2019), and Iris K. Shim's *Umma* (2022). Horror's therapeutic turn has not only led filmmakers to parody the conceit—Cody Callahan's high concept horror comedy *Vicious Fun* (2020) is about a group-therapy session for horror's most cliched killers—it has also created a separate genre focused on when the therapeutic narrative fails. In films like Ruth Paxton's *A Banquet* (2021), Mattie

Do's *The Long Walk (Bor Mi Vanh Chark)* (2019), Hanna Bergholm's *Hatching (Pahanhautoja)* (2022), and Jane Schoenbrun's *We're All Going to the World's Fair* (2021), characters discover the emptiness of the therapeutic narrative. As we will see, Marxism will help us to find in these two approaches to the therapeutic narrative the ways that capitalism demands workers manage the bad feelings created by its inequities. First, though, we need to understand how the therapeutic narrative works.

The Babadook and the Therapeutic Narrative

As the cycle's inaugurator, *The Babadook* shows us most clearly how horror makes use of the therapeutic narrative. A little top-hatted monster modeled on Lon Chaney's character in *London After Midnight* (1927), the Babadook embodies the range of feelings that make up Amelia's depression, from grief and sadness to resentment and rage. Why is Amelia depressed? She has repressed all the feelings brought on by her husband's death in an auto accident. And not just any auto accident; the couple were on their way to the hospital for Amelia to give birth to their son, Samuel. In one blow, then, Amelia lost a partner and gained a dependent. As a result, she's been forced to give up her career as a writer for full-time caregiving. She ekes out a meager living as a retirement home caregiver and spends her evenings tending to Samuel. While Amelia loves Samuel, he reminds her of all she has lost—her partner, her career, economic stability, even sexual expression. She's never allowed Samuel to celebrate his birthday on his birthday because she can't extricate her losses from his gain. It is no coincidence, then, that the Babadook arrives as Samuel's birthday approaches. He is the film's irreal figure for Amelia's mental and emotional distress. An anagram of *a bad book*, the Babadook is the book of Amelia's frustrations and distress, and makes his first appearance in a book that Samuel discovers in his room. This bad book may seem to come out of nowhere, but it's been with Samuel his entire life.

The oppressions of the nuclear family are responsible for Amelia's depression. Yet Kent's film doesn't rely on coldness and distance for her horror so much as metaphor. What has proven influential in *The Babadook* is the way it uses the terror of the Babadook to represent the terror of a parent's mental illness. Amelia's mental state dictates what Samuel can and can't do. He wants to know about his father, but she won't talk about him no matter how much Samuel asks. She panics if he goes into the basement to look at his father's old things. Since she won't talk, Samuel tries to get her attention in other ways. He follows her around the house. He breaks things. He acts out at school. And when he gets suspended, their newly enforced time together precipitates a crisis that the film depicts as Amelia's possession by the Babadook. Now escaped from its book, the creature crawls across Amelia's bedroom ceiling and plunges into her mouth. If this possession narrative is typical of demonic possession horror, the Babadook doesn't show its control using possession's typical signifiers. Amelia doesn't arch her back, crab walk, vomit everywhere, develop horrible skin, or talk in strange voices. She's possessed only by a violent depressive state, unable to stay awake and sometimes sitting in the bath fully clothed. Still, her depression does have a point of violent focus: Samuel. Like *The Shining*, *The Babadook* relies on a climactic battle between parent and child. However, Samuel doesn't trick and abandon his possessed parent. Instead, he captures her and pleads for her help. They promised to protect one another, he implores. This is enough for Amelia to expel the Babadook by vomiting up a pint of black ink, but it isn't enough to escape the Babadook's wrath. The creature now pursues them through the house, cornering them in her bedroom. Amelia only understands what she must do after Samuel repeats the book's opening lines: "If it's in a word, or it's in a look, you can't get rid of The Babadook." If she can't get rid of it, she realizes, then she can't ignore it. When it raves and collapses to the floor after she tells it that it can't have Samuel, she approaches it with concern. Her care and attention drive the Babadook into the basement, and she locks the door on it. But Amelia understands now that she can't keep it locked down there forever. It must be tended to, cared for, *dealt with*. And so, in an allegory of self-care, Amelia carves out time for her monster. Only when she has created space for her depression, grief, and loss, can she calmly relay the story of Samuel's father's death and Samuel's birth or celebrate Samuel's birthday on the day of and be happy while she does it.

You may not be able to get rid of the Babadook, the film says, but you can learn to manage it.

If all this sounds like behavioral therapy, it should. The links between behavioral psychology and capitalism begin with what capitalists claim they do best: manage. When Marx describes the importance of revolutionizing production for capital in his account of relative surplus-value, he writes that "the work of directing, superintending and adjusting becomes one of the functions of capital, from the moment that the labor under capital's control becomes cooperative."[17] The early twentieth century gave birth to an ideology for capitalism's vaunted organizational skills, Frederick Winslow Taylor's theory of scientific management. Taylor used labor time studies to make claims about the best ways to rationalize labor.[18] Taylor didn't come up with this idea on his own, of course. In the eighteenth century, Adam Smith used rudimentary versions of time studies to show how the division of labor could increase productivity, and Taylor draws on Smith's example of a pin factory in the opening chapter of *The Wealth of Nations*. However, Taylor avoids an argument that Smith made about the division of labor in book 4 of *The Wealth of Nations*, that it stultifies workers' minds.[19] Taylor had no such concerns. He used time studies to extend the rationalization of labor into every aspect of work that he could touch. His aim wasn't simply to maximize output but to manage workers' uncooperative bodies. Technology could determine how many pins the division of labor could make in an hour, but it couldn't eliminate the recalcitrance of the workers themselves. Taylor's rationalizations looked for ways to push workers to work harder. In his study of Taylorism, Harry Braverman argues that this more intensive division of head and hand work wound up creating two classes of workers, "those whose time is infinitely valuable and those whose time is worth almost nothing."[20] These results wouldn't have surprised Adam Smith. Deprived of thought in their labor, workers become bored, angry, and depressed.

And here's where psychology comes in. To manage the ugly feelings wrought by these more intensive divisions of labor, capitalism needed what Braverman calls a "maintenance crew for the human machinery."[21] It is found in industrial psychology. At first, industrial psychologists relied on psychoanalysis. Management theorists like Elton Mayo pitched workplace struggles as Freudian conflicts, in Eve Illouz's words, of "tangled emotions, personality factors, and unresolved psychological problems."[22] However, behavioral psychology quickly dethroned Mayo's daddy-boss workplace analysis. Perhaps that's to be expected. From its beginning, behavioral psychology was closely attuned to capitalism's needs. It found its earliest proponents in advertising, not academia. Behaviorism is, after all, about changing what people do, not explaining why they do it. When behaviorism entered the workplace in the mid-twentieth century, employers weren't wrestling with a definable set of problems. Workers were suffering from an apparently aimless anomie.[23] As William Davies puts it, although they were depressed, they "were not speaking in [Freudian] terms of shame or repressed desires any longer, but merely in terms of their own weakness and inadequacy."[24] This didn't pose a problem for behavioral psychology. If workers were acting unhappy, behavioral psychology would find ways to get them to act differently, and it offered employers an array of tools to manage unhappiness, from cognitive behavioral therapy and positive psychology to the pharmaceutical industry's new "psychic energizers," what we know today as antidepressants.[25]

In the process, behavioral psychology radically altered how people understood what it meant to be mentally well or ill. As Davies explains, "humanistic psychology, as advanced by Abraham Maslow and Carl Rogers, attempted to reorient psychology—and society at large—away from principles of normalization and towards the quest for ever greater fulfillment."[26] To be well came to mean *being fulfilled*. And the positive ideal of a fully actualized self also created a contrasting negative ideal, the unfulfilled self. Illness no longer had to be present to be redressed. It could appear as an absence of self-actualization or even as behaviors that don't seem to lead to self-actualization, whatever that might be. The appearance of a negative ideal of psychological wellness had another, even more perverse effect. It altered the very idea of wellness. To be healthy, people now had to overcome whatever was holding them back.

Here we see the rise of the therapeutic narrative. Self-actualization becomes the narrative endpoint for a properly adjusted worker. The result, as Eve Illouz explains, makes "suffering the central 'knot' of the narrative, what initiates and motivates it, helps it unfold and makes it 'work.'"[27] Suffering's many possible sources suddenly become narratively important. You can't narrate your life as a process of overcoming obstacles unless you have obstacles to hold you back. Amelia's story follows this therapeutic structure. At first, her suffering seems unresolvable, the result of sheer contingency. Her husband has died, and her life has changed in ways she cannot control. The Babadook gives her suffering meaning, both at the level of the story where she is pursued by a supernatural entity and at the level of narrative as a metaphor for her depression. Capitalism relies on this narrativization of suffering to help people reimagine their political, economic, and social problems as personal ones. These stories make workers' trials, in sociologist Jennifer M. Silva's words, "a psychic *struggle to triumph over the demons of their past*."[28] That's what therapeutic horror is: stories about how characters struggle to triumph over the demons of their past. The key lesson in Kent's film is you can't overcome your demons without accepting them. The Babadook's book doesn't just tell Amelia and Samuel "you can't get rid of the Babadook." The next line underscores the film's therapeutic point: "If you're a really clever one, and you know what it is to see . . . Then you can make friends with a special one, a friend of you and me." Amelia's downward spiral is the result of her refusal to recognize her depression. Only when she perceives her suffering as an obstacle she must "make friends with" can Amelia create a new coherent story of the self.

The aim of the therapeutic narrative, then, is to create new selves out of tales in which the teller can be at once a passive victim and the active agent in her own "self-transformation."[29] It is the sort of story people need to tell themselves in a world subject to capitalism's management. You can't change the world around you. You just have to learn to accept things the way they are. From this Marxist perspective, the lesson of *The Babadook* is one of capitalist realism. There's no alternative. You have to learn to live with your monsters.

Midsommar and *Men*: Therapeutic Horror and the Woman's Film

This isn't to say that therapeutic horror means to be about capitalism's demands for emotional management. Like other films in this cycle, *The Babadook* is more interested in reimagining horror to better capture women's experiences. That's not only because a substantial number of the filmmakers in this subgenre are women but because many therapeutic horrors are also women's films, a genre with female leads and narratives focused on stereotypically women's issues and experiences.[30] In an interview, Kent highlighted her interest in reframing film's representations of women, explaining,

We're all, as women, educated and conditioned to think that motherhood is an easy thing that just happens. But it's not always the case. I wanted to show a real woman who was drowning in that environment. I thought that maybe I would be criticized by women, by mothers, because I'm not a mother. The opposite has happened; I've experienced a collective sigh of relief that women are seeing a mother up there that's human. Sure, it's an extreme situation but what I realize is that a lot of women have felt those feelings that Amelia goes through at some point along the way.[31]

Kent's "collective sigh of relief" points toward the importance of feminist film theory and criticism for this cycle of films. At first, we should hear echoes of Adrienne Rich's *Of Woman Born*. In the opening chapter, Rich describes a group of female poets discussing a murder case: "a local woman, a mother of eight, who had been in a severe depression since the birth of her third child . . . had recently murdered and decapitated her two youngest, on her front lawn."[32] Instead of horror, Rich explains, "every woman in that room who had children, every poet, could identify with her."[33] Kent's film aims for a similar form of recognition and does so in dialogue with Linda Williams's influential essay "When a Woman Looks." When a Babadook-struck Amelia watches television, a scene from *Phantom of the Opera* (1925) appears briefly on screen (Figure 27). This scene is central to Williams's argument that horror treats women and monsters as equivalents. When Christine unmasks the Phantom,

Figure 27. A flash of recognition between woman and monster in *The Phantom of the Opera* flickers onscreen before a depressed Amelia. *The Babadook*, directed by Jennifer Kent. IFC Midnight, 2014.

Williams explains, viewers can spot "between the monster and the girl . . . a flash of sympathetic recognition."[34] Kent's film encourages a similar flash of recognition. Amelia's story means to unravel the equivalence of women and monsters by showing what Rich calls "our own moments of murderous anger at our children, because there was no one and nothing else on which to discharge anger."[35]

This flash of recognition also aims to link female audiences with female characters, and takes us to perhaps the strongest connection between therapeutic horror, the women's film, and feminist film criticism: their focus on gender's role in spectatorship. Between the genre's longstanding reputation as made by men and for men, its often exploitative scenes of female nudity, and its use of male characters to enact violence on female ones, horror would seem to exemplify what Laura Mulvey calls the male gaze. For Mulvey, the gaze lacquers three distinct forms of looking: how the male director looks, how the camera looks, and how the lead male character looks. The gaze puts men in command of looking and doing and relegates women to the status of sexualized spectacles or objects to be punished. Foundational to later feminist film criticism, Mulvey's idea led critics to ask what happens when women control the narrative, whether as filmmakers or as a narrative's central character. From the perspective Mulvey lays out in "Visual Pleasure and Narrative Cinema," female spectators of the woman's film face a dilemma. They should identify with the female characters on screen, or so the theory goes, but the very way the camera looks in narrative cinema forces female spectators to act like male ones, sexualizing or punishing the very women on screen they are supposed to identify with. Later, Mulvey would suggest that female spectators might navigate this difficulty by taking up a kind of "trans-sex identification"[36]—that is, they might take on some of the agency offered by the male gaze yet also distance themselves from its demands to sexualize or punish. However, Mulvey admitted that Hollywood's narrative structures and formal construction would make it difficult for spectators to shift between these active and passive roles.

In Mary Ann Doane's study of the woman's film of the 1940s, Doane examines how the narratives in this genre account for the problem. In many respects, Doane follows Mulvey. For Doane, the woman's film denudes the male gaze of its sexualized demands while blocking female spectators' recognition or identification with the women on screen. What the woman's film offers female spectators is, in Doane's words, a "masochistic fantasy" that turns "the look violently against itself."[37] The woman's film aims to catch its female spectators between the violent objectification of the camera's gaze and a narrative antipathy to women's existence. The films that Doane examines turn spaces that were historically gendered female into hostile territory, and feature characters who deploy intellectual and scientific discourses that reduce women to objects to be studied or operated on. The results, Doane argues, explain why these films were often called "weepies." The male gaze is the basis for the genre's violent emotional appeals to its spectators. By immobilizing female spectators, the gaze forces them to turn from its deflected violence to the relief of "violent emotionalism."[38] If the male gaze and its gender norms affect how female spectators view the woman's film, Doane also describes fleeting moments of resistance. In its displays of what Doane calls *"stylized"* femininity,[39] the woman's film offers moments that denaturalize the genre's otherwise pervasive appeal to dominant gender norms. In films like *Gaslight* (1944), *Dark Victory* (1939), and *The Gay Sisters* (1942), Doane describes how doubling allows characters to parody the norms of femininity by pretending to be overbearing mothers, mad wives, and narcissists. As Doane puts it, the woman's film "[makes] these gestures and poses *fantastic,* literally *incredible.*"[40]

A number of filmmakers of therapeutic horror take Doane at her word. In these tales, fantastic metaphors double and distort emotions that past representations of women's experiences elided, making the gestures and poses of femininity literally incredible. The demonic Babadook is the irreal double of Amelia's depression; the fairy-swapped mother of *You Are Not My Mother* doubles the emotional experiences of living with a parent with bipolar disorder; the haunted house nightmare of *Relic* doubles the mind of a parent with dementia; the demons who torment the grieving mother of *A Dark Song* double her unwillingness to forgive; and the violent Korean ghost-mother who haunts and possesses her Americanized daughter in *Umma* doubles the violence and guilt of her feelings about cultural assimilation. For many therapeutic horrors, the therapeutic narrative takes up Mulvey's challenge to uncover "the transformative power of telling one's own story."[41] The result has been the creation of a new woman's horror film. Its appeal resides not simply in the management of bad feelings but in the recognition that feelings long treated as unspeakable or unworthy of representation are in fact *shared*.

Such recognition forms the plot of Ari Aster's folk horror *Midsommar* (2019). Its story follows Dani, a grief-stricken young woman whose boyfriend, Christian, barely tolerates her feelings about her family's murder-suicide. During a sojourn to a Nordic Midsomer festival, their relationship unravels. Why? Because the folk cult they meet recognizes and celebrates death as central to the making and remaking of their community. Instead of studiously ignoring Dani's feelings, they celebrate them. That's especially clear after Dani discovers Christian engaged in a ritualistic sex act with another cult member. Now Dani doesn't cry alone. The women of the community gather round and wail with her as well. When Dani is chosen as the cult's May Queen, she's allowed to select one of the festival's human sacrifices, and Christian finds himself stitched into a bear skin and burnt alive, an offering to, as one of the cult members intones, "purge our most unholy affekts" (Figure 28).[42] *Midsommar* tries to unsettle its therapeutic narrative with the cult's violence. They murder all of the men who have come with Dani to the festival and a few of their own as well. Dani shouldn't be happy to be part of this community, the film implies, but she is. And so were audiences, who received *Midsommar* as a film about Dani overcoming her grief and leaving her shitty boyfriend. Film critic Beatrice Loayza grouped

Figure 28. Even the cult sees Christian's sacrifice in therapeutic terms. *Midsommar*, directed by Ari Aster. A24 Films, 2019.

it with *The Brood, Possession, Antichrist*, and *The Invitation* as "breakup horror," a subgenre she defines as "often [capitalizing] on female madness and rage."[43] Aster himself described the film in similar terms to the *Washington Post*.[44] For Loayza, these films are a "way of articulating the emotional inadequacies of a partner unwilling to see us and our suffering for what it truly means."[45] These films may veer into misogynist stereotypes, as Loayza notes, but they also encourage audiences to pick up the therapeutic narrative and imagine themselves as a character like Dani, overcoming their bad feelings and worse partners by becoming flower queens, their exes stitched up in bear suits ready for the flames.

Midsommar helps us to see that therapeutic horror doesn't just evoke bad feelings for audiences to recognize and vibe with; it relies on a recognizable narrative form in which characters confront their bad feelings and ameliorate them. We shouldn't mistake this amelioration for catharsis, the purgation of negative feelings. It is a way of learning to live with bad feelings. No film makes that clearer than Alex Garland's *Men* (2022). After Harper's abusive husband completes suicide, she decides she needs a vacation. Harper rents a remote house in the English countryside to process her conflicting emotions, only to find herself pursued by the Green Man, a pre-Christian nature figure of death and rebirth often found in medieval architecture in the United Kingdom. The village offers her no help. Every man there is the Green Man, albeit in different forms. Each accuses her of indifference to her husband's death. Eventually, the Green Man attacks her, running through his various incarnations in a bit of cosmic horror until he arrives at his final form, Harper's dead husband. Although Harper has fought the Green Man for much of this sequence, the film doesn't show her destroying him. Instead, it cuts from Harper sitting next to her Green Man husband on the sofa to a shot of her sitting happily alone outside. Some viewers took this as evidence that Harper overcame her past trauma, but the film's star, Jessie Buckley, offered a different interpretation. When asked by an interviewer if playing Harper felt "cathartic," Buckley replied, "I wouldn't say cathartic . . . I think she went to come to terms with the kind of monsters within herself and monsters outside of herself, and to meet them and for them to meet each other. . . . [The film] doesn't follow the horror trope where the damsel in distress slays the dragon, you know? She meets the dragon, and she still has to live with the thing. She's come to learn how to live with the thing and learn from the thing."[46] One might well encapsulate all of therapeutic horror with Buckley's words. It's not about catharsis. It's about learning to live with and from your bad feelings.

The Vigil: Managing Professionalized Demons

Although the therapeutic horror cycle is global, most of these films originate from developed service economies: Australia (*The Babadook*, *Relic*), the United States (*Midsommar*, *The Vigil*, *Umma*), and Ireland and the United Kingdom (*A Dark Song, You Are Not My Mother, Men*). The focus on women's elided emotional experiences, then, comes largely from cultures with service-centered economies—that is, a mix of social reproduction work, professional services, and finance. That's no mistake. Workplaces in these economies prioritize emotional management. In *The Managed Heart*, Arlie Hochschild suggested that white-collar professionals weren't all that different from other emotional laborers like flight attendants and grocery store clerks. Instead of managers to supervise their emotional labor, professionals had an idea, *professionalism*. Hochschild saw professionalism emerge in the 1980s as a watchword, not for the actions of someone in an established profession but for a particular kind of middle-class emotional management. Feelings should be expressed at work but only within a limited range of acceptable social norms. To act otherwise is to be *unprofessional*. Middle-class children, she argued, were trained by their parents in the art of self-directed limited emotional expression. Working-class parents emphasized simple obedience, Hochschild explained, while professionalized parents taught their children to "learn to manage [their] feelings, and learn to attune [themselves] to feeling rules because doing this well will get [them] places."[47] Hochschild believed the rise of service-centered economies, which would force more workers to engage in this practice of what she termed *emotion work*, could bring a wider cultural application of middle-class emotional management techniques.[48]

Thirty years later, Richard Sennett shows Hochschild was right. In *Together*, Sennet contrasts his studies of work relations in mid-twentieth-century manufacturing with studies of work in twenty-first-century services. In manufacturing, Sennet found, expressions of anger were typical.

Obedience to authority would follow sometimes violent disagreements, Sennett notes, but workers and foremen recognized each other as autonomous human beings through these fights. These workers weren't responsible for emotion work, but their work nonetheless gave rise to a form of workplace civility. Workers and foremen crafted what Sennett calls a kind of "mutual acknowledgement" in these disputes, one that was based on authority earned by working together.[49] By contrast, workers in twenty-first-century services at all levels—whether white collar, pink collar, food services, or janitorial staff—cannot escape the demands of emotion work, in large part because employers now emphasize the importance of cooperation, as Luc Boltanski and Eve Chiapello show.[50] However, Sennett demonstrates that service-sector employers' lack of long-term commitment to their employees makes actual workplace cooperation impossible. Because employers churn through employees, the earned authority and mutual acknowledgment of more stable workplaces never emerges. Instead, the modern workplace encourages mere displays of cooperation. "Underneath the surface of working cooperatively," Sennett writes, "team-members are showing off personally, usually to a manager or superior who is judging team performance."[51] Employers reward people for the cynical performance of cooperation, displays of emotional labor that require no real negotiation with others. Demands for emotional management at work thus perversely create workplaces where no one truly cooperates, and no one recognizes the value of anyone else.[52]

We see here a result of the pervasive precarity of twenty-first-century capitalism that we discussed in chapter 1. It breeds cynicism, a drive to find and manipulate the rules. This cynicism affects workers' psyches as they manage and manipulate their emotions to suit capital's demands. While occupational psychology has spent the last thirty years looking for the positive aspects of service workers' emotional labor, it has also documented the toll that emotion work takes on them in stress, burnout, and the loss of job satisfaction.[53] No account of working-class life illustrates the importance of therapeutic narratives to the precarious workers of the twenty-first century better than Jennifer Silva's study of working-class people's passage from adolescence to adulthood. When the economy gives working people little control over their lives, the therapeutic narrative allows them to put themselves in the driver's seat. As

Silva recounts, "the men and women I spoke with cope with their disappointments in the labor market by actively fostering a kind of flexibility within themselves, bending with the constant disruptions and disappointments in the labor market, and staunchly willing themselves to be unbreakable."[54] The therapeutic narrative isn't just about overcoming one's traumas, then. It helps people to create an inner flexibility about their emotional responses and a rigid emotional shell about everyone else's. The therapeutic narrative thus has a perverse effect on its practitioners. It isn't enough to do work on yourself to get ahead. The economic environment teaches you "that depending on, trusting, and investing in others will only hurt [you] in the end."[55] The resulting "mood economy," Silva writes, makes "*emotional management* . . . the new currency of working-class adulthood."[56] Not only do people have to work on themselves to be flexible and prepared for whatever the economy throws at them, they also have to maintain boundaries so others can't drag them down. And this reveals another crucial component of the therapeutic narrative. It's incomplete without an audience. You've got to show the reworking you've done to others to prove you've gotten past them as obstacles. The therapeutic narrative is, as Eve Illouz explains, a performative utterance—that is, a speech act that changes the world in its enunciation. It doesn't matter if it hurts others' feelings as long as it redounds to your therapeutic growth.

Therapeutic horror turns this confrontation and recognition into a narrative structure readily divorced from questions of gender norms or women's elided experiences. Its irreal doubles give characters something to confront, recognize, and overcome. Consider Keith Thomas's *The Vigil*. A therapeutic horror about grief and faith, *The Vigil* reaches its climax when Yakov, its protagonist, recognizes himself in the demon that is tormenting him. The plot involves various complications and specifics, of course. Yakov has left a Hasidic community after his brother died in an antisemitic assault. Lost and alone, Yakov hasn't even enough money to pay for his anxiety medication. His former rabbi hires him to watch over Mr. Litvak, a recently deceased man without blood relations, to perform the task. Yakov doesn't want to, but he has little choice. That night, he discovers a mazzik, a grief-eating demon of Jewish folklore, has fed on Litvak since his days in a German concentration camp. With Litvak dead, the mazzik needs a new host to torment, and Yakov, still devastated by his failure to protect his brother, is a perfect target. To escape, he must burn the mazzik's true face the first night it appears. This face is hard to see, he is told, because the demon always looks away. Nonetheless, Yakov manages it, and the face he sees is his own. The allegory is clear enough. Grief and shame are demons that feed on your traumas. You can't move forward if you're always looking back into the past.

The Vigil makes no bones about its therapeutic intentions. Early on, the mazzik calls Yakov pretending to be his therapist. But in a way, it is. Yakov needs this supernatural element to create a story that will make sense of his suffering. The mazzik allows Yakov to re-narrate his past as meaningful but also past. He does this by conjuring the mazzik's true face with his knowledge of esoteric Judaica, donning *tefillin*, phylacteries on the arms and forehead containing scrolls from the Torah, and praying in Hebrew to hold the mazzik in check. This isn't a return to the past, either. Yakov keeps the past firmly in the past. When the rabbi appears the next morning to take Litvak's body away, Yakov doesn't go with them to the synagogue as the rabbi asks. Instead, he makes a clean break with the rabbi and calls another former Hasid to make a date. From the perspective of the therapeutic narrative, this makes sense. He's performed his new self for the rabbi and now he wants a new audience to listen to his successful narrative. The lesson of *The Vigil* is clear: It's not enough to confront your demons or even to recognize them as part of yourself. You must re-narrate them for someone else to recognize. Only then will your past be past. This is what the therapeutic narrative offers. Told in the right way, anything that occurred in the past can become a blessing to your new self. It's your job to show off how you manage your demons.

Anti-Therapy Horror: Ungovernable Feelings

What does it mean, then, to refuse capitalism's demands to manage your emotions? We can see this refusal in action in a set of horrors that subvert the therapeutic narrative. At first glance, Ruth Paxton's *A Banquet* (2021), Mattie Do's *The Long Walk* (2019), and Hanna Bergholm's *Hatching* (2022) seem to elicit bad feelings about women's elided emotions to work them through. Their conclusions, however, pull the therapeutic rug out from under viewers. In these films, people don't learn to manage their feelings; they are consumed by them. These refusals of the therapeutic narrative might seem mere extensions of horror's love for unresolved suspense, from final scares like hands reaching out of the grave in *Carrie* (1976) or bursting from a body in *A Nightmare on Elm Street 2: Freddy's Revenge* (1985), to purposefully open-ended conclusions like the cycle of zombie pollution beginning again after the nuclear blast in *The Return of the Living Dead* (1985) or the copying and sending of the cursed tape in *The Ring* (2002), to the dead ends of found-footage horror from *The Blair Witch Project* (1999) on.[57] However, in anti-therapy horror, the genre's love for thwarted resolutions serves to thwart the therapeutic narrative itself. Instead of creating a new self, confrontation and recognition produce literal dead ends. In *A Banquet*, a mother and daughter are caught up in punishing narratives of the self. Following the suicide of her terminally ill husband, Holly must tend to her daughter, Betsey, after she claims to have had a religious experience. The end of the world is coming, Betsey insists, then refuses to eat. Holly is torn. Betsey needs help, but Holly remembers her own trauma after her mother institutionalized her as a teenager. Desperate not to injure Betsey in the same way, Holly struggles to make sense of her affliction. Is it a religious experience, mental illness, demonic possession? She doesn't know. The answer Holly comes to is a therapeutic one. She will recognize her daughter as she wishes to be seen. Yet this recognition doesn't remake Betsey or Holly. Instead, Betsey dies of starvation, and Holly, overcome with grief, runs outside, where she is consumed in a sudden blast of light. Betsey's foretold apocalypse is her mother's grief.

Nor is there redemption in recognition in *The Long Walk*. The story follows an old man desperate to save his mother from a terminal illness. With the help of an enslaved ghost, he travels back in time to intervene at different moments in his childhood. Yet nothing he does works. His mother still dies, and his interventions deform and destroy him. From an idealistic, caring child, he devolves into a brutal killer. *The Long Walk* suggests that the old man must recognize his inability to change the past, yet when he does, it brings no transformation. He frees the ghosts of the women he has killed, yet he refuses to free the ghost who has helped him all these many years, and when he dies of old age, she takes her revenge by traveling back in time to start another loop of destruction and despair.

Hatching takes this refusal of recognition the furthest by making it altogether impossible. Everything in the life of Tinja, the daughter of a mommy-vlogger, has been shaped for appearance. Her mother's job is to present herself as the knowing matriarch of a happy and successful family, but the film's opening peels back her cheerful façade after a bird flies into the house during one of her social media posts. Angry about her ruined video and dirty house, Tinja's mother snaps the bird's neck and tells Tinja to dispose of it. That night, Tinja hears the bird drag itself away to die and follows it. In the woods, she discovers the bird's now-motherless egg, and takes it home out of guilt. The egg isn't nourished by Tinja's attentions but by her sadness. Fed on her tears, it swells to massive proportions, hatching an enormous, deformed bird-like creature that immediately imprints itself on Tinja. Tinja doesn't understand the nature of this psychic bond, but when someone makes her feel inadequate, the creature feels it too. Tinja suppresses her rage as her mother insists, but the creature acts it out, feeding on those who make her feel misrecognized. As it grows, it becomes Tinja's uncanny double. When her mother discovers its existence, she's incensed, more for the doubling than for the bird's violence. There's only one answer: kill it. Tinja pleads for its life, but her mother refuses to listen. In the ensuing fight, she kills Tinja, mistaking her for her double. The film ends with a final scene of bad recognition. The supernatural cuckoo turns to the grieving woman and utters her first word: "Mother."

However, the film that cuts most deeply at horror's use of therapeutic narratives doesn't rely on irreal entities at all. In trans filmmaker Jane Schoenbrun's *We Are All Going to the World's Fair* (2021), we see how people try to use horror to ameliorate capitalism's bad feelings and fail. Casey, a deeply depressed and socially isolated young woman, starts playing a collaborative online game called the World's Fair Challenge. Players begin by recording themselves watching a "cursed" video, chanting "I want to go to the World's Fair" three times, then smearing blood on their screens. This act is supposed to initiate unpredictable personal changes, and players are to document them in videos that rely on horror's elements, narratives, and aesthetics, from levitation and body horror to blue-green lighting and jump scares. In effect, the World's Fair offers players a therapeutic remaking of the self through genre play. It is literally horror as therapy.

There's no liberation here, though. What we see in *We're All Going to the World's Fair* is that using genre to manage capitalism's bad feelings may be curdling humanity's imaginative capacity to make and remake itself. Media theory would agree. In *Gamer Theory*, McKenzie Wark describes the demise of liberatory narratives about play and games. Video games in capitalism, Wark argues, mean

> play is no longer a counter to work. Play becomes work; work becomes play. Play outside of work found itself captured by the rise of the digital game, which responds to the boredom of the player with endless rounds of repetition, level after level of difference as more of the same. Play no longer functions as a foil for a critical theory. The utopian dream of liberating play from the game, of a pure play beyond the game, merely opened the way for the extension of gamespace into every aspect of everyday life. While the counter-culture wanted worlds of play outside the game, the military entertainment complex countered in turn by expanding the game to the whole world, containing play forever within it.[58]

The World's Fair is one instance of this extension of gamespace into everyday life, and we see that Casey is drawn to it out of boredom. As a character, she seems the result of twenty-first-century parenting's political-economic turn to emotion work, her feelings so tightly controlled that they can find almost no expression at all. Here we encounter one of Mark Fisher's reasons for capitalism's pervasive feeling of depression. Depression privatizes the stresses of capitalism through what Fisher describes as "a sneering 'inner' voice which accuses you of self-indulgence."[59] This voice brings with it anhedonia—the loss of interest, pleasure, and feeling. Anhedonia, we might say, is feeling management taken to its furthest extreme.

And Casey is at this limit. Withdrawn from all social interaction, she spends her days in the attic of her father's exurban house staring at a computer screen or skulking in the woods. The World's Fair seems to offer a path out of depression. It is an interest, it offers community, and it promises personal transformation. Yet Casey discovers in the World's Fair just another version of the attention economy. Its players are content creators clamoring for eyeballs, whether they understand that or not. Instead of transformation, Casey experiences indifference.

Staying up late waiting for the play-counts on her videos to change, she goes to her father's rec room barn to listen to ASMR videos and try to sleep. First, though, she stops to examine her father's assault rifle. The film makes no bones about where depression can lead. At last, however, someone recognizes her. A player named JLB sends her a message. Over a distorted image of her face, he says she is "in trouble." They need to talk. After a bit of web sleuthing, Casey discovers JLB runs a World's Fair YouTube channel and claims to often collaborate with other players. However, he admonishes viewers that "this channel is for serious players only." His channel is exclusively "in-game"—that is, in every conversation, JLB will act like the World's Fair is real.

In an interview, Schoenbrun explained that the World's Fair Challenge was inspired by an internet phenomenon called "creepypasta." Schoenbrun described it as "a very internet idea . . . that you will never really know whether what you're reading is true or false."[60] For JLB, the game's blurred lines between reality and fantasy allow a middle-aged man to cross younger players' personal boundaries. He says he can only keep Casey safe if she films herself sleeping and sends him the videos. When this attention draws Casey out of her shell, JLB tries to close his trap with another video. He can "feel the forces of the Fair pulling [her] in closer with each new video [she] uploads" and he wants to "save" her. When JLB delivers this message, though, Schoenbrun doesn't show JLB's video, only his screen as he reads from a script. He's done this before. Casey may be naïve, but she's not oblivious. In her next video, she responds to JLB, calling him a "lonely person" with "a lot of mental issues" who is "trying to deceive people." But she can't stop posting. In her next video, she walks toward a New Year's Eve celebration while murmuring into the microphone in a quiet monotone: "My father needs to go. I know this. I'll wait until the morning. It will be a long time, but I won't be nervous. And at 6 am, when he gets up for his first job of the day, I'll be ready for him. Three shots to the stomach. And I'll stand there and watch him bleed. I don't want to do it. But I don't think I'll be able to control myself. I don't know. Maybe I'll just kill myself instead." When she approaches a crowd counting down the ball drop, her voice shifts. "Why won't you help me?" she implores.

At this point in the film, it isn't clear who is manipulating whom. Casey may be turning the tables on JLB, or the game may have unleashed feelings that she can either no longer manage or no longer wishes to. In her next video, she claims she has become possessed by the World's Fair. Covering her face in blacklight paint, she glows green under an ultraviolet lamp as she mocks her favorite stuffed animal. She has had it since she was five days old, she explains, then rips it to shreds and stomps it mercilessly. At last, she toys with its eyeball, looking directly into the camera (Figure 29). The sequence seems an oblique reference to voodoo and zombism, a perverse revision of the chicken sacrifices in Jean Rouch's *The Mad Masters (Les Maitres Fous)* (1955). Whether Casey is not in control of herself, or pretending not to be for the camera, she's clearly distraught when she comes out of her trance, and JLB, the only person paying attention, is concerned. On Skype, she tells him she's about to die. She asks how long he thinks she has before she does "it." JLB says he needs to ask her something and "we need to go out of game first." "Sure," Casey replies blankly. "What's that?" "It means outside the margins of the game, the MMORPG," JLB replies. "I didn't know that term," Casey says, sounding muddled. "A massive multiplayer online role-playing game. You know it's just a game we're playing, right?" "Oh." Casey shakes her head in confusion, looking around the room. "I

Figure 29. Casey poses with a doll's eye, as if asking who is watching who. *We Are All Going to the World's Fair*, directed by Jane Schoenbrun. Utopia, 2021.

mean, yeah," she adds. JLB presses on. Her videos have become "intense," he says. Casey's affect suddenly changes: "Well, it's a horror game, right?" JLB tries to reframe his interest by acting parental. He knows what it's like to be young and to think about doing . . . He can't say. He wonders aloud if he should call the police. But he doesn't know her last name or where she lives. Now Casey is defensive. They're just videos. Pretend. Besides, her name isn't even Casey, she says, and ends the call. The film's perspective suddenly shifts from Casey to JLB. Panicked, he wanders through his cavernous suburban house. What can he do? He sits in his living room for a moment, rehearsing lines to talk Casey down, then returns to his office and calls again. She doesn't answer. He messages her: "Please don't do it." No response. In despair, he puts his hand on the screen and lays his head on the desk as the camera retreats from the room.

If the film ended here, the game's collapse of fiction and reality might simply be the unresolved suspense that people expect of horror. Whether Casey is playing an elaborate hoax on JLB or not, the violent feelings the game has helped Casey to shape have de-realized reality. The video is a fake, but so is all of this, she says. Killing her father or herself or somebody else or no one becomes equally meaningless. The game has made nothing real except the world of the game. And that is where Casey seems to be headed, to be absorbed one way or another by the game and its cursed video. And in a way, she is. After this call, she disappears from the film, never to return.

The film's final scenes offer us perhaps the most sustained attack on the therapeutic narrative. In voice-over, JLB gives his audience an update on Casey, one year later. But has it really been a year? The film offers nothing to indicate the passage of time. It could be the next year. It could be the next morning. No matter. The story JLB tells is a therapeutic one: Casey went to a psychiatric facility after that night, he says, and contacted him much later. They told each other their real names, then, even later, he visited her in Manhattan where she's enrolled in a theater program. He asks her about that night, and she tells him she got to the heart of the Fair, but something brought her back. Only then does JLB reveal he spent the night praying in front of his screen. Yes, she says. She felt it. He brought her back. They hug, he claims, and she rode the subway off into her new life.

While JLB's tale may be therapeutic, what the film shows isn't. There's no evidence they ever met. No photos, no text messages, no videos. All we see is JLB staring blankly into his computer screen. "I couldn't believe I was actually there," he says, "that I was touching her." And the way the camera holds on his face after he finishes indicates maybe we shouldn't either (Figure 30). After all, JLB's narratives are in-game. While his story of Casey's turn to therapy and remaking of herself could be true, his expression, silent and on the verge of tears, suggest it isn't.

Whatever has happened to Casey remains unknown. In some respects, the film can be read as a trans narrative much like Schoenbrun's next, and more explicitly trans-focused, film, *I Saw the TV Glow* (2024). Where the main character of *I Saw the TV Glow* uses fiction to escape the constrictions of gender, Casey turns to fiction to escape a more loosely defined but equally destructive reality. In both instances, these characters discover that fiction is not enough. Its satisfactions cannot replace real change. Instead, these fictions can become merely another narrative imposed by others, another attempt to manage who you are by telling you that *this* is who you should be. In these films, we glimpse another way to think about Mulvey's idea of a "trans-sex identification"

Figure 30. JLB's audience would find his story harder to believe if they could see the look on his face. *We Are All Going to the World's Fair*, directed by Jane Schoenbrun. Utopia, 2021.

for spectators. Perhaps it can be understood as a refusal to accept that feelings can and should be controlled by others. From a Marxist perspective, we might add, managing our feelings can't resolve the material constraints posed by capitalism. And this shows, I think, why horror matters now. It gives us ways to feel bad, together, and at its best, it does so without the promise that these bad feelings or their causes can be easily resolved, or even kept in the realm of fiction. If we mean to deal with capitalism's bad feelings, we'll need solidarity and revolution, not therapy.

CONCLUSION

As we have seen, horror in the twenty-first century is an expansive and diverse genre, one that extends beyond slashers and meat movies, and is made for audiences wider than young white men looking for cheap thrills or stories to ameliorate their castration anxiety. I've argued that the diversity of contemporary horror helps us to see that, as a genre, horror is the result of shared judgments about what terrifies. Its pleasures come from joining with others in the recognition that these terrors are and can be shared. Because those judgments are deeply bound up with our experience of everyday life, horror's terrors reflect the wider experiences of its audiences and its creators. After all, genre creators are part of the audience too. Horror gives these terrors narrative and generic form, often quite knowingly. Much of contemporary horror understands itself as a critique of contemporary life, whether of work, climate change, anti-Black racism, mass culture and consumerism, patriarchy, or women's representation in film.

Marxism helps us to analyze these shared judgments about what is terrifying in modern life and to unearth from these critiques some of the forms of common sense that keep capitalism going. Hidden under commonsense views of work as punishment or as endeavors of love, Marxism can find in horror's representations of work the violence that capitalism directs at labor, a violence that has less interest in labor's destruction than in the intensification of its exploitation. Marxism can discover in horror's fears of the Anthropocene the metabolic rifts opened by capitalism's robbery of the biosphere. In new Black horror's tales of anti-Black spaces, it can uncover the realities of racial capitalism's uneven development, and in its critiques of mass culture, commodification's terrifying activity. It can disclose capitalism's exploitation of reproductive labor in elevated family horror, and its demands to police our emotions in therapeutic horror. In short, horror gives our conjuncture's terrors narrative form, and Marxism teaches us how to read those forms.

For the majority of this book, then, my argument has been that horror needs Marxism. We can't make sense of it otherwise. Here, I want to argue that Marxism needs horror. Consider Lorcan Finnegan's *Nocebo* (2022), a revenge horror based on the 2015 Kentex factory fire in the Philippines that killed seventy-four people. Its story follows a British high-end children's fashion designer, Christine, whose career and health collapse after a subcontractor's Philippines factory catches fire and kills the workers inside.[1] She begins to recover only when Diana, a Filipino woman, appears on her doorstep. At first, Diana simply cares for her daughter, Bobs, but it isn't long before she's offering Christine folk remedies to treat her guilt-induced illnesses. Her husband, Felix, doesn't trust Diana, and rightly so. Diana worked in Christine's factory, and while she escaped the fire, her daughter didn't. She's come for revenge.

Viewers don't need Marxism to grasp *Nocebo*'s critique. Its credits declare "Justice for all Kentex fire victims," echoing the language of labor organizers in the fire's aftermath. They called for improved labor and safety standards, higher wages, and an end to working conditions that Filipino labor advocacy organization Migrante International called "slave-like."[2] The film lays the blame for these working conditions squarely at Christine's feet. In flashback, it shows her demanding that the factory overseers lock the doors from the outside. Loss prevention, as it were. Diana exacts her vengeance through supernatural means, transporting Christine back in time to the factory fire where she's forced to witness the suffering and death she caused before the flames consume her too (Figure 31). While it is tempting to read the film's visceral depiction of capitalism's violence as an attempt to incite viewers to act, *Nocebo* understands its project as commentary, albeit commentary on capitalism, exploitation, and consumerism. Indeed, that's how Lorcan Finnegan speaks about the film in interviews. He explained to *Film Int.*:

> as contemporary film makers we try to make sense of the world around us now by tackling issues that are affecting us and society as a whole. On this project we knew we wanted to delve into exploitation, but our

starting point was actually just around the general interest in placebos and nocebos, and how they relate to shamanism first of all and how shamanism has been affected by the arrival of Christianity both into Ireland and into Philippines and how that has been further compounded by the introduction of colonialism and then capitalism and this kind of consumerist culture.³

We don't need Marxist analysis to grasp the film's broad anticapitalist perspective, even if Marxism could help us to unravel the film's depiction of uneven development, racialization, and trend form commodities. Finnegan's account underscores what I've said throughout this book. As a genre, horror aims to organize and capitalize on the suffering that permeates our conjuncture. How people use those ordered feelings isn't and can't be predetermined, politically or otherwise. What horror offers audiences is a sociality built around shared experiences of displeasure. At its best, a film like *Nocebo* offers filmmakers a way to express their horror at capitalism's injustices in a way that can organize and express a larger *social* disapprobation.

It is this sociality that shows why Marxism needs horror. Horror underscores that capitalism isn't just an economic system but a social

Figure 31. Christine is trapped in her own burning factory. *Nocebo*, directed by Lorcan Finnegan. RLJE Films, 2022.

one. Horror's shared judgments show us that what terrifies in capitalism is its use of violence and domination to produce value. Throughout this book, horror has forced us to account for capitalism's violence in ways that illustrate a larger shift in Marxist research toward an understanding of capitalism as a social, political, and economic system. Throughout, I've drawn on an array of Marxisms to describe this violence, from value theory, materialist feminist research on social reproduction and ecology, and work on uneven development, racial capitalism, and commodification to materialist feminist work on family abolition and twenty-first-century capitalism's demands for emotion work. Taken together, these different perspectives show us that capitalism extends beyond the exploitation of workers in production—itself a violent process—to the direct appropriation of land, labor, food, energy, and raw materials, and that its appropriations often draw on prior forms of domination, from patriarchy and the family structure to racial hierarchies and nature's reduction to raw material. Violence and domination aren't outside capitalism but integral to it, from settler colonialism's violent dispossessions of Indigenous peoples, the transatlantic slave trade, and the subjugation of women, to the neoliberal era's use of accumulation by dispossession to give capital new sources of value.

No one knows this better than Nancy Fraser. As Fraser explains, when we talk about capitalism, we have to talk about "capitalist *society*."[4] For Fraser, Marxism needs to connect social reproduction theory, ecosocialism, Black Marxism, and Marxist political theory. At the crux of Fraser's reimagined Marxism is the understanding that capitalism is a system of appropriation and exploitation that lives parasitically off what she calls its "background conditions of possibility": the biosphere, systems of social reproduction, and political systems.[5] Fraser's account helps us to understand why people think of capitalism as an economic system rather than a social one. What makes capitalism unique is its use of economics to naturalize the social separation of life from its conditions of reproduction. Søren Mau also emphasizes this point. Capitalism exploits humanity's "ontological fragility," Mau explains, by "inserting [itself] in the gap between life and its conditions."[6] Marx himself made this point, of course. For Marx, the separation of life from its conditions of reproduction is the conflict between the realms of freedom and necessity. A communist society can attain freedom from necessity, Marx explains, by "bringing [the human metabolism] under their collective control instead of being dominated by it as a blind power."[7] This doesn't mean a free society ever leaves behind its material needs. As Marx observes, there "always remains a realm of necessity. The realm of true freedom, the development of human powers as an end in itself, begins beyond it, though it can only flourish with this realm of necessity as its basis."[8] Why, then, have we so long overlooked appropriation's role in capitalism? We can find the answer in Marx's very next sentence: "The reduction of the working day is the basic prerequisite."[9] For Marx, freedom comes from the reduction of *necessary* work, and the only way to satisfy the realm of necessity while reducing necessary work seems to be technological innovation.[10] Marx hoped that technological change would free labor from its exploitation, and twentieth-century communism focused on modernization and industrialization with this end at least ostensibly in mind. However, as the failures of actually existing communism and our conjuncture amply show, technology won't open the realm of freedom on its own, and it certainly won't deliver us from the climate catastrophes that capital has wrought. Why? Because when we focus solely on technology's ability to reduce necessary labor time, we don't address its rapacious appropriations of labor, food, energy, and raw materials. Attempts to overcome capitalism without addressing its uses of appropriation will leave in place its most destructive processes and activities.[11]

Understood as a social system rather than a purely economic one, capitalism reveals itself to be more than a ceaseless process of commodification. Capitalism can try to commodify whatever it likes, but we will miss everything about how capitalism functions if we take the commodity form as an inexorable monster that simply subsumes culture, society, nature, and subjectivity in a homogeneous mass of value. Capitalism isn't a smoothly functioning set of economic processes that readily transform the striated spaces of noncapitalist life into the smooth space of capitalist relations. If we view capitalism in this functionalist way, it appears to be a perpetual-motion machine for accumulation, one that we have to master and subdue to find a way out.[12] Capitalism's subsumptions are always partial, subject to struggle, and indicate the existence of spheres outside capital's control. "Commodification is far from universal in capitalist society," Fraser explains. "On the contrary, where it is present, it depends for its very existence on zones of non-commodification, which capital systematically cannibalizes."[13] I'd avoid *cannibalize* for less racialized and historically freighted language. As C. Richard King documents, the term originates in the racist colonial imaginary, and cultural critics shouldn't adopt it. We can say more simply that what capitalism does is live off the destructive consumption of its conditions of existence.[14] In its search for new resources to exploit, capital continually contests whatever falls outside its circuits of exploitation and exchange in what Fraser terms "boundary struggles."[15] These are battles over which relations and objects outside capitalist exchange will be commodified and which won't. Some of these struggles are about what gets commodified, but others are about what gets held outside of commodity exchange and how it's held out of commodity exchange. Capital would prefer to keep some relations outside of commodification to appropriate them directly and others to hold them in reserve for later use. Those preferences don't dictate what happens. They are part of the grounds for struggle as people contest capital's depredations. As a social system, then, capitalism is constantly made and remade through social, political, and economic struggles. The outcomes of these struggles aren't simply dictated by the forces and relations of production through some functionalist capitalist logic but through active contestations of the ways people want to use the law of value and the forces and relations of production to shape our social world.

Not only does horror help us to see how capitalism functions as a social system based in appropriation and exploitation, it also helps us to redress one of the most damaging criticisms lobbed at Marxism, that it can't account for difference. As Vivek Chibber details, postcolonial critics of Marxism fault it for being unable to account for the persistence of racial, social, and labor-based hierarchies, or for differences in the trajectory of political-economic development, especially in regions outside Europe. Cultural difference, they argue, matters. And they're not wrong. Twentieth-century historical materialists claimed industrialization would bring the freedoms of bourgeois progress, yet all over the globe, industrialization and modernization only intensified regimes of social and racial domination. According to Chibber, for postcolonial critics, the problem with Marxism isn't just that it maintains that capitalism always develops into European-style industrial society, but that its homogenization of historical development is baked into its analysis of capital itself.[16] Marx's theory of abstract labor, they argue, makes every form of labor as interchangeable as the different stages of so-called historical development. For these reasons, postcolonial critics argue that culture and history shape development in ways that Marxism can't adequately address. And if we embraced historical materialism's creaky theory that capitalism always follows the same social, political, and economic stages of development, we'd have to agree.

But horror has led us to a Marxism that can account for the importance of difference to capitalism. As we saw in chapter 1, Marx's notion of abstract labor does not mean that all concrete labor in capitalism is interchangeable, only that it is calculable for exchange and that employers view it as socially productive—that is, that it produces at a rate that will allow capitalists to sell the fruits of their workers' labor on the market. As Chibber notes, and as we discussed in chapters 1 and 4, social and racial hierarchies can be used by employers to sort employees into different parts of the labor process, with its different determinations of socially productive abstract labor; to intensify the production process by putting different social or racial groups in competition with one another; and, most importantly, to maintain capital's control over its workforce by pitting different groups against each other. "*Capital*," Chibber explains, "*can reproduce social hierarchies just as readily as it can dissolve them.*"[17] In other words, difference is part of how capitalism functions.[18] As Chibber shows, capitalism uses cultural differences to create new social and political hierarchies and to extract more value from racialized or ethnicized populations.[19]

Marxism needs horror, then, because it helps us to create a fuller account of capitalism. In the process, it reveals that capitalism's crises extend beyond the economic. For Marx, economic crisis is a persistent internal feature of capitalism. The basics of his account are fairly simple: As competition encourages individual firms to produce more for less, it creates a drive for each capitalist to revolutionize production in order to increase profit margins. The result is a system-wide problem of overproduction that drives down the rate of profit for everyone. We needn't reopen arguments about whether the law of the falling rate of profit is the basis of capitalism's economic crises. The important point is this: Marx understood that capitalism's internal tendencies made it a fundamentally unstable system that could be readily thrown into crisis by contingent events.[20] He also understood that economic crises don't auger capitalism's end. In fact, they're its solution to the problem of overproduction, a form of what Friedrich Hayek famously called creative destruction. As Søren Mau explains, in crises, the "depreciation and destruction" of existing capital purges some firms while allowing others to accumulate at a higher rate of profit.[21] When we approach capitalism as a social system, rather than an economic one, we see that it is shot through with other internal tendencies that render it unstable. Those tendencies are the result of boundary struggles over social reproduction, political systems, and the environment.

In the prior chapters, we saw how horror gives affective shape to our conjuncture's manifold struggles over social and ecological reproduction. Our ongoing political crisis is harder to locate. Yet we can find intimations of capitalism's destructive parasitism on the political systems it needs to survive in the ignorant violence of Sustin, the patriarch of *Jug Face*. "The pit wants what it wants," Sustin declares, hoping that his sacrifices of family and community will maintain his cult's tenuous social and religious order. But Sustin is trapped in an unsustainable situation. There's no way to satisfy the pit they've built their society around except by destroying themselves. Such is the nature of our political crisis. As Fraser explains, in the 2010s the social and political blocs that maintained the neoliberal era crumbled, leaving behind disparate demands for progressive action and violent counterreaction that no power bloc has yet managed to cohere. For Fraser, our moment can be neatly summed up by an aphorism from Antonio Gramsci describing fascism's rise in the 1920s. He declared: "The old is dying and the new cannot be born; in this interregnum, a great variety of morbid symptoms appear."[22]

Perhaps, then, contemporary horror tells us more about our political crisis than we might expect. In its foregrounding of violence and appropriation, twenty-first-century horror reflects the morbid symptoms of our political-economic impasse. It is perhaps no surprise that we see this most clearly in new Black horror. Black Marxism has long been most attentive to what Dylan Rodriguez calls "the *primary and productive*" role that violence plays for both capitalism and fascism, an insight he draws from the work of Frantz Fanon, George Jackson, and Angela Davis.[23] In its focus on the creation of anti-Black spaces and the state's violent policing of those spaces, new Black horror amply illustrates how primary and productive violence can be for capitalism. As a whole, horror offers Marxism the opportunity to uncover violence's role in capitalism's domination, and how violence marks capitalism's continual struggles over what it means to consume or destroy. Horror lets us see why capitalism hates us. We're in it but never entirely of it. Even though we must navigate its demands every day, our lives are not and can never be reduced to purely capitalist relations. Its structures constrain our actions, but they cannot keep us from choosing another way. And its manifold crises show that we must.

If Marxism needs horror, horror also needs Marxism. Marxism holds out the promise that we can stop being subject to the market's blind domination, and determine, communally and democratically, what we value and how those values should structure how we live. Marxism insists that we can have the material wealth we need to live fulfilling lives and the free time to live lives of our choosing. It doesn't predicate this better world on industrial society or technological breakthroughs, only on a thorough reassessment of the ways we inhabit the world and how we use the limited amount of time we have on it. As we have seen, Marxism unravels the role of value in capitalist society. Behind its discussion of value in capitalism lies a larger question about values, our values as human beings. Capitalism may insist that only one kind of value matters. Marxism allows us to conceive of other kinds. As philosopher Martin Hägglund argues, Marx's thought is fundamentally concerned with questions of life and time.[24] We saw this in chapter 3 in terms of labor and ecology. Capitalism's focus on extracting labor-time from workers means it's always robbing them of the limited time they have to be alive. In a similar sense, it robs the biosphere by taking from it faster than it can replenish itself. The horror of capitalism is that its endless search for value raises one kind of value over all others. Instead of humane values, we have capitalist value, which is interested only in robbing us of life, individually and collectively. What we gain by confronting this horror is a deeper understanding of what feminist scholar Lynn Seagall calls our "shared vulnerability."[25] Horror allows us to feel our shared vulnerability as precisely that, *shared*, and Marxism allows us to understand how we might reorder society around that vulnerability. Together, they can help us conceive of more human and humane lives and relations—with ourselves, with one another, and with the Earth.

ACKNOWLEDGMENTS

Growing up, I thought horror wasn't my thing. My father had a library of VHS cassettes and laser discs, and we watched pretty much everything else—Welles, Hitchcock, Kurosawa, noir, westerns, screwball comedies, and musicals. For whatever reason, we didn't think of films like *Alien*, *Re-Animator*, or even *Evil Dead 2* as horror. I didn't pay any more attention to it when Wes Craven came to Sonoma, California, to film *Scream*. That was big news for a small town, but I was too busy playing in a punk band to notice. It wasn't until I started dating a film studies PhD student that I really paid attention to horror. She lured me in with a respectable screening of *The Battle of Algiers*, but soon enough it was art horror like *Eyes without a Face* and *Eraserhead*, then we were on to the Italians and everything else. Twenty years on and we still watch horror together and talk deeply about film, theory, and, well, everything. I couldn't have written this book without her insight and support, and I wouldn't have written it at all if I hadn't met her. It's likely no surprise that our son loves scary stories too.

    I am grateful for the support I have received from friends and colleagues. Douglas Dowland encouraged me to pursue the weirdest possible version of this project. Marge McGeachy helped me bring the book into focus, and my family suffered through rough drafts. I was fortunate to be able to present portions of this work as I completed it, and I would like to thank Jeffrey Weinstock, Alexandra Brown and the Marxist Reading Group, and Molly Henderson for giving me the time and space to present portions of this material. When William Thomas McBride accepted my piece on Dracula for MLA's *Approaches to Teaching Bram Stoker's Dracula*, he unwittingly started me down the path to this book. I could not have written this book without the librarians of D'Youville University and of the Buffalo/Erie public library system, or the music of the Necks, Blue Lake, Mary Lattimore, Pharoah Sanders, and the Bitchin Bajas.

FILMOGRAPHY

Alice in Wonderland. Directed by Clyde Geronimi, Wilfred Jackson, and Hamilton Luske. Disney, 1951.
Alice, Sweet Alice. Directed by Alfred Sole. Allied Artists Pictures, 1976.
American Horror Story, season 1. Created by Brad Falchuk and Ryan Murphy. FX, 2011.
The Amityville Horror. Directed by Stuart Rosenberg. American International Pictures, 1979.
The Angry Black Girl and Her Monster. Directed by Bomani J. Story. RLJE Films, 2023.
Annihilation. Directed by Alex Garland. Paramount, 2018.
Antichrist. Directed by Lars von Trier. IFC, 2006.
Antlers. Directed by Scott Cooper. Searchlight, 2021.
The Babadook. Directed by Jennifer Kent. IFC Midnight, 2014.
The Baby. Created by Lucy Gaymer and Sian Robbins-Grace. HBO, 2022.
The Bad Seed. Directed by Mervyn LeRoy. Warner Bros., 1956.
A Banquet. Directed by Ruth Paxton. IFC Midnight, 2021.
Barbarian. Directed by Zach Cregger. 20th Century Studios, 2022.
Battle Royale. Original title: *Batoru rowaiaru.* Directed by Kinji Fukasaku. Anchor Bay, 2000.
Beetlejuice. Directed by Tim Burton. Warner Bros., 1988.
Berberian Sound Studio. Directed by Peter Strickland. IFC Midnight, 2012.
The Blackcoat's Daughter. Directed by Oz Perkins. A24 Films, 2015.
The Blackening. Directed by Tim Story. Lionsgate, 2023.
Blade Runner. Directed by Ridley Scott. Warner Bros., 1982.
The Blair Witch Project. Directed by Daniel Myrick and Eduardo Sánchez. Artisan Entertainment, 1999.
Bleed with Me. Directed by Amelia Moses. Shudder, 2020.
Blood and Black Lace. Original title: *6 donne per l'assassino.* Directed by Mario Bava. VCI Entertainment, 1964.
Blood Conscious. Directed by Timothy Covell. Dark Sky Films, 2021.
The Brood. Directed by David Cronenberg. New World Pictures, 1979.

The Burning. Directed by Tony Maylam. Miramax, 1981.
Candyman. Directed by Bernard Rose, Columbia Tristar, 1992.
Candyman. Directed by Nia DaCosta, Universal, 2021.
Cannibal Holocaust. Directed by Ruggero Deodato. F.D. Cinematografica, 1980.
Carrie. Directed by Brian De Palma. United Artists, 1976.
Censor. Directed by Prano Bailey-Bond, Magnolia Pictures, 2021.
Child's Play 3. Directed by Jack Bender. Universal, 1991.
Christine. Directed by John Carpenter. Columbia Pictures, 1983.
The Conference. Original title: *Konferensen.* Directed by Patrik Eklund. Netflix, 2023.
Creep. Directed by Patrick Brice. Blumhouse Productions, 2014.
Damn! Directed by Aaron Fisher-Cohen. Fantastic Relationship Filmmaking, 2011.
A Dark Song. Directed by Liam Gavin. IFC Midnight, 2016.
Dark Victory. Directed by Edmund Goulding. Warner Bros., 1939.
Dawn of the Dead. Directed by George Romero. United Film Distribution Company, 1978.
The Day after Tomorrow. Directed by Roland Emmerich. Twentieth-Century Fox, 2004.
Death Bed: The Bed That Eats. Directed by George Barry, 1977.
Demons. Original title: *Dèmoni.* Directed by Lamberti Bava. Synapse Films, 1985.
Dog Star Man. Directed by Stan Brakhage. Criterion, 2021.
Dogville. Directed by Lars von Trier. Lions Gate Films, 2003.
Don't Look Now. Directed by Nicholas Roeg. Paramount, 1973.
Dracula. Directed by Todd Browning. Universal, 1931.
Drag Me to Hell. Directed by Sam Raimi. Universal, 2009.
Dressed to Kill. Directed by Brian DePalma. Filmways Pictures, 1980.
Dr. Jekyll and Mr. Hyde. Directed by Rouben Mamoulian. Paramount, 1931.
El Topo. Directed by Alejandro Jodorwsky. Anchor Bay, 1970,
El Valley Centro. Directed by James Benning. 1999.
The Empty Man. Directed by David Prior. Walt Disney Studios, 2020.
The Evil Dead. Directed by Sam Raimi. New Line Cinema, 1981.
Evil Dead 2. Directed by Sam Raimi. Anchor Bay, 1987.
Eyes without a Face. Original title: *Les yeux sans visage.* Directed by Georges Franjou. Criterion, 1960.
Frankenstein. Directed by James Whale. Universal, 1931.
Friday the 13th. Directed by Sean S. Cunningham. Paramount, 1980.
Funny Games. Directed by Michael Haneke 1997.
Funny Games. Directed by Michael Haneke. 2007.
Gaia. Directed by Jaco Bouwer. Neon, 2021.
Gaslight. Directed by George Cukor. MGM, 1944.
The Gay Sisters. Directed by Irving Rapper. Warner Bros., 1942.
Get Out. Directed by Jordan Peele. Universal, 2017.
Ghosts. Created by Mathew Baynton, Jim Howick, and Laurence Rickard. BBC, 2019.

Ghosts. Created by Joe Port and Joe Wiseman. CBS, 2021.
The Girl with All the Gifts. Directed by Colm McCarthy. Saban Films, 2016.
Good Madam. Original title: *Mlungu Wam.* Directed by Jenna Cato Bass. Shudder, 2021.
Goodnight Mommy. Directed by Severin Fiala and Veronika Franz. Anchor Bay, 2014.
Halloween. Directed by John Carpenter. Compass, 1978.
Halloween III: Season of the Witch. Directed by Tommy Lee Wallace. Universal Pictures, 1982.
The Happening. Directed by M. Night Shyamalan. Twentieth-Century Fox, 2008.
Harbinger. Directed by Cody Duckworth. Summer Hill Films, 2015.
Hatchet for Honeymoon. Original title: *Il rosso segno della follia.* Directed by Mario Bava. Redemption, 1970.
Hatching. Original title: *Pahanhautoja.* Directed by Hanna Bergholm. IFC Midnight, 2022.
The Haunting. Directed by Robert Wise. MGM, 1963.
The Haunting of Hill House. Directed by Mike Flanagan. Netflix, 2018.
Hell Baby. Directed by Robert Ben Garant and Thomas Lennon. Millennium Entertainment, 2013.
Hellraiser. Directed by Clive Barker. New World Pictures, 1987.
Hereditary. Directed by Ari Aster. A24, 2017.
High Rise. Directed by Ben Wheatley. Magnet, 2015.
Host. Directed by Rob Savage. Shudder, 2020.
Huesera: The Bone Woman. Directed by Michelle Garza Cevera. XYZ Films, 2022.
I Blame Society. Directed by Gillian Wallace Horvat. Cranked Up Films, 2020.
I Saw the TV Glow. Directed by Jane Schoenbrun. A24, 2024.
Ichi the Killer. Original title: *Koroshiya 1.* Directed by Takashi Miike. Media Blasters, 2001.
In Fabric. Directed by Peter Strickland. A24, 2018.
Inferno. Directed by Dario Argento. 20th Century Fox, 1980.
Inside. Original title: *À L'Interieur.* Directed by Alexandre Bustillo and Julien Maury. Dimension Extreme, 2007.
In the Earth. Directed by Ben Wheatley. Neon, 2021.
Invasion of the Body Snatchers. Directed by Philip Kaufman. United Artists, 1978.
The Invitation. Directed by Karyn Kusama. Drafthouse Films, 2015.
It Follows. Directed David Robert Mitchell. RADiUS-TWC, 2014.
It's Alive. Directed by Larry Cohen. Warner Bros., 1974.
I Walked with a Zombie. Directed by Jacques Tourneur. RKO Pictures, 1943.
Jug Face. Directed by Chad Crawford Kinkle. Modern Distributors, 2013.
Kill List. Directed by Ben Wheatley. IFC Films, 2011.
The Last of Us. Created by Neil Druckmann and Craig Mazin. HBO, 2023.
The Last Winter. Directed by Larry Fessenden. IFC Films, 2006.
The Legend of Hell House. Directed by John Hough. Twentieth-Century Fox, 1973.

Lockdown Tower. Original title: *La Tour*. Directed by Gauillaume Nicloux. Wild Bunch, 2022.
The Lodge. Directed by Severin Fiala and Veronika Franz. Neon, 2019.
London after Midnight. Directed by Todd Browning. MGM, 1927.
The Long Walk. Original title: *Bor Mi Vanh Chark*. Directed by Matti Do. Yellow Veil Films, 2019.
Los. Directed by James Benning. 2001.
Lovecraft Country. Created by Misha Green. HBO, 2020.
The Mad Masters. Original title: *Les Maitres Fous*. Directed by Jean Rouch. Icarus Films, 1955.
Man Bites Dog. Original title: *C'est arrivé près de chez vous*. Directed by Rémy Belvaux, André Bonzel, and Benoît Poelvoorde. Criterion, 1992.
Martyrs. Directed by Pascal Laugier. Weinstein Company, 2008.
Master. Directed by Mariame Diallo. Amazon Studios, 2022.
Matango. Directed by Ishirô Honda. Toho, 1963.
Mayhem. Directed by Joe Lynch. RLJE Films, 2017.
Melancholia. Directed by Lars von Trier. Magnolia, 2011.
Men. Directed by Alex Garland. A24, 2022.
Midsommar. Directed by Ari Aster, A24, 2019.
The Mirror. Original title: Zerkalo. Directed by Andrei Tarkovsky. Mosfilm, 1975.
Murder Party. Directed by Jeremy Saulnier. Magnet, 2007.
My Heart Can't Beat Unless You Tell It To. Directed by Jonathan Cuartas. Dark Sky Films, 2020.
Nanny. Directed by Nikyatu Jusu. Amazon Studios, 2022.
Night of the Living Dead. Directed by George Romero. Image Ten, 1968.
Nightmare on Elm Street. Directed by Wes Craven. New Line, 1984.
A Nightmare on Elm Street 2: Freddy's Revenge. Directed by Jack Sholder. New Line, 1985.
Nocebo. Directed by Lorcan Finnegan. RLJE Films, 2022.
Nope. Directed by Jordan Peele. Universal Pictures, 2022.
Nosferatu. Directed by F. W. Murnau. Kino, 1922.
The Omen. Directed by Richard Donner. Twentieth-Century Fox, 1976.
Paranormal Activity. Directed by Oren Poll. Paramount, 2007.
The People Under the Stairs. Directed by Wes Craven. Universal, 1991.
A Perfect Host. Directed by C. Bailey Werner. Dark Star Pictures, 2020.
Personal Shopper. Directed by Oliver Assayas. IFC Films, 2016.
Phantom of the Opera. Directed by Rupert Julian. Universal, 1925.
The Platform. Original title: *El Hoyo*. Directed by Galder Gaztelu-Urru. Netflix, 2019.
Poltergeist. Directed by Tobe Hooper. MGM, 1982.
Possession. Directed by Andrzej Żuławski. Gaumont, 1981.
The Power. Directed by Corinna Faith. RLJE Films, 2021.
Prevenge. Directed by Alice Lowe. RLJE, 2016.
Psycho. Directed by Alfred Hitchcock. Paramount, 1960.
Pyewacket. Directed by Adam MacDonald. IFC Midnight, 2017.

Relic. Directed by Natalie Erika James. IFC Midnight, 2020.
The Rental. Directed by Dave Franco. IFC, 2020.
The Return of the Living Dead. Directed by Dan O'Bannon. Orion, 1985.
The Ring. Directed by Gore Verbinski. DreamWorks, 2002.
The Road. Directed by John Hillcoat. Magnolia Pictures, 2009.
Rosemary's Baby. Directed by Roman Polanski. Paramount, 1968.
The Sadness. Original title: *Ku bei*. Directed by Rob Jabbaz. Shudder, 2021.
Saint Maud. Directed by Rose Glass. A24, 2019.
Satanic Panic. Directed by Chelsea Stardust. RLJE, 2019.
Scream. Directed by Wes Craven. Dimension, 1996.
The Seventh Victim. Directed by Mark Robson. RKO, 1943.
Severance. Directed by Christopher Smith. Magnolia, 2006.
She Dies Tomorrow. Directed by Amy Seimetz. Neon, 2020.
Shelley. Directed by Ali Abbasi. Scream Factory, 2016.
The Shining. Directed by Stanley Kubrick. Warner Bros, 1980.
Sight Seers. Directed by Ben Wheatley. IFC Films, 2012.
Sin City. Directed by Frank Miller, Quentin Tarantino, and Roberto Rodriguez. Dimension Films, 2005.
Slaxx. Directed by Elza Kephart. The Horror Collective, 2020.
Snowpiercer. Directed by Bong Joon Ho. Weinstein Company, 2013.
Sogobi. Directed by James Benning. 2002.
Stan Against Evil. Created by Dana Gould. IFC, 2016-18.
The Stepford Wives. Directed by Bryan Forbes. Columbia Pictures, 1975.
The Strangers. Directed by Bryan Bertino. Universal, 2008.
The Stuff. Directed by Larry Cohen. New World Pictures, 1985.
Superhost. Directed by Brandon Christensen. Shudder, 2021.
Take Shelter. Directed by Jeff Nichols. Sony Pictures Classics, 2011.
The Texas Chainsaw Massacre. Directed by Tobe Hooper. New Line Cinema, 1974.
Them. Created by Little Marvin. Amazon Studios, 2021.
Them. Original title: *Ils*. Directed by David Moreau and Xavier Palud. StudioCanal, 2006.
They Live! Directed by John Carpenter. Universal, 1988.
"Treehouse of Horror IV." *The Simpsons*, season 5, episode 4. Directed by David Silverman. Fox Entertainment, 1993.
Tucker and Dale vs. Evil. Directed by Eli Craig. Magnet, 2010.
28 Days Later. Directed by Danny Boyle. 20th Century Fox, 2002.
28 Weeks Later. Directed by Juan Carlos Fresnadillo. 20th Century Fox, 2007.
The Twilight Zone. Created by Simon Kinberg, Jordan Peele, and Marco Ramirez. Paramount, 2019–20.
2001: A Space Odyssey. Directed by Stanley Kubrick. Warner Bros., 1968.
2012. Directed by Roland Emmerich. Columbia, 2009.
Umma. Directed by Iris K. Shim. Sony Pictures, 2022.
Under the Skin. Directed Jonathan Glazer. A24, 2013.
Unearth. Directed by John C. Lyons and Dorota Swies. Cinedigm Entertainment Group, 2020.

Unfriended. Directed by Levan Gabriadze. Blumhouse, 2014.
The Uninvited. Directed by Lewis Allen. Paramount, 1944.
Us. Directed by Jordan Peele. Universal, 2019.
Van Helsing. Directed by Stephen Sommers. Universal, 2004.
Vicious Fun. Directed by Cody Calahan. Breakthrough Entertainment, 2020.
Videodrome. Directed by David Cronenberg. Universal, 1983.
The Vigil. Directed by Keith Thomas. IFC Midnight, 2019.
The Void. Directed by Jeremy Gillespie and Steven Kostanski. Screen Media Films, 2016.
The Walking Dead. Created by Frank Darabont. AMC, 2010–22.
Wavelength. Directed by Michael Snow. 1967.
We Are All Going to the World's Fair. Directed by Jane Schoenbrun. Utopia, 2021.
Wellington Paranormal. Created by Taika Waititi, Jemaine Clement, and Paul Yates, TVNZ2, 2018–22.
What We Do in the Shadows. Created by Jermaine Clement. FX, 2019–22.
White Zombie. Directed by Victor Halperin. United Artists, 1932.
The Wicker Man. Directed by Robin Hardy. Anchor Bay, 1973.
The Witch. Directed by Robert Eggers. A24, 2015.
You Are Not My Mother. Directed by Kate Dolan. Magnet Releasing, 2021.
Zombie. Original title: *Zombi 2*. Directed by Lucio Fulci. Blue Underground, 1979.
Zombieland. Directed by Ruben Fleischer. Columbia, 2009.

NOTES

Introduction

1. *Maintenance Phase*, "Olestra," April 13, 2021, Apple Podcasts, at 1:02:40.
2. S. A. Bradley, *Screaming for Pleasure: How Horror Makes You Happy and Healthy* (San Leandro, Calif.: Coal Cracker Press, 2018), 257.
3. Abby Moss, "Why Some Anxious People Find Comfort in Horror Movies," *Vice*, November 8, 2017, https://www.vice.com/en/article/a3wdzk/why-some-anxious-people-find-comfort-in-horror-movies.
4. Coltan Scrivner, John A. Johnson, Jens Kjeldgaard-Christiansen, and Mathias Clasen, "Pandemic Practice: Horror Fans and Morbidly Curious Individuals Are More Psychologically Resilient during the COVID-19 Pandemic," *Personality and Individual Differences* 168 (January 1, 2021), https://doi.org/10.1016/j.paid.2020.110397.
5. Bethony Butler and Travis M. Andrews, "19 Scary Movies to Take Your Mind Off Real-World Horrors," *The Washington Post*, May 12, 2020, https://www.washingtonpost.com/arts-entertainment/2020/05/12/horror-movies-streaming/. See Nicole Johnson, "How Horror Movies Can Help People Overcome Real-World Trauma," *National Geographic*, October 30, 2020, https://www.nationalgeographic.com/science/article/how-horror-movies-can-help-overcome-trauma-and-relieve-stress; Coltan Scrivner, "How You Could Use Horror to Overcome Anxiety," *Psychology Today*, October 26, 2021, https://www.psychologytoday.com/us/blog/morbid-minds/202110/how-you-could-use-horror-overcome-anxiety; and Bryony Porteous-Sebouhian, "Releasing Fear: How Horror Films Can Help to Ease Anxiety," *Mental Health Today*, January 20, 2022, https://www.mentalhealthtoday.co.uk/innovations/releasing-fear-how-horror-films-can-help-to-ease-anxiety.
6. See Sara Ahmed, *The Cultural Politics of Emotion*, 2nd ed. (London: Routledge, 2014). On affect and politics, see also Sara Ahmed, *The Promise of Happiness* (Durham, N.C.: Duke University Press, 2010), Lauren Berlant, *Cruel Optimism* (Durham, N.C.: Duke University Press, 2011), Sianne Ngai, *Ugly Feelings* (Cambridge, Mass.: Harvard University Press, 2007), Kathleen Stewart, *Ordinary Affects* (Durham, N.C.: Duke University Press, 2007), and Jason Read, *The Politics of Transindividuality* (Chicago: Haymarket Books, 2017).

7. Frédéric Lordon, *Imperium: Structures and Affects of Political Bodies* (London: Verso, 2022), 9; see also 229.

8. For another demonstration of the importance of Marxism to film theory and the world, see Anna Kornbluh, *Marxist Film Theory and Fight Club* (New York: Bloomsbury, 2019).

9. See Fredric Jameson, *Representing 'Capital': A Reading of Volume One* (New York: Verso, 2011); Anna Kornbluh, *Realizing Capital: Financial and Psychic Economies in Victorian Form* (New York: Fordham University Press, 2014); Terrell Carver, *The Postmodern Marx* (Manchester, UK: Manchester University Press, 1998); Jacques Derrida, *Spectres of Marx* (New York: Routledge, 2006); Stanley Edgar Hyman, *The Tangled Bank: Darwin, Marx, Frazer, and Freud as Imaginative Writers* (New York: Atheneum, 1962); Margaret Cohen, *Profane Illumination: Walter Benjamin and the Paris of Surrealist Revolution* (Berkeley, Calif.: University of California Press, 1993); Richard Dienst, *The Bonds of Debt* (New York: Verso, 2011).

10. On vampires and accumulation, see Franco Moretti, *Signs Taken for Wonders* (New York: Verso, 2005); on social parasitism, see Robert Paul Wolff, *Moneybags Must Be So Lucky: On the Literary Structure of 'Capital'* (Amherst: University of Massachusetts Press, 1988).

11. Mark Neocleous, "The Political Economy of the Dead: Marx's Vampires," *History of Political Thought* 24, no. 4 (Winter 2003): 684. See also Mark Neocleous, *The Monstrous and the Dead: Burke, Marx, Fascism* (Cardiff: University of Wales Press, 2005).

12. Karl Marx, *Capital*, vol. 1, trans. Ben Fowkes (London: Penguin, 1976), 165, and Karl Marx, *Das Kapital: Kritik der politischen Ökonomie. Buch I: Der Produktionsprozeß des Kapitals*, volume 23 of *Marx Engels Werke* (Berlin: Dietz Verlag, 1962), 48.

13. Marx, *Capital* 1:86. In *The Arcades Project*, Walter Benjamin followed the implication of this phrase, describing the rise of nineteenth-century commodity culture as an experience of two distinct phantasmagorias, one of the flaneur's distracted experience of the market, another of the collector's heightened experience of a private interior separate from the market. See Walter Benjamin, *The Arcades Project*, trans. Howard Eiland and Kevin McLaughlin (Cambridge, Mass.: Belknap Press, 1999), 14. For further discussion of Benjamin and the phantasmagoria, see chapter 4.

14. Phantasmagorias were part of an emerging commodity culture. As literary scholar E. J. Clery notes, eighteenth-century phantasmagoria shows "freed [ghosts] from the service of doctrinal proof . . . to be caught up in the machine of the economy; [the ghost] was available to be processed, reproduced, packaged, marketed, and distributed by the engines of cultural production." See E. J. Clery, *The Rise of Supernatural Fiction* (Cambridge: Cambridge University Press, 1995), 17.

15. See Michael Heinrich, *How to Read Marx's Capital*, trans. Alexander Locasio (New York: Monthly Review Press, 2021), 150.

16. Marx, *Capital*, 1:128.
17. See translator's note, Heinrich, *How to Read Marx's Capital*, 64.
18. See Linda Williams, "When a Woman Looks," in *The Dread of Difference*, 2nd ed., ed. Barry Keith Grant, 17–36 (Austin: University of Texas Press, 2015); Barbara Creed, *Monstrous Feminine: Film, Feminism, and Psychoanalysis* (New York: Routledge, 1993); and Carol Clover, *Men, Women, and Chainsaws: Gender in the Modern Horror Film* (Princeton, N.J.: Princeton University Press, 1992), 202. More recently, Eugenie Brinkema has put the body in horror at the center of her apparently nonpolitical argument for "radical formalism." See Eugenie Brinkema, *Life Destroying Diagrams* (Durham, N.C.: Duke University Press, 2022), 22.
19. See Jack (published as Judith) Halberstam, *Skin Shows: Gothic Horror and the Technology of Monsters* (Durham, N.C.: Duke University Press, 1995), 1–27.
20. See Xavier Aldana-Reyes, *Body Gothic: Corporeal Transgression in Contemporary Literature and Horror* (Cardiff: University of Wales Press, 2014), 7.
21. On *Gallerte* in Marx, see Keston Sutherland, "Marx in Jargon," *World Picture* 1 (2008), https://www.worldpicturejournal.com/WP_1.1/KSutherland.html.
22. Mark Steven, *Splatter Capital* (London: Repeater Books, 2017), 14.
23. David McNally, *Monsters of the Market: Zombies, Vampires, and Global Capitalism*. (Chicago: Haymarket Books, 2012).
24. Jules Joanne Gleeson and Elle O'Rourke, "Introduction," to *Transgender Marxism*, ed. Jules Joanne Gleeson and Elle O'Rourke (London: Pluto Press, 2021), 18.
25. Second-wave feminism sometimes framed horror film as coeval with pornography, treating both as expressions of male sadism. See Williams, "When a Woman Looks," and Creed, *Monstrous Feminine*.
26. See Noel Carroll, *The Philosophy of Horror* (New York: Routledge, 1990), 27.
27. Xavier Aldana-Reyes, "Gothic Affect: An Alternative Approach to Critical Models of the Contemporary Gothic." *New Directions in 21st Century Gothic: The Gothic Compass*, ed. Lorna Piatti-Farnell and Donna Lee Brien (New York: Routledge, 2015), 17.
28. Mathias Clasen, *Why Horror Seduces* (Oxford: Oxford University Press, 2017), 29.
29. See Teresa De Lauretis, *Alice Doesn't: Feminism, Semiotics, Cinema* (Bloomington: Indiana University Press, 1984), 141–44 and 151. For Mulvey on masochism, see Laura Mulvey, *Visual and Other Pleasures*, 2nd ed. (New York: Palgrave Macmillan, 2009), 25.
30. Clover, *Men, Women, and Chainsaws*, 202.
31. Marco Abel, *Violent Affect: Literature, Cinema, and Critique after Representation* (Lincoln: University of Nebraska Press, 2008), 22.
32. See Edmund Burke, *A Philosophical Enquiry into the Sublime and the Beautiful*, ed. David Womersley (New York: Penguin, 2004), 164–65.

33. Burke, 164. Tom Furniss, *Edmund Burke's Aesthetic Ideology: Language, Gender, and Political Economy in Revolution* (Cambridge: Cambridge University Press, 1993), 27. Furniss highlights that Burke's sublime offers readers a masculinized notion of self-creation and mastery that helped middle-class eighteenth-century men like Burke reconcile themselves to their new political and economic power. The sublime provided a way for men like Burke to see themselves as self-determining (the economically powerful middle class) and dominated by an outside force (subservient to the monarchy). I would argue that the affective experience of structural position may lead to individual reworkings but does not necessitate changes in subjectivity.

34. Burke, *A Philosophical Enquiry*, 164.

35. See Clasen, *Why Horror Seduces*, 28–30.

36. Andrew Schopp, "Transgressing the Safe Space: Generation X Horror in *The Blair Witch Project* and *Scream*," in *Nothing That Is: Millennial Cinema and the Blair Witch Controversies*, ed. Sarah L. Higley and Jeffrey Andrew Weinstock (Detroit, Mich.: Wayne State University Press, 2004), 130.

37. See Neocleous, *The Monstrous and the Dead*, 33.

38. Jeffrey Andrew Weinstock, *Gothic Things: Dark Enchantment and Anthropocene Anxiety* (New York: Fordham University Press, 2023), 42.

39. Ngai, *Our Aesthetic Categories* (Cambridge, Mass.: Harvard University Press, 2012), 188.

40. In this respect, my approach to contemporary horror has much in common with Aviva Briefel and Jason Middleton's in their edited collection *Labors of Fear*. They approach "work not as a marker of monstrous difference from 'normality' (as it is for such figures as the Caribbean zombie, *The Brood*'s Nola, Leatherface, and Freddy Krueger) but as the painful and often fearsome obligation to sustain a fleeting sense of normality or to try to create a better one, a burden disproportionately borne by women and people of color." See Aviva Briefel and Jason Middleton, "Introduction," to *Labors of Fear* (Austin: University of Texas Press, 2023), 6.

41. Ngai, *Our Aesthetic Categories*, 231.

42. See Sianne Ngai, *Theory of the Gimmick* (Cambridge, Mass.: Harvard University Press, 2020).

43. Horror sometimes draws on the zany to create a mix of horror and zaniness in horror-comedies like *Mayhem, Satanic Panic, Tucker and Dale vs. Evil*, and *Vicious Fun*, as well as in horror-comedy television shows like *What We Do in the Shadows, Wellington Paranormal*, and *Stan Against Evil*.

44. See Johanna Isaacson, *Stepford Daughters: Weapons for Feminists in Contemporary Horror* (New York: Common Notions, 2022).

45. See Camilla Fojas, *Zombies, Migrants, and Queers: Race and Crisis Capitalism in Pop Culture* (Champaign: University of Illinois Press, 2017); Annalee Newitz, *Pretend We're Dead: Capitalist Monsters in American Pop Culture* (Durham, N.C.: Duke University Press, 2006); Mark Selzer, *Serial Killers: Death and Life in America's Wound Culture* (New York: Routledge, 1998).

46. See Aldana-Reyes, "Gothic Affect," and Isaacson, *Stepford Daughters*.

Notes to Introduction | 221

47. Linda Williams. "Discipline and Fun," in *Psycho: A Casebook*, ed. Robert Kolker, 164–204 (Oxford: Oxford University Press, 2001). For discussion of feminist film theory and its problems with gender essentialism, see chapter 6.

48. Ralph Cohen, *Genre Theory and Historical Change: Theoretical Essays of Ralph Cohen*, ed. John L. Rowlett (Charlottesville: University of Virginia Press, 2017), 86.

49. Rick Altman, *Film/Genre* (London: BFI Publishing, 1998), 208.

50. See Abigail De Kosnik, "Fandom as Free Labor," in *Digital Labor: The Internet as Factory and Playground*, ed Trevor Scholz, 98–111 (New York: Routledge, 2013).

51. This approach differs from Fredric Jameson's treatment of genre in twentieth-century culture as a set of elements to be mixed and recombined in postmodernity's continual churn of nostalgia and pastiche. The culture industry undoubtedly relies on generic play to produce its products and produces texts for the market. Yet the continued production and development of genres because of negotiations between creators, audiences, and institutions is not unique to postmodernity. The history of the Gothic illustrates these continued negotiations in the late eighteenth and early nineteenth centuries, for instance. One might argue this idea of genre development is particular to capitalism, at least in terms of the interaction of audiences and institutions on genres. Scholars have mapped the Gothic's many waves and modes onto changes in the production, distribution, and reception of texts in different mediums and for different audiences. Franz Potter's work on chapbooks and bluebooks illustrates the ways in which the Gothic moved through distinct phases of form and production, with a substantial shift from novel production to bluebooks and chapbooks during the period from 1810 to 1830. These different phases of production entailed shifts in institutional power, distribution of cultural texts, and audience. Similarly, Diane Hoeveler's work on Sarah Wilkinson shows how one creator navigated different institutions and audiences in her work. See Franz Potter, *Gothic Chapbooks, Bluebooks, and Shilling Shockers, 1797–1830* (Cardiff: University of Wales Press, 2021), and Diane Hoeveler, "Sarah Wilkinson: Female Gothic Entrepreneur." *Gothic Archive: Related Scholarship*. 7 (2015), https://epublications.marquette.edu/gothic_scholar/7. Accessed May 23, 2022.

52. Stuart Hall, "The Problem of Ideology: Marxism without Guarantees," in *Selected Writings on Marxism*, ed. Gregor McLennan (Durham N.C.: Duke University Press, 2021), 154.

53. This method of analysis also has roots in Marxism, specifically in Althusserian Marxism and the work of Pierre Macherey. See Pierre Macherey, *Theory of Literary Production* (London: Routledge, 1978); Warren Montag, *Althusser and His Contemporaries* (Durham, N.C.: Duke University Press, 2013); and Warren Montag and Audrey Wasser, ed., *Pierre Macherey and the Case of Literary Production*, (Evanston, Ill.: Northwestern University Press, 2022).

54. Ryan Faughnder, "How Horror Became Hollywood's Safe Bet in a Scary Box Office Climate," *Los Angeles Times*, October 28, 2022, https://www.la

times.com/entertainment-arts/business/story/2022-10-28/horror-films-become-hollywoods-safe-bet.

55. Faughnder.

56. On the role of corporatization in fiction, see Dan Sinykin, *Big Fiction: How Conglomeration Changed the Publishing Industry and American Literature* (New York: Columbia University Press, 2023).

57. See Amanda Lotz, *Netflix and Streaming Video: The Business of Subscriber-Funded Video on Demand* (Cambridge: Polity, 2022); Roman Lobado, *Netflix Nations: The Geography of Digital Distribution* (New York: NYU Press, 2019); Mattias Frey, *Algorithms, Film Choice, and the History of Taste* (Berkeley: University of California Press, 2021); and Colin Jon Mark Crawford, *Netflix's Speculative Fictions: Financializing Platform Television* (London: Lexington Books, 2021).

58. Crawford, *Netflix's Speculative Fictions*, 1.

59. Josef Adalian and Lane Brown, "The Binge Purge TV's Streaming Model Is Broken. It's Also Not Going Away. For Hollywood, Figuring That Out Will Be a Horror Show," *Vulture*, June 6, 2023, https://www.vulture.com/2023/06/streaming-industry-netflix-max-disney-hulu-apple-tv-prime-video-peacock-paramount.html.

60. See Martha M. Lauzen, "Living Archive: The Celluloid Ceiling, Documenting 25 Years of Women's Employment in U.S. Films," *SDSU Center for the Study of Women in Television and Film*, 2023, https://womenintvfilm.sdsu.edu/wp-content/uploads/2023/08/25-years-of-womens-employment-in-film-report.pdf.

61. See Allison Picurro and Liam Mathews, "Netflix, HBO, BET, and More Companies Voice Support for Black Lives Matter amid Protests over George Floyd's Death," *TV Guide*, June 1, 2020, https://www.tvguide.com/news/netflix-hbo-hulu-amazon-starz-black-lives-matter/.

62. Jeremy Rosen identifies a similar tendency to elevate genre in contemporary literary fiction. See Jeremy Rosen, "Literary Fiction and the Genres of Genre Fiction," *Post45*, August 7, 2018, https://post45.org/2018/07/literary-fiction-and-the-genres-of-genre-fiction/#identifier_9_8848.

63. David Church, *Post-Horror: Art, Genre, and Cultural Elevation* (Edinburgh: Edinburgh University Press, 2021), 10.

64. See Brigid Cherry, "Refusing to Refuse to Look: Female Viewers of the Horror Film," in *Horror, the Film Reader*, ed. Mark Jancovich (New York: Routledge, 2002), 173.

65. See Alison Pierse, ed., *Women Make Horror: Filmmaking, Feminism, Genre* (New Brunswick, N.J.: Rutgers University Press, 2020).

66. See Adalian and Brown, "The Binge Purge TV's Streaming Model Is Broken."

67. See Danielle Broadway, "Hollywood's Minority Writers Fear Diversity to Fall Farther Down the Agenda after Strike," *Reuters*, October 10, 2023, https://www.reuters.com/world/us/hollywoods-minority-writers-fear-diversity-fall-farther-down-agenda-after-strike-2023-10-10/.

68. Michael Löwy, "The Current of Critical Irrealism: 'A Moonlit Enchanted Night,'" in *Adventures in Realism*, ed. Matthew Beaumont (Oxford:

Blackwell, 2007), 196. Löwy's concept is important to the account of world literature offered by the Warwick Research Collective, which includes Shapiro. See Warwick Research Collective, *Combined and Uneven Development: Towards a Theory of World Literature* (Liverpool, UK: Liverpool University Press, 2015).

69. Löwy, "The Current of Critical Irrealism," 197.

70. Sheri-Marie Harrison, "New Black Gothic," *Los Angeles Review of Books*, June 23, 2018, https://lareviewofbooks.org/article/new-black-gothic/.

71. Marx, *Capital*, 1:381.

72. Max Abelson and Harry Wilson. "HSBC Suspends Executive Who Downplayed Climate Change Risks." *Bloomberg.com*, May 22, 2022, https://www.bloomberg.com/news/articles/2022-05-22/hsbc-suspends-executive-who-downplayed-climate-change-risks-ft.

73. See Silvia Federici, *Re-Enchanting the World: Feminism and the Politics of the Common* (Oakland, Calif.: PM Press, 2019), 26–33; Paul Burkett, *Marx and Nature: A Red and Green Perspective* (Chicago: Haymarket Books, 2014), 70–78; Jason W. Moore, *Capitalism in the Web of Life* (New York: Verso, 2015), 8–18; and Jason Read, *The Production of Subjectivity: Marx and Philosophy* (Chicago: Haymarket Books, 2022), 9–90; Michael Hardt and Antonio Negri, *Empire* (Cambridge, Mass.: Harvard University Press, 2000), 256–59; Antonio Negri, *Insurgencies: Constituent Power and the Modern State* (Minneapolis: University of Minnesota Press, 1999), 1–25. For further discussion of appropriation, see chapters 2 and 3 of this book.

74. Marx, *Capital*, 1:915.

75. Marx, 1:926.

76. See Burkett, *Marx and Nature*, 33–47.

77. See Moore, *Capitalism in the Web of Life*. On the role of political systems, see Nancy Fraser, *Cannibal Capitalism* (New York: Verso, 2022), 115–40.

78. Cedric Robinson, *Black Marxism: The Making of the Black Radical Tradition*, 3rd ed. (Charlottesville: University of North Carolina Press, 2006), 26.

79. Ruth Wilson Gilmore, *The Golden Gulag* (Berkeley: University of California Press, 2008), 247.

80. Ruth Wilson Gilmore, *Abolition Geographies* (New York: Verso, 2022), 303.

81. See Leopoldina Fortunati, *Arcane of Reproduction: Housework, Prostitution, Labor, and Capital* (Brooklyn, N.Y.: Autonomedia, 1989); Maria Mies, *Patriarchy and Accumulation on a World Scale* (London: Zed Books, 2014); Claudia von Werlhof, "Women's Work: The Blind Spot in the Critique of Political Economy," in *Women: The Last Colony*, ed. Maria Mies, Veronika Bennholdt-Thomsen, and Claudia von Werlhof, 13–26 (London: Zed Books, 1988); Silvia Federici, *Caliban and the Witch: Women, the Body, and Primitive Accumulation* (Brooklyn, N.Y.: Autonomedia, 2004).

82. Christopher Chitty, *Sexual Hegemony*, ed. Max Fox (Durham, N.C.: Duke University Press, 2020).

83. Louis Althusser, *For Marx*, trans. Ben Brewster (New York: Verso, 2005), 205.

84. See Étienne Balibar, *Politics of the Other Scene* (New York: Verso, 2012). On capitalism's use of differences and their continued autonomy, see Søren Mau, *Mute Compulsion: A Marxist Theory of the Economic Power of Capital* (London: Verso, 2023), 172.

85. Maurizio Lazzarato, *Capitalism Hates Everyone* (Cambridge, Mass.: MIT Press, 2021), 183.

86. See Moishe Postone, *Time, Labor, and Social Domination* (Cambridge: Cambridge University Press, 1993).

87. For more on the contradictory positions and class divisions of what John and Barbara Ehrenreich called the professional managerial class, see Erik Olin Wright, *Classes* (New York: Verso, 2023).

88. Kozo Uno's analysis of Marx usefully brings forward money as value's key form. See Makoto Itoh, *Value and Crisis: Essays on Marxian Economics in Japan*. 2nd edition (New York: Monthly Review Press, 2021), 90–96.

89. Mau, *Mute Compulsion*, 114.

90. Mau, 134.

91. Fraser, *Cannibal Capitalism*, 17.

92. Baruch Spinoza, *The Essential Spinoza*, ed. Michael L. Morgan, trans. Samuel Shirley (Indianapolis: Hackett, 2006), 69. On the importance of hate as a political affect in Spinoza, see Jason Read, *The Politics of Transindividuality* (Chicago: Haymarket Books, 2017), 20–38.

93. Karl Marx, *Grundrisse*, trans. Martin Nicolaus (London: Penguin, 1973), 334.

94. Fraser, *Cannibal Capitalism*, 24.

95. George Lipsitz, "The Racialization of Space and the Spatialization of Race: Theorizing the Hidden Architecture of Landscape," *Landscape Journal* 26, no. 1 (2007): 10.

1. Work Hates You

1. See "Employment Situation Summary," U.S. Bureau of Labor Statistics, November 3, 2023, https://www.bls.gov/news.release/empsit.nr0.htm.

2. Kathi Weeks, *The Problem with Work: Feminism, Marxism, Antiwork Politics, and Postwork Imaginaries* (Durham, N.C.: Duke University Press, 2011), 100. On the history of the refusal of work in Italian Marxism, see Steve Wright, *Storming Heaven: Class Composition and Struggle in Italian Autonomist Marxism*, 2nd ed. (London: Pluto Press, 2017). For the most famous articulation of the refusal of work, see Mario Tronti, "The Strategy of Refusal," in *Workers and Capital*, trans. David Broder (New York: Verso, 2019), 241–62. For a contemporary account of the refusal of work, see David Frayne, *The Refusal of Work: The Theory and Practice of Resistance to Work* (London: Zed Books, 2015).

3. Thomson Reuters Newsfoundation. "It's not just people on lower incomes who are part of the antiwork community. We spoke to 'Roger', an r/antiwork subscriber who earns $300,000 per year as a computer programmer.

He explains why he supports their aims." Twitter, January 21, 2021, https://twitter.com/TRF_Stories/status/1484561942752776195?s=20.

4. Mark Fisher, *Capitalist Realism* (London: Zero Books, 2008).

5. Thomson Reuters Newsfoundation. "🌀 The final straw came when he was told his pay would be cut from $15 to $12 an hour. 🌀 'I just finally realized I'm worth more than this,' he told us. 🌀 He told us what he thinks the antiwork movement could achieve." Twitter, January 21, 2022, https://twitter.com/TRF_Stories/status/1484562027016339460?s=20

6. Genesis 3:19.

7. William Stanley Jevons, *Theory of Political Economy*, 3rd ed. (London: Macmillan & Co, 1888), 32.

8. Max Weber, *The Protestant Ethic and the Spirit of Capitalism*, trans. Talcott Parsons (New York: Routledge, 2001).

9. On the role of feeling in economics, see William Davies, *The Happiness Industry* (New York: Verso, 2015); Regenia Gagnier, *The Insatiability of Human Wants: Economics and Aesthetics in Market Society* (Chicago: University Chicago Press, 2000); and Catherine Gallagher, *The Body Economic: Life, Death, and Sensation in Political Economy and the Victorian Novel* (Princeton, N.J.: Princeton University Press, 2006).

10. Weeks, *The Problem with Work*, 8.

11. See John Locke, *Two Treatises of Government*, ed. Peter Laslett (Cambridge: Cambridge University Press, 1968).

12. On Marx's political project as based on the republican idea of freedom as freedom from domination, see J. G. A. Pocock, *The Machiavellian Moment: Florentine Political Thought and the Atlantic Republican Tradition* (Princeton, N.J.: Princeton University Press, 1975), 457–62 and 502–505, and William Clare Roberts, *Marx's Inferno: The Political Theory of Capital* (Princeton, N.J.: Princeton University Press, 2017), 1–19.

13. Karl Marx, *Capital*, vol. 1, trans. Ben Fowkes (London: Penguin, 1976), 128.

14. Diane Elson, "The Value Theory of Labor," in *Value: The Representation of Labor in Capitalism*, ed. Diane Elson (New York: Verso, 2015), 148.

15. This is a contested point in Marxism. I'm taking sides here when I assert that value is not a transhistorical phenomenon but constituted through the linkage of production and circulation in a particular historical context. Elson is unclear on this point. Other value-form theorists discussed here, e.g., Heinrich, Itoh, and Banaji, support this point.

16. Elson, "The Value Theory of Labor," 150.

17. Marx, *Capital*, 1:274.

18. Marx, 1:129.

19. For instance, see Althusser's discussion of production in Louis Althusser et al., *Reading Capital: The Complete Edition*, trans. Ben Brewster and David Fernbach (New York: Verso, 2015), 324–28.

20. Michael Heinrich, *How to Read Marx's Capital: Commentary and Explanations on the Beginning Chapters*, trans. Alexander Locasio (New York: Monthly Review Press, 2021), 164.

21. Makoto Itoh, "Marx's Theory of Market Value," in *Value: The Representation of Labor in Capitalism*, ed. Diane Elson (New York: Verso, 2015), 110

22. Alfred Sohn-Rethel, *Intellectual and Manual Labor*, trans. Martin Sohn-Rethel (Chicago: Haymarket, 2021), 16.

23. See Slavoj Žižek, *The Sublime Object of Ideology* (New York: Verso, 1989), 31–33.

24. Søren Mau, *Mute Compulsion: A Marxist Theory of the Economic Power of Capital* (New York: Verso, 2023).

25. See Plato, *The Republic*, 2nd ed., trans. Desmond Lee (Penguin, 1987), IX.575a: 312.

26. Bram Stoker, *Dracula*, ed. Nina Auerbach and David J. Skal (New York: Norton, 1996), 297.

27. Stoker, 202.

28. Stoker, 325.

29. The film's central themes of domination and corruption by an outside force are conjunctural. J. Hoberman rightly asserts the film shouldn't be read as an overt expression of antisemitism; he notes that the screenwriter, Henrik Galeen, and actor Alexander Granach, were Jewish and that Jewish critics like Kracauer and Eisner didn't receive it as antisemitic. Hoberman suggests the film reflects fears produced by the Spanish flu epidemic. Kracauer, however, saw the film in terms of domination as much as disease. Nosferatu is the first figure in a chapter that Kracauer titles "Procession of Tyrants." "Like Attila, Nosferatu is a 'scourge of God,' and only as such identifiable with the pestilence," Kracauer writes. "He is a blood-thirsty, blood-sucking tyrant figure looming in those regions where myths and fairy tales meet." See J. Hoberman, "The Twinned Evils of *Nosferatu*." *Tablet*, May 19, 2020, https://www.tabletmag.com/sections/arts-letters/articles/nosferatu-hoberman-murnau, and Siegfried Kracauer, *From Caligari to Hitler: A Psychological History of the German Film* (Princeton, N.J.: Princeton University Press, 1974), 79.

30. "Treehouse of Horror IV." *The Simpsons*, season 5, episode 4, directed by David Silverman (Fox Entertainment, 1993).

31. On critical irrealism and Löwy, see the Introduction.

32. Paolo Virno, "The Ambivalence of Disenchantment," in *Radical Thought in Italy*, ed. Paolo Virno and Michael Hardt (Minneapolis: University of Minnesota Press, 1996), 19.

33. Virno, 17.

34. Virno, 18.

35. Paolo Virno later uses "exodus" to describe a complete exit from labor and capitalism. See Paolo Virno, "Virtuosity and Revolution: The Political Theory of Exodus," in *Radical Thought in Italy*, ed. Virno and Hardt, 189–212.

36. See Tiffany Besana, Dalal Katsiaficas, and Aerika Brittian Loyd, "Asian American Media Representation: A Film Analysis and Implications for Identity Development," *Research in Human Development* 16, no. 3–4 (2019): 214.

37. Besana, Katsiaficas, and Loyd, 217.

2. Love Hates You

1. Sam Allen, "The Good News about the Great Resignation," *Fortune*, November 15, 2021, https://fortune.com/2021/11/15/great-resignation-retaining-talent-purpose-driven-work/.
2. Emphasis in original. Olivia Harrison, "What If the New Dream Job Is No Job at All?" *Refinery29.com*, March 4, 2022, https://www.refinery29.com/en-us/2021/03/10344736/why-people-quitting-jobs-covid.
3. On the complexities that lead people to refuse to work, see David Frayne, *The Refusal of Work: The Theory and Practice of Resistance to Work* (London: Zed Books, 2015).
4. Sarah Jaffe, *Work Won't Love You Back* (New York: Bold Type Books, 2021).
5. Frédéric Lordon, *Willing Slaves of Capital*, trans. Gabriel Ash (New York: Verso, 2014), 52.
6. Patricia Stuelke, "Horror and the Arts of Feminist Assembly," *Post45: Contemporaries*, April 4, 2019, https://post45.org/2019/04/horror-and-the-arts-of-feminist-assembly/.
7. Horror is intimately linked with the emergence of the woman's film as a genre, a link that Mary Ann Doane argues, following the work of Linda Williams and Julia Kristeva, is due to women's exclusion from cultural symbolic systems. See Mary Ann Doane, *The Desire to Desire: The Woman's Film of the 1940s* (Bloomington: University of Indiana Press, 1984), 141–42. It is also useful to understand the woman's film as a genre created in response to feminist film criticism; see Rick Altman, *Film/Genre* (London: BFI Publishing, 1998), 73–75.
8. Silvia Federici, *Revolution at Point Zero: Housework, Reproduction, and Feminist Struggle* (Oakland, Calif.: PM Press, 2012), 16; emphasis added.
9. It is necessary to note that my citation of Federici is in no way an endorsement of the gender essentialism she espouses in *Beyond the Periphery of the Skin* (Berkeley, Calif.: PM Press, 2020). One of the most striking and unfortunate experiences of reading 1970s and 1980s materialist feminism is the use of biology to ground arguments. Arguments about the naturalization of the social division of labor, of the appropriation of reproductive work, and the exploitation of biological capacities simply does not need to rely on biological essentialism. I would hope my discussion throughout makes that clear: biology is not determinative. Federici, like Mariarosa Dalla Costa, are influenced by Italian feminism, and biological essentialism runs throughout Italian feminism, whether materialist or not. See Paolo Bono and Sandra Kemp, ed., *Italian Feminist Thought* (Oxford: Blackwell, 1991).
10. See Michael Hardt and Antonio Negri, *Empire* (Cambridge, Mass.: Harvard University Press, 2000).
11. See Karl Marx, *Theories of Surplus Value* (Amherst, N.Y.: Prometheus Books, 2000), 411. This point is made by social reproduction theorists such as Silvia Federici and Marxian economists such as Jason W. Smith. See Silvia Federici, *Patriarchy of the Wage* (Oakland, Calif.: PM Press, 2021), 59–64; and

Jason E. Smith, *Smart Machines and Service Work: Automation in an Age of Stagnation* (London: Reaktion Books, 2020), 72–91.

12. See Federici, *Patriarchy of the Wage*, 76–91, and Joshua Gooch, *The Victorian Novel, Service Work, and the Nineteenth-Century Economy* (New York: Palgrave, 2015), 42–44.

13. See Karl Marx, *Capital*, vol. 1, trans. Ben Fowkes (London: Penguin, 1976), 492–508. Jason E. Smith has made this argument more recently in *Smart Machines and Service Work*, 129–49.

14. For a useful overview of the origins-of-capitalism debate as a debate between Brenner and Wallerstein, see Evgeny Morozov, "Critique of Techno-Feudal Reason," *New Left Review*, no. 133–34 (January/April 2022): 97–102.

15. Ellen Meisken Wood, *The Origin of Capital* (New York: Verso, 2017), 70.

16. See Immanuel Wallerstein, *The Origins of the Modern World-System*, vol. 1 (Berkeley: University of California Press, 2011), 16–20.

17. For the foundational intervention, see Claudia von Werlhof, "Women's Work: The Blind Spot of the Critique of Political Economy," in *Women: The Last Colony*, ed. Maria Mies, Veronika Bennholdt-Thomsen, and Claudia von Werlhof, 13–26 (London: Zed Books, 1988).

18. As ecosocialists such as Paul Burkett later demonstrate, Marx's value-form theory does not rely simply on labor to produce value. Capital "freely appropriates" (71), as Burkett puts it, "conditions serving as material or social vehicles of value production and accumulation" (73), from natural resources to family life, social and technical knowledge, whatever. See Paul Burkett, *Marx and Nature: A Red and Green Perspective* (Chicago: Haymarket Books, 2014). David Harvey would later use a variant of this notion of appropriation to describe what he initially took as a feature unique to capitalism during the neoliberal era. See David Harvey, *The New Imperialism* (Oxford: Oxford University Press, 2005), 137–82. Harvey qualifies this position with more economic analysis in *Seventeen Contradictions and the End of Capitalism* (Oxford: Oxford University Press, 2015). For further discussion of appropriation and Harvey's concept of "accumulation by dispossession," see chapters 3 and 4.

19. Note: Zombi films dramatize Haitain folklore and religious beliefs. By contrast, zombie films begin with Romero's flesh-eating monsters.

20. See Sarah Juliet Lauro, *The Transatlantic Zombie: Slavery, Rebellion, and Living Death* (New Brunswick, N.J.: Rutgers University Press, 2015).

21. Johanna Isaacson, *Stepford Daughters: Weapons for Feminists in Contemporary Horror* (New York: Common Notions, 2022), 130. This use of "emotional labor" encompasses more than its definition and discussion by Arlie Hochschild, the term's originator. For Hochschild, emotional labor is public-facing work that evokes an emotion in clients or customers and is supervised. Emotional labor, as Isaacson uses it, is more a question of emotional regulation in professional settings, a related but distinct concern for its lack of direct management by employers. For more on emotional regulation in modern capitalism, see my discussion in chapter 7, "Feelings Hate You."

22. The hospital appears modeled on the long-running London Hospital, now the Royal London Hospital, in the East End.

23. William Davies, "The New Neoliberalism," *New Left Review*, no. 101 (September/October 2016): 124.

24. For discussion of the video nasties moral panic, see Martin Barker, "The UK 'Video Nasties' Campaign Revisited: Panics, Claims-Making, Risks, and Politics," in *Discourses of Anxiety over Childhood and Youth across Cultures*, ed. L. Tsaliki and D. Chronaki, 29–50 (New York: Palgrave, 2020). For a history of video nasties and their constitution as a genre, see Jennifer Egan, *Trash or Treasure? Censorship and the Changing Meanings of the Video Nasties* (Manchester, U.K.: Manchester University Press, 2007), 1–15.

25. Julian Petley, "The British Critics and Horror Cinema," in *British Horror Cinema*, ed. Steve Chibnall and Julian Petley (London: Routledge, 2001), 39

26. Julian Petley, "In Defense of Video Nasties," *British Journalism Review* 5, no. 3 (1994): 52.

27. On neoliberalism as a political project, see Wendy Brown, *Undoing the Demos: Neoliberalism's Stealth Revolution* (Cambridge, Mass.: Zone Books, 2015). On the problems of this approach, see Adam Kotsko, *Neoliberalism's Demons* (Stanford, Calif.: Stanford University Press, 2018), esp. 39–68.

28. See William Davies, *The Limits of Neoliberalism* (London: Sage Publishing, 2017), 1–36. Elsewhere, Davies argues that these assaults can be periodized. See Davies, "The New Neoliberalism."

29. Harvey makes a similar point. See David Harvey, *A Brief History of Neoliberalism* (Oxford: Oxford University Press, 2007), 76.

30. See Davies, "The New Neoliberalism," 127. Foucault makes a related claim in his discussion of human capital. See Michel Foucault, *Birth of Biopolitics: Lectures at the Collège de France 1978–79*, trans. Graham Burchell (New York: Picador, 2008), 227–32.

31. While the film shown in *Censor* bears little resemblance to it, the film's title seems a nod to Alfred Sole's *Alice, Sweet Alice* (1976), an English-language *giallo*, which has a plot similar to *Censor*: one sister is suspected of murdering the other in a church.

32. Candice Frederick, "*Saint Maud* Examines a Crisis of Faith through Unmitigated Horror," *Elle.com*, February 19, 2021, https://www.elle.com/culture/movies-tv/a35552831/saint-maud-rose-glass-interview/ or https://news.yahoo.com/saint-maud-examines-crisis-faith-233000726.html.

33. See Emma Dowling, *The Care Crisis* (New York: Verso, 2021), 133.

34. This kind of exploitation is rife in the UK care sector. Sweating care work relies in large part on the goodwill and intentions of the carers themselves. Trained carers tend to choose the work because it is work that will do well by others. When they are asked to do more with less, they do, or try. Intensification of care work is a sweating of workers' goodwill. See Dowling, 116–18 and 135–38.

35. See Dowling, 118.

3. Nature Hates You

1. On the history of the term, see Christophe Bonneuil and Jean-Baptiste Fressoz, *The Shock of the Anthropocene: The Earth, History, and Us*, trans. David Fernbach (London: Verso, 2016), 47–64, and Jebediah Purdy, *After Nature: A Politics for the Anthropocene* (Cambridge, Mass: Harvard University Press, 2015), 11–50. For Marxist titles, see Kohei Saito, *Marx in the Anthropocene: Towards the Idea of Degrowth Communism* (Cambridge: Cambridge University Press, 2023), and John Bellamy Foster, *Capitalism in the Anthropocene: Ecological Ruin or Ecological Revolution* (New York: Monthly Review Press, 2022).

2. Bonneuil and Fressoz, *The Shock of the Anthropocene*, 224.

3. Jason W. Moore, *Capitalism in the Web of Life* (London: Verso, 2015), 173.

4. Allison R. Crimmins et al., "Fifth National Climate Assessment." *U.S. Global Change Research Program*, Washington, D.C., https://doi.org/10.7930/NCA5.2023.

5. Andreas Malm, *How to Blow Up a Pipeline* (London: Verso, 2021), 142–43.

6. Crimmins et al., "Fifth National Climate Assessment."

7. Matthew T. Huber, *Climate Change as Class War: Building Socialism on a Warming Planet* (London: Verso, 2022), 16.

8. See Saito, *Marx in the Anthropocene*. For other degrowth Marxists, see Foster, *Capitalism in the Anthropocene*; Kristin Ross, *Communal Luxury: The Political Imaginary of the Paris Commune* (London: Verso, 2015); Kate Soper, *Post-Growth Living: For an Alternative Hedonism* (London: Verso, 2020); Matthias Schmelzer, Aaron Vansintjan, and Andrea Vetter, *The Future Is Degrowth* (London: Verso, 2022). Naomi Klein may not be a Marxist per se but offers a similar argument; see *This Changes Everything* (New York: Simon and Schuster, 2014). This strain of thought stands opposed to accelerationist Marxism that argues changes in consumption will be unnecessary as the result of continued technological innovation. For accelerationists, see Aaron Bastani, *Fully Automated Luxury Communism* (London: Verso, 2019), and Nick Srnicek and Alex Williams, *Inventing the Future: Postcapitalism and a World without Work* (London: Verso, 2015).

9. My use of the term "Capitalocene" with this group of thinkers means to bridge a theoretical difficulty. Saito, along with Foster, Burkett, Andreas Malm, and Kate Soper, strongly disagrees with Moore's work for its "monism"—in effect, Moore argues that capitalism reshapes the web of life as one vast ecology, while they insist on the distinction between capitalism's metabolic processes and nature's. I agree on the need to distinguish metabolic processes but believe Capitalocene better articulates the political economic and ecological antagonisms of our moment, even with its monistic implication. Nancy Fraser's contribution to this debate of three forms of nature—nature's metabolism, capitalism's metabolism, and the resulting altered nature-society metabolism—resolves the difficulties here, at least for me. See Fraser, *Cannibal Capitalism*, 90–92.

10. E. Ann Kaplan, *Climate Trauma: Foreseeing the Future in Dystopian Film and Fiction* (Newark, N.J.: Rutgers University Press, 2015), 28.

11. Fredric Jameson, "Future City," *New Left Review* 21 (May-June 2003): 76.

12. Fredric Jameson, *Postmodernism, or The Cultural Logic of Late Capitalism* (Durham, N.C.: Duke University Press, 1992), 46.

13. Amitav Ghosh, *The Great Derangement* (Chicago: University of Chicago Press, 2017), 32.

14. Ghosh, 32. Ghosh puts the value of nonhuman beings at the center of his subsequent call for a "vitalist politics." Amitav Ghosh, *The Nutmeg's Curse* (Chicago: University of Chicago Press, 2022), 235. The only way to resist the depredations of climate change, he maintains, is to defend a vision of a living and interconnected world and to fight modernity's reduction of nature and non-Western peoples to raw materials it can appropriate. Ghosh's argument echoes eco-Marxism's analysis of capitalism and nature, but Ghosh himself resists the use of Marxism, insisting that capitalism doesn't explain global warming because imperialism "retarded the onset of the climate crisis." See Ghosh, *Great Derangement*, 110. For Ghosh, Marxism can be reduced to a Promethean view of modernity and demand for a revolutionary industrial proletariat, claims that Foster and Burkett dismantle at length. In *Nutmeg's Curse*, Ghosh similarly avoids Marxist work on ecology, uneven development, or imperialism even as he shows how deeply entwined are ecological destruction, the violence of imperialism, and white settler colonialism. See Paul Burkett, *Marx and Nature: A Red-Green Perspective* (Chicago: Haymarket Books, 2014), 250–56, and John Bellamy Foster and Paul Burkett, *Marx and the Earth: An Anti-Critique* (Chicago: Haymarket Books, 2016).

15. Claudia von Werlhof, "On the Concept of Nature and Society in Capitalism," in *Women: The Last Colony*, ed. Maria Mies, Veronika Bennholdt-Thomsen, and Claudia von Werlhof (London: Zed Books, 1988), 105. Carolyn Merchant makes a similar argument in *Death of Nature: Women, Ecology, and the Scientific Revolution* (San Francisco: HarperSanFrancisco, 1990).

16. More recently Françoise Vergès connects colonialism, racialization, and the domination of nature in her decolonial feminism. See Françoise Vergès, "Decolonize the City," *E-flux*, May 2023, https://www.e-flux.com/architecture/appropriations/533423/decolonize-the-city/.

17. William Clare Roberts, *Marx's Inferno: The Political Theory of Capital* (Princeton, N.J.: Princeton University Press, 2017), 207.

18. Werlhof, Mies, Federici, and others supported this contention by offering a variety of analyses of women's unpaid labor in the global South. See Claudia von Werlhof, "Production Relations without Wage Labor and Labor Division by Sex: Collective Cooperatives in New Irrigated Farming Systems in Venezuela," *Review (Fernand Braudel Center)* 7, no. 2 (1983): 315–59; Maria Mies, *Patriarchy and Accumulation* (London: Zed Books, 2014), 74–144; Silvia Federici, *Re-Enchanting the World* (Oakland, Calif.: PM Press, 2017), 13–77.

19. David Harvey, *The New Imperialism* (Oxford: Oxford University Press, 2006), 145.

20. Harvey, 145.

21. Harvey, 137.
22. Moore, *Capitalism in the Web of Life*, 17.
23. Harvey, *The New Imperialism*, 149.
24. Neil Smith, *Uneven Development: Nature, Capital, and the Production of Space*, 3rd ed. (Athens: University of Georgia Press, 2008), 197.
25. Karl Marx, *Capital*, vol. 1, trans. Ben Fowkes (London: Penguin, 1976), 290.
26. See John Bellamy Foster, *Marx's Ecology: Materialism and Nature* (New York: Monthly Review Press, 2000).
27. Marx, *Capital*, 1:638.
28. Burkett, *Marx and Nature*, 37.
29. Foster, *Marx's Ecology*, 156.
30. See Karl Marx and Friedrich Engels, *The German Ideology* (Amherst, N.Y.: Prometheus Books, 1998), 72.
31. Karl Marx, *Capital*, vol. 3, trans. David Fernbach (London: Penguin, 1981), 195.
32. Marx, *Capital*, 1:638.
33. See Saito, *Marx in the Anthropocene*, 23–28.
34. See Saito, 29–34.
35. Moore, *Capitalism in the Web of Life*, 53.
36. See Andreas Malm, *Fossil Capital: The Rise of Steam Power and the Roots of Global Warming* (London: Verso, 2016).
37. Marx, *Capital*, 3:959.
38. See Manisha Mishra and Deepa Srivastava, "Mycoremediation: An Emerging Technology for Mitigating Environmental Contaminants," *Revisiting the Rhizosphere Eco-System*, ed. Udai B. Singh, Jai P. Rai, and Anil K. Sharma (New York: Springer, 2022), 225–44.
39. See Richard Grant, "Do Trees Talk to Each Other?" *The Smithsonian Magazine*, March 2018, https://www.smithsonianmag.com/science-nature/the-whispering-trees-180968084/
40. See Edgar Allan Poe, "The Fall of the House of Usher," in *The Complete Tales and Poems of Edgar Allan Poe* (New York: Vintage, 1975), 231–45, and William Hope Hodgson, *The Weird Tales of William Hope Hodgson*, ed. Xavier Aldana Reyes (London: British Library Publishing, 2019), 27–42. Hodgson's story was adapted in the Japanese film *Matango* (1963).
41. A noninclusive list of other works would include the fungal landscapes and mushroom people in Vandermeer's Southern Reach trilogy (collected in *Area X* [New York: FSG, 2012]) and its 2018 film adaptation *Annihilation*; the mutated zombie ant fungus, *Ophiocordyceps*, of M. R. Carey's zombie tale, *The Girl with All the Gifts* (New York: Orbit, 2014) and its 2016 film adaptation; the alien spores intent on humanity's destruction in Caitlin Kiernan's Lovecraftian *Agents of Dreamland* (New York: Tordotcom, 2017); the mushroom women that sprout from graves in Aliya Whiteley's *The Beauty* (London: Titan Books, 2018); the assorted fungal creatures in the collection *Fungi*, edited by Moreno-Garcia

and Orrin Grey (n.p.: Innsmouth Free Press, 2012); and the video game–cum–HBO series *The Last of Us* (2023). An important literary precursor for climate-based fungal horror is Michael Shea's short story "Fill It with Regular," first published in the *Magazine of Fantasy & Science Fiction* in 1986 and collected in Michael Shea, *The Autopsy*, ed. S. T. Joshi (New York: Hippocampus Press, 2022).

42. Anna Lowenhaupt Tsing, *The Mushroom at the End of the World: On the Possibility of Life in Capitalist Ruins* (Princeton, N.J.: Princeton University Press, 2015), 3.

43. Harry M. Benshoff, "The Short-Lived Life of the Hollywood LSD Film," *Velvet Light Trap*, no. 47 (2001): 31.

44. Benshoff, 31.

45. Unfortunately, these psychedelic effects are nearly impossible to capture in still images, especially the use of montage, rapid cutting, strobing lights, and afterimages, all of which are central to the effects of *Gaia* and *In the Earth*.

46. Barry Keith Grant, "Science Fiction Double Feature: Ideology in the Cult Film," in *The Cult Film Reader*, ed. Ernest Mathijs and Xavier Mendik (Berkshire, UK: Open University Press, 2008), 78.

47. James Lovelock, *The Vanishing Face of Gaia* (New York: Basic Books, 2009), 254–55. For an overview of Lovelock's work, see Bonneuil and Fressoz, *The Shock of the Anthropocene*, 56–60. For a refutation of the Gaia hypothesis, see Toby Tyrell, *On Gaia: A Critical Investigation of the Relationship between Life and Earth* (Princeton, N.J.: Princeton University Press, 2013).

48. Sam Moore and Alex Roberts. *The Rise of Ecofascism*. (Cambridge, UK: Polity, 2022), 11.

49. Moore and Roberts, 11.

50. Moore and Roberts, 42.

51. Janet Biehl and Peter Staudenmaier, *Ecofascism Revisited: Lessons from The German Experience* (Porsgrunn, Norway: New Compass Press, 2011), 11. While Moore and Roberts argue that "ecofascism" is an imprecise term because contemporary far-right ecology has not currently coalesced into paramilitary political operations to seize state power, I use the term in the sense offered by Biehls and Staudenmaier, and most famously deployed by Murray Bookchin to decry reactionary Malthusianism in the Green movement. See Moore and Roberts, *Rise of Ecofascism* 1–13.

52. The production design of *Gaia* bears substantial debts to Alex Garland's *Annihilation*, most especially the collapsed fungal human body in the swimming pool.

53. Werlhof, "On the Concept of Nature," 103.

54. On *Gaia*'s production history, see Graeme Guttman, "Jaco Bouwer Interview: Gaia," *Screen Rant*, October 26, 2021, https://screenrant.com/gaia-movie-jaco-bouwer-interview/. On the production history of *In the Earth*, see Phil Nobile Jr., "Interview: Ben Wheatley on *In the Earth*," *Fangoria*, April 14, 2021, https://www.fangoria.com/original/ben-wheatley-interview/.

55. Nobile Jr., "Interview: Ben Wheatley on *In the Earth*."

56. See M. John Harrison, *The Sunken Land Begins to Rise Again* (London: Gollancz, 2020), and Sarah Moss, *Ghost Wall* (London: Picador, 2018).

57. Quoted in Robert Hullot-Kentor, *Things beyond Resemblance: Essays on Theodor Adorno* (New York: Columbia University Press, 2006), 6.

58. I'm extrapolating a little here. Robinson describes this in the past tense: "Western culture, constituting the structure from which European consciousness was appropriated, the structure in which social identities and perceptions were grounded in the past, transmitted a racialism that adapted to the political and material exigencies of the moment." Cedric Robinson, *Black Marxism: The Making of the Black Radical Tradition*, 3rd ed. (Chapel Hill: University of North Carolina Press, 2006), 64.

59. This scene also seems a play on Matthew 7:3 "And why beholdest thou the mote that is in thy brother's eye, but considerest not the beam that is in thine own eye?"

60. Carlos Aguilar, "In Conversation: Amy Seimetz: On the Fears behind her Unsettling Film *She Dies Tomorrow*," *Flood Magazine*, August 10, 2020, https://floodmagazine.com/80087/in-conversation-amy-seimetz-she-dies-tomorrow/. Accessed December 4, 2020.

61. Qtd. in Jonathan Rosenbaum, "James Benning's California Trilogy." JonathanRosenbaum.net. Originally published in *Chicago Reader*, March 15, 2002, https://www.jonathanrosenbaum.net/2019/12/california-trilogy/. Accessed December 2, 2020.

62. William Morris, *News from Nowhere* (New York: Roberts Brothers, 1890), 134.

63. Burkett, *Marx and Nature*, 256.

64. Foster, *Capitalism in the Anthropocene*, 372.

65. Foster, 372.

66. Jason Hickel, "The Double Objective of Democratic Ecosocialism," *Monthly Review* 70, no. 4 (September 2023): 15.

67. Foster, *Capitalism in the Anthropocene*, 372.

68. Kate Soper, *Post-Growth Living* (London: Verso, 2020), 146.

69. Soper, 146.

70. Soper, 102.

71. See George Bataille, *The Accursed Share*, vol. 1, trans. Robert Hurley (Cambridge, Mass.: Zone Books, 1988), 189–90.

72. Soper, *Post-Growth Living*, 158

73. Bini Adamczak, *Communism for Kids* (Cambridge, Mass.: MIT Press, 2017), 73.

4. The Neighborhood Hates You

1. See Adam Howard, "'Rent Is Too Damn High' Guy Retires: Jimmy McMillan Faults 'Brainwashed' Voters," *MSNBC*, December 10, 2018, https://www.msnbc.com/msnbc/rent-too-damn-high-guy-retires-jimmy-mcmillan-faults-brainwashed-voters-msna747586.

2. Sarah Maslin Nir, "Opposing Excessive Rent, but Vague about His Own," *New York Times*, October 19, 2010, https://www.nytimes.com/2010/10/20/nyregion/20rent.html.

3. For instance, see Zackariah Farah, "Op-Ed: The Rent Is Too Damn High," *Michigan Daily*, September 7, 2023, https://www.michigandaily.com/opinion/op-ed-the-rent-is-too-damn-high/; "Why Is the Rent So Damn High?" *NPR*, February 9, 2022, https://www.npr.org/2022/02/09/1079645680/why-is-the-rent-so-damn-high; Katy O'Donnell and Victoria Guida, "Biden's Next Inflation Threat: The Rent Is Too Damn High," *Politico*, November 10, 2021, https://www.politico.com/news/2021/11/10/rent-inflation-biden-520642. Janell Ross, "Breaking: The Rent Is Indeed Too Damn High," *Washington Post*, July 8, 2015, https://www.washingtonpost.com/news/the-fix/wp/2015/07/08/breaking-the-rent-is-indeed-too-damn-high/.

4. Shaye Weaver, "Will Rent Stop Being Too Damn High in 2024?" *Time Out*, December 23, 2023, https://www.timeout.com/newyork/news/will-rent-stop-being-too-damn-high-in-2024-122823.

5. Emily Peck, "Data Shows the Rent Is (Still) Too Damn High," *Axios*, January 23, 2023, https://www.axios.com/2023/01/23/data-shows-the-rent-is-still-too-damn-high.

6. Derek Thompson, "Why the Rent Inflation Is So Damn High," *The Atlantic*, August 18, 2022, https://www.theatlantic.com/ideas/archive/2022/08/rent-inflation-housing-demand-prices/671179/.

7. See Balakrishnan Rajagopal, *Adequate Housing as a Component of the Right to an Adequate Standard of Living, and On the Right to Non-discrimination in This Context* (New York: United Nations Headquarters, 2023), https://documents-dds-ny.un.org/doc/UNDOC/GEN/N23/240/69/PDF/N2324069.pdf.

8. Leslie Kern, *Gentrification Is Inevitable and Other Lies* (New York: Verso, 2022), 14.

9. Kern, 24.

10. Fredric Jameson, *An American Utopia: Dual Power and the Universal Army* (New York: Verso, 2016), 13. However, we needn't accept Jameson's proposed solution to this problem, a service-based institution he calls "the universal army" that bears more than a passing resemblance to Hegel's account of universal bureaucrats in *Philosophy of Right*. See Jameson, *American Utopia*, 20.

11. Neil Smith, *The New Urban Frontier* (New York: Routledge, 1996), 65.

12. Smith, 73. Smith usefully defines uneven development as "two contradictory tendencies" in capitalism: "on the one hand, the equalization of conditions and levels of development and, on the other, their differentiation" (*New Urban Frontier*, 74).

13. For a useful overview, see David Harvey, *The Limits to Capital* (New York: Verso, 2007), 413–45.

14. See Rosa Luxemburg, *The Complete Works of Rosa Luxemburg*, vol. 2, *The Economic Writings*, ed. Peter Hudis and Paul Le Blanc (New York: Verso, 2016).

15. Postcolonial theory has sometimes argued against Marxist analysis on the basis of this claim, insisting that Marx's understanding of capitalism entails

one trajectory for development independent of political economic context. For an overview of this position and a Marxist rebuttal, see Vivek Chibber, *Postcolonial Theory and the Specter of Capital* (London: Verso, 2013), 1–27. For more discussion, see the Conclusion of this book.

16. For instance, see Chibber, *Postcolonial Theory and the Specter of Capital*; Nancy Fraser, *Cannibal Capitalism* (London: Verso, 2022); and Immanuel Wallerstein, *The Modern World System I* (Berkeley: University of California Press, 2011).

17. David Harvey, *The New Imperialism* (Oxford: Oxford University Press, 2005), 145. For more on this concept in Harvey, see chapter 3. On regional capital flight, see Smith, *New Urban Frontier*, 197–200.

18. For a case study in deindustrialization, see Gabriel Winant, *The Next Shift* (Cambridge, Mass.: Harvard University Press, 2021), 179–217.

19. Mark Neocleous, *A Critical Theory of Police Power* (London: Verso, 2021), introduction.

20. Kern, *Gentrification Is Inevitable and Other Lies*, 184.

21. Neville Alexander, "Nation and Ethnicity in South Africa," in *Against Racial Capitalism: Selected Writings*, ed. Salim Vally and Enver Motala (London: Pluto Press, 2023), 102.

22. For more on racial capitalism see the Introduction in this volume.

23. Alexander, "Nation and Ethnicity in South Africa," 104.

24. George Lipsitz, "The Racialization of Space and the Spatialization of Race: Theorizing the Hidden Architecture of Landscape," *Landscape Journal* 26, no. 1 (2007): 10.

25. Lipsitz, 15.

26. David Roediger, *The Wages of Whiteness* (New York: Verso, 2007), 12.

27. Étienne Balibar, "Class Racism," in *Race, Nation, Class: Ambiguous Identities*, by Étienne Balibar and Immanuel Wallerstein (New York: Verso, 1991), 215.

28. In contemporary horror, the battle over real estate might seem most pronounced in the emerging subgenre of murderous Airbnb hosts. Films like *Barbarian* (2022), *The Rental* (2020), *Superhost* (2021), and *A Perfect Host* (2020) use the Gothic plot of the murderous innkeeper—think of Don Raymond's tale in Matthew Lewis's *The Monk*—by way of Hitchcock's *Psycho*. *Barbarian* provides the strongest example. Like *Psycho*, *Barbarian* is set in a region caught in a cycle of capital disinvestment. In *Psycho*, the highway moved. In *Barbarian*, the people did. The Airbnb here is smack in the middle of one of Detroit's abandoned neighborhoods. For the film, this is less a gesture toward gentrification than a commentary on misogyny. The film's villains, the rental unit's landlord, a Hollywood actor recently #MeToo'd, and an ancient serial killer who lives in tunnels beneath the house, prey on women. Investment or disinvestment in the built environment doesn't matter, the film suggests. Women are never safe in any space, whether in their own homes, vacation rentals, cars, the streets, or when asking for help from the police.

29. Robin R. Means Coleman, *Horror Noire: Blacks in American Horror Films from the 1890s to Present* (New York: Routledge, 2011), 12.

30. Jordan Peele, Foreword to *Out There Screaming: An Anthology of New Black Horror*, ed. Jordan Peele and John Joseph Adams (New York: Random House, 2023), viii.

31. Mark Jerng, *Racial Worldmaking* (New York: Fordham University Press, 2017), 2.

32. We should note that some Indigenous horror creators share this concern with space. In Jeff Barnaby's *Blood Quantum* (2019), the Red Crow are protected from a zombie virus that infects white people and must protect their reservation from the encroaching hordes. In Warwick Thornton's television series *Firebite* (2021–22), Indigenous vampire hunters must protect their people from the depredations of vampires.

33. "Get Out," *Box Office Mojo*, February 15, 2018, https://www.boxoffice mojo.com/release/rl256280065/.

34. One testament to Peele's auteur status is the extensive array of critical commentary around his work. Of particular interest for *Get Out* are the essays in Dawn Keetley's edited collection *Jordan Peele's Get Out: Political Horror* (Columbus: Ohio State University Press, 2020); Elizabeth Patton, "*Get Out* and the Legacy of Sundown Suburbs in Post-racial America," *New Review of Film and Television Studies* (2019), https//doi.10.1080/17400309.2019.1622889; and Ryan Poll, "Can One 'Get Out'?" The Aesthetics of Afro-Pessimism," *Journal of the Midwest Modern Language Association* 51, no. 2 (Fall 2018): 69–102.

35. See Frank Wilderson, *Red, White, and Black: Cinema and the Structure of U.S. Antagonisms* (Durham, N.C.: Duke University Press, 2010), 21–23.

36. Wilderson, 115.

37. See The Hollywood Reporter, "Full Writers Roundtable: Jordan Peele, Darren Aronofsky, Emily V. Gordon | Close Up with THR," *YouTube*, February 21, 2018, https://www.youtube.com/watch?v=nB3nfc1tQ0E.

38. On the cultural connection between water imagery and the Middle Passage, see Christina Sharpe, *In the Wake: On Blackness and Being* (Durham, N.C.: Duke University Press, 2016).

39. Jordan Peele, [@JordanPeele], March 17, 2017, *Twitter*, https://twitter.com/JordanPeele/status/842589407521595393.

40. Smith, *The New Urban Frontier*, 84.

41. See Kern, *Gentrification Is Inevitable and Other Lies*.

42. Katherine McKittrick, "Plantation Futures," *Small Axe* 17, no. 3 (November 2013): 11

43. McKittrick, 8.

44. McKittrick, 11.

45. Robin D. G. Kelley, "The Rest of Us: Rethinking Settler and Native," *American Quarterly* 69, no. 2 (June 2017): 268.

46. See Stuart Hall with Chas Critcher, Tony Jefferson, John Clarke, and Brian Roberts, "Policing the Crisis: Preface to the 35th Anniversary Edition," in *Essential Essays*, vol. 1, ed. David Morley, 362–73 (Durham, N.C.: Duke University Press, 2019).

47. Ruth Wilson Gilmore, *Abolition Geography: Essays toward Liberation* (New York: Verso, 2022), 474.

48. Its narrative operates more like a mainstream home-invasion thriller such as *Panic Room* (2002) or true crime home-invasion films like *In Cold Blood* (1968) or *The Honeymoon Killers* (1970).

49. Kinitra D. Brooks, *Searching for Sycorax: Black Women's Hauntings of Contemporary Horror* (New Brunswick, N.J.: Rutgers University Press, 2018), 8. For another useful study of Black female characters in speculative fiction, see Diana Adesola Mape, *Where No Black Woman Has Gone Before: Subversive Portrayals in Speculative Film and TV* (Austin: University of Texas Press, 2018).

50. See Frantz Fanon, *The Wretched of the Earth* (New York: Grove, 1968).

51. Aisha Harris, "*Candyman* and What's Making Us Happy." *Pop Culture Happy Hour*, NPR, August 27, 2021, Apple app.

52. The character's name is another metatextual reference, here to the actor who played Candyman in the 1990s, Tony Todd.

53. Coleman, *Horror Noire*, 6.

54. Coleman, 189.

55. Karen E. Fields and Barbara J. Fields, *Racecraft: The Soul of Inequality in American Life* (New York: Verso, 2014), 17.

56. Frantz Fanon, *Black Skin, White Masks*, trans. Charles Lam Markmann (New York: Grove Press, 1967), 155.

57. Coleman, *Horror Noire*, 190–91.

58. Aviva Briefel and Sianne Ngai, "'How Much Did You Pay for This Place?' Fear, Entitlement, and Urban Space in Bernard Rose's *Candyman*," *Camera Obscura* 13, no. 1 (1996): 85.

59. Gilmore, *Abolition Geography*, 307

60. See Frank Wilderson III, *Afropessimism* (New York: Liveright, 2021).

61. Stuart Hall, *Selected Writings on Race and Difference*, ed. Paul Gilroy and Ruth Wilson Gilmore (Durham, N.C.: Duke University Press, 2021), 239

62. Adolph L. Reed, *The South: Jim Crow and Its Afterlives* (New York: Verso, 2022), chapter 5.

63. Gilmore, *Abolition Geography*, 481.

5. Commodities Hate You

1. See Gillian Rose, *The Melancholy Science: An Introduction to the Thought of Theodor W. Adorno* (New York: Verso, 2014), 38.

2. Georg Lukàcs, *History and Class Consciousness*, trans. Rodney Livingstone (Cambridge, Mass.: MIT Press, 1972), 89.

3. Lukàcs, *History and Class Consciousness*, 91.

4. Lukàcs, 149.

5. On the turn to Hegel in Marxism, see Perry Anderson, *Considerations of Western Marxism* (New York: Verso, 1976), especially chapter 3 for discussion of Lukács and Marcuse. On the rise of interest in Hegel in France, see Susan M.

Ruddick, "Translators Introduction," in *Hegel or Spinoza* by Pierre Macherey, v–xxi (Minneapolis: University of Minnesota Press, 2011).

6. Lukács, *History and Class Consciousness*, xxiiii. For an expressly Hegelian Lukács, see Georg Lukács, *The Theory of the Novel*, trans. Anna Bostock (Cambridge, Mass.: MIT Press, 1974).

7. See Herbert Marcuse, *One-Dimensional Man* (New York: Routledge Classics, 2002), and Guy Debord, *Society of the Spectacle*, trans. Donald Nicholson-Smith (Cambridge, Mass.: Zone Books, 1995); Fredric Jameson, *The Political Unconscious* (Ithaca, N.Y.: Cornell University Press, 1981).

8. Thomas Frank, *The Conquest of Cool: Business, Counter-Culture, and the Rise of Hip Consumerism* (Chicago: University of Chicago Press, 1997), 11.

9. *The Pervert's Guide to Ideology*, starring Slavoj Zizek, directed by Sophie Fiennes, Zeitgeist Films, 2012.

10. Barry K. Grant, "Science Fiction Double Feature: Ideology in the Cult Film," in *The Cult Film Reader*, ed. Ernest Mathijs and Xavier Mendik (Berkshire, UK: Open University Press, 2008), 78.

11. Grant, 87.

12. Stuart Hall, "Encoding and Decoding in the Television Discourse," in *Essential Essays*, vol. 1, ed. David Morley (Durham, N.C.: Duke University Press, 2019), 269.

13. Horror loves to comment on its own genre status and its history of construction, but I'm trying to locate here films focused directly on the experience of spectatorship itself. Other films bring up questions of apparatus, the making of the film. There's a strong case to be made that Jordan Peele's *Nope* (2022) is a cult film for its affect and for its focus on the process of filmmaking, a focus that implicates audiences without drawing them into it directly.

14. This lockdown was announced on March 23, 2020, and ran until April 16, 2020.

15. *Host* doesn't aim to show a recorded Zoom call, either. It aims for the sort of open-ended terror that Shane Denson describes in another pseudo–found-footage horror, *Unfriended* (2014). The images of these films, Denson explains, are "no longer fixed or determined by past events but opened up to an indeterminate becoming-in-time." For the film's viewers, this can seem to imbue the film's characters with more narrative possibilities than toward death or disappearance, the two endings the genre usually requires for footage to be found. See Shane Denson, *Discorrelated Images* (Durham, N.C.: Duke University Press, 2020), 159.

16. Alfred Sohn-Rethel, *Intellectual and Manual Labor*, trans. Martin Sohn-Rethel (Chicago: Haymarket, 2021), 43.

17. Sohn-Rethel, 16. For further discussion of real abstraction, see chapter 1.

18. Karl Marx, *Capital*, vol. 1, trans. Ben Fowkes (London: Penguin, 1976), 126.

19. Michael Heinrich, *An Introduction to the Three Volumes of Karl Marx's Capital*, trans. Alexander Locasio (New York: Monthly Review Press, 2012), 63.

20. Luca Basso, *Marx and the Common: From Capital to the Late Writings*, trans. David Broder (Chicago: Haymarket, 2015), 44.

21. Basso, 44.

22. Although literal masks often appear in horror, I won't argue here that the mask's varied uses in horror could somehow cohere into a commentary on commodification as such. In her study of masks in horror, Alexandra Heller-Nicholas documents the extensive use of masks in transnational horror but treats their role in the genre as a result of a broad human interest in ritual and shamanistic thought. We might argue that the depersonalization of the mask, an integral part of its ability to evoke horror, captures the violence of commodification, the aimless destruction of whatever is in front of or underneath the mask, but this is general. Even the horror film that most directly connects masks and commodification, *Halloween III: The Season of the Witch* (1982), is at best a satire of the terrors of mass production. Little kids will put on mass-produced masks and be turned into goo by enchanted television commercials! See Alexandra Heller-Nicholas, *Masks in Horror Cinema: Eyes without Faces* (Cardiff: University of Wales Press, 2020).

23. Basso prefers this translation of *"gepenstige Gegenständlichkeit."* For more discussion of the phrase's translation, see the Introduction to this book.

24. Pietz shows through his historical analysis of the term *fetishism* that the word was widely treated as a cognate for the misrecognition of social relationships. For Marx, the fetish is not misrecognition but a kind of veiling. He begins from French philosophy's creation of an equivalence between, in Pietz's words, "exploitive fetish priests and greedy merchants as equal embodiments of the essentially antisocial motive of 'interest.'" William Pietz, "The Problem of the Fetish, IIIa: Bosman's Guinea and the Enlightenment Theory of Fetishism," *RES: Anthropology and Aesthetics*, no. 16 (Autumn 1988): 106. Pietz's three essays on fetishism have been published together as *The Problem of the Fetish* (Chicago: University of Chicago Press, 2022).

25. Basso, 19.

26. Marx, *Capital*, 1:163–64.

27. See Sohn-Rethel, *Intellectual and Manual Labor*, 115.

28. Luc Boltanski and Pierre Esquerre, *Enrichment: A Critique of Commodities*, trans. Catherine Porter (Cambridge: Polity, 2020), 271.

29. See Jarius Banaji, *Theory as History: Essays on Modes of Production and Exploitation* (Chicago: Haymarket Press, 2011), 45–102, especially 61–72. On the articulation of forms of capitalism, see Banaji, 349–60.

30. Boltanski and Esquerre, *Enrichment*, 271. One might fairly object that Boltanski and Esquerre's idea of value isn't Marx's. In their discussion, value is a "metaprice" (94) that allows people to make judgments about prices of goods and services. Different commodity forms demand different determinations of metaprices. From a Marxist perspective, however, Boltanski and Esquerre's commodity forms allow us to expand our analysis of value and labor. The exploitation of labor in mass production is just one of capitalism's forms of labor exploitation now. What Boltanski and Esquerre's commodity forms emphasize is that, at least in integral capitalism, new commodity forms entail new forms of work, and that all this is the result of people constantly making judgments about what kind of

commodity an object is and how they should relate to it. In essence—and this is like Marx, at least in the abstract—a commodity's value is inextricable from its form.

31. Boltanski and Esquerre, 135.
32. An important aspect of this spectrum of commodity forms is that it allows Boltanski and Esquerre to describe what they call "enrichment economies," economies based on the extraction of value from history and culture typically focused on tourism and luxury goods. See Boltanski and Esquerre, 42–67.
33. Boltanski and Esquerre, 135.
34. Boltanski and Esquerre, 234.
35. Walter Benjamin, *The Arcades Project*, trans. Howard Eiland and Kevin McLaughlin (Cambridge, Mass.: Belknap Press, 1999), 19.
36. Benjamin, 14.
37. Walter Benjamin, "The Work of Art in the Age of Mechanical Reproduction," in *Selected Writings, Volume 4, 1938–1940*, trans. Howard Eiland and Michael W. Jennings (Cambridge, Mass.: Belknap Press, 2006), 221.
38. Boltanski and Esquerre, 221.
39. Boltanski and Esquerre, 234.
40. Boltanski and Esquerre, 236.
41. Karl Marx, *Capital*, vol. 2, trans. David Fernbach (London: Penguin, 1978), 205.
42. Marx, *Capital* 2:205.
43. Boltanski and Esquerre, 126.
44. See Hayden White, *Metahistory* (Baltimore: Johns Hopkins University Press, 2014), 1–44.
45. Brian Price and Meghan Sutherland, "On Debord, Now and Then: An Interview with Oliver Assayas," *World Picture* 1 (Spring 2008), http://www.worldpicturejournal.com/WP_1.1/Assayas.html. Accessed December 9, 2020.
46. On the difference between Spiritualist and Theosophist views of mediums, see Gary Lachman, *Madame Blavatsky: The Mother of Modern Spiritualism* (New York: Penguin, 2012), chapters 4 and 5.
47. Boltanski and Esquerre, 241.
48. Boltanski and Esquerre, 249.
49. Andrew Ross, *No-Collar: The Hidden Costs of the Humane Workplace* (New York: Basic Books, 2002), 161.

6. The Family Hates You

1. Karl Marx, *Capital*, vol. 1, trans. Ben Fowkes (London: Penguin, 1976), 928.
2. Marx, 1:929.
3. See Giovanni Cadioli, "Soviet Planning in Theory and Practice: From Marxist Economics to the Command System," *Scienza & Politica* 32, no. 62 (2020): 17–39, and Mark Harrison, "Coercion, Compliance, and the Collapse of the Soviet Command Economy," *Economic History Review* 55, no. 3 (2002): 397–433.

4. Karl Marx and Friedrich Engels, "Manifesto of the Communist Party," in Karl Marx, *The Political Writings*, vol. 1, *The Revolutions of 1848*, ed. David Fernbach (New York: Vintage Books, 1974), 83.

5. See Kristen Ghodsee, *Red Valkyries: Feminist Lessons from Five Revolutionary Women* (London: Verso, 2022).

6. M. E. O'Brien, *Family Abolition: Capitalism and the Communizing of Care* (London: Pluto Press, 2023), 39–40.

7. See Sophie Lewis, *Abolish the Family* (New York: Verso, 2022), 36–49.

8. Marx and Engels, "Manifesto of the Communist Party," 83.

9. Lewis, *Abolish the Family*, 1.

10. O'Brien, *Family Abolition*, 37.

11. Lewis, *Abolish the Family*, 4.

12. Marx and Engels, "Manifesto of the Communist Party," 83.

13. Nancy F. Cott, *The Bonds of Womanhood: "Woman's Sphere" in New England 1780–1835* (New Haven, Conn.: Yale University Press, 1977), 60.

14. On slavery and family structure, see W. E. B. Du Bois, *The Negro American Family* (Atlanta, Ga.: Atlanta University Press, 1909); Barbara J. Fields, *Slavery and Freedom on the Middle Ground: Maryland during the Nineteenth Century* (New Haven, Conn.: Yale University Press, 1985); and Wilma A. Dunaway, *Slavery in the American Mountain South* (Cambridge: Cambridge University Press, 2003).

15. O'Brien, *Family Abolition*, 26.

16. O'Brien, 28.

17. Friedrich Engels, *Origin of the Family, Private Property, and the State*, ed. Eleanor Burke Leacock (New York: International Publishers, 1972), 121.

18. On Roman property law, see Orlando Patterson, *Slavery and Social Death* (Cambridge, Mass.: Harvard University Press, 1982), 28–32. On usufruct and the family, see David Graeber and David Wengrow, *The Dawn of Everything: A New History of Humanity* (New York: FSG, 2021), 508–10. Engels's discussion of the monogamous family effectively reiterates many of these points. See Engels, *Origin of the Family*, 125–46.

19. Erin Harrington, *Women, Monstrosity, and Horror Film: Gynaehorror* (New York: Routledge, 2018), 7.

20. Elevated horror certainly isn't the only instance of high culture using the stuff of genre while giving it an intellectual sheen. Jeremy Rosen identifies a similar dynamic in literary fiction, writing: "Esteemed writers of contemporary literary fiction use the frameworks of genres that have flourished in popular culture, but want to maintain their distance from the subfield of genre fiction." See Jeremy Rosen, "Literary Fiction and the Genres of Genre Fiction," *Post-45*, August 7, 2018, https://post45.org/2018/08/literary-fiction-and-the-genres-of-genre-fiction/.

21. Richard Nowell, "'A Kind of Bacall Quality': Jamie Lee Curtis, Stardom, and Gentrifying Non-Hollywood Horror," in *Merchants of Menace*, ed. Richard Nowell (New York: Bloomsbury, 2014), 133.

22. David Church, *Post-Horror: Art, Genre, and Cultural Elevation* (Edinburgh: Edinburgh University Press, 2021), 11.

23. Church, 12.
24. Church, 11.
25. See Tony Williams, *Hearths of Darkness: The Family in American Horror Film*, updated edition (Jackson: University of Mississippi Press, 2014).
26. Johanna Isaacson, *Stepford Daughters: Weapons for Feminists in Contemporary Horror* (New York: Common Notions, 2022), 5.
27. Isaacson, 9.
28. See "Salem Panel Q&A with Cast and Crew." DVD extra. *The Witch*, directed by Robert Eggers (A24, 2016); Anton Bitel, "Voices of the Undead: Robert Eggers on *The Witch*," *Sight and Sound*, July 11, 2016, https://www2.bfi.org.uk/news-opinion/sight-sound-magazine/interviews/robert-eggers-witch.
29. Bitel, "Voices of the Undead."
30. Aviva Briefel, "Devil in the Details: The Uncanny History of *The Witch* (2015)," *Film & History: An Interdisciplinary Journal* 49, no. 1 (Summer 2019): 4–20.
31. See Amanda Howell and Lucy Baker, "'I Am That Very Witch': Claiming Monstrosity, Claiming Desire in *The Witch*," in *Monstrous Possibilities: The Female Monster in 21st Century Screen Horror* (New York: Palgrave, 2022), pp. 65–82.
32. This is how Joho summarizes Taylor-Joy's response, not an exact quote. See Jess Joho, "The Witch Isn't an Empowerment Narrative and That's Why It's Great," *Kill Screen*, February 23, 2016, https://killscreen.com/previously/articles/the-witch-isnt-an-empowerment-narrative-and-thats-why-its-great/.
33. See Jess Joho and David Sims, "Female Freedom and Fury in *The Witch*," *The Atlantic*, February 24, 2016, https://www.theatlantic.com/entertainment/archive/2016/02/robert-eggers-the-witch-female-empowerment/470844/.
34. See Silvia Federici, *Caliban and the Witch: Women, the Body, and Primitive Accumulation*. (Brooklyn, N.Y.: Autonomedia, 2004), esp. 86–87, and Maria Mies, *Patriarchy and Accumulation on a World Scale* (London: Zed Books, 2014), 78–90.
35. See also Mies, *Patriarchy and Accumulation*, 66–70, and Claudia von Werlhof, "On the Concept of Nature and Society in Capitalism," in *Women: The Last Colony*, ed. Maria Mies, Veronika Bennholdt-Thomsen, and Claudia von Werlhof (London: Zed Books), 98–99.
36. Federici, *Caliban and the Witch*, 220; italics in original.
37. See Sven Lindqvist, *The Dead Do Not Die: "Exterminate All the Brutes" and Terra Nullius* (New York: The New Press, 2014), and Roxanne Dunbar-Ortiz, *An Indigenous People's History of the United States* (Boston, Mass.: Beacon Press, 2015), 45–55.
38. *Mourt's Relation: A Journal of The Pilgrims at Plymouth*, ed. Dwight B Heath (Bedford, Mass.: Applewood Books, 1963), 64. On the pervasive cultivation of North America by Native Americans prior to the arrival of Europeans, see Charles C. Mann, *1491: New Revelations of the Americas before Columbus*. 2nd edition (New York: Vintage, 2011), 277–378. On Indian settlements in New England and the effects of plague on the population in the seventeenth century,

see David J. Silverman, *This Land Is Their Land: The Wampanoag Indians, Plymouth Colony, and the Troubled History of Thanksgiving* (New York: Bloomsbury, 2019), 23–59.

39. See Charles C. Mann, *1493: Uncovering the New World Columbus Created* (New York: Vintage Books, 2011), 359–499.

40. See Dunbar-Ortiz, *An Indigenous People's History of the United States*, 25–27, and Graeber and Wengrow, *The Dawn of Everything*, 27–59.

41. For an overview of the history of reproductive struggles, see Jenny Brown, *Birth Strike: The Hidden Fight over Women's Work* (Oakland, Calif.: PM Press, 2019), esp. 29–41 and 70–80.

42. For a detailed account of the history of birth control and abortion, see Jenny Brown, *Without Apology: The Abortion Struggle Now* (New York: Verso, 2019). On women's role in supporting collapsing household incomes, see Gabriel Winant, *The Next Shift* (Cambridge, Mass.: Harvard University Press, 2023). On the entrance of women in the workforce, see Julian E. Zelizer and Kevin M. Kruse, *Fault Lines: A History of the United States since 1974* (New York: W. W. Norton, 2019).

43. Mariarosa Dalla Costa, *Women and the Subversion of the Community: A Mariarosa Dalla Costa Reader* (Oakland, Calif.: PM Press, 2019), 42.

44. See Arlene Hochschild, *The Second Shift*, rev. ed. (New York: Penguin, 2012), 4–10.

45. See Brown, *Birth Strike* 143.

46. Brown, *Without Apology*, 118.

47. Angela McRobbie, "Feminism, the Family, and the New 'Mediated' Maternalism," *New Formations*, no. 80–81 (Winter 2013), 128, https://doi.org/10.3898/newF.80/81.07.20133.

48. See Isaacson, *Stepford Daughters*, 40–41.

49. See Shulamith Firestone, *The Dialectic of Sex* (New York: Farrar, Straus, & Giroux, 2003), and Marge Piercy, *Woman on the Edge of Time* (New York: Ballantine Books, 1976).

50. Alexandra Kollontai, *"Theses on Communist Morality in the Sphere of Marital Relations."* Marxists.org. Originally published 1921, trans. Alix Holt, https://www.marxists.org/archive/kollonta/1921/theses-morality.htm.

51. Angela Davis, *Women, Race, Class* (New York: Random House, 1981), 223.

52. Audre Lorde, *Sister Outsider: Essays and Speeches* (Berkeley, Calif.: Crossing Press, 2007), 74.

53. Lorde, 173.

54. Alexis Pauline Gumbs, "M/other ourselves: A Black Queer Feminist Genealogy for Radical Mothering," in *Revolutionary Mothering*, ed Alexis Pauline Gumbs, China Martens, and Mai'a Williams (Oakland, Calif.: PM Press, 2016), 20.

55. Weeks, "Abolition of the Family," 14.

56. Sophie Lewis, *Full Surrogacy Now: Feminism against Family* (New York: Verso, 2019), 153.

57. Lewis, 20.
58. Lewis, 19.
59. Kathryn Russell, "A Value-Theoretic Approach to Childbirth and Reproductive Engineering," in *Materialist Feminism*, ed. Rosemary Hennessy and Chrys Ingraham (New York: Routledge, 1997), 335.
60. Lewis, *Full Surrogacy Now*, 59.
61. This point is made most forcefully by Cedric Robinson and Immanuel Wallerstein. See Cedric Robinson, *Black Marxism, revised and updated third edition* (Chapel Hill: University of North Carolina Press, 2021), 9–28, and Immanuel Wallerstein, *Historical Capitalism* (New York: Verso, 2011), 75–93.
62. See G. W. F. Hegel, *Philosophy of Right*, trans. S. W. Dyde (Amherst, N.Y.: Prometheus Books, 1996), ¶173:176,
63. Sometimes referred to as "baby brain," neuroscientists have recently suggested this idea may have biological reality. See Eliseline Hoekzema, Henk van Steenbergen, Milou Straathof, et al., "Mapping the Effects of Pregnancy on Resting State Brain Activity, White Matter Microstructure, Neural Metabolite Concentrations and Grey Matter Architecture," *Nature Communication* 13 (2022), https://doi.org/10.1038/s41467-022-33884-8.
64. Amy Chambers, "The (Re)birth of Pregnancy Horror in Alice Lowe's *Prevenge*." in *Women Make Horror: Filmmaking, Feminism, Genre*, ed, Alison Pierse (New Brunswick, N.J.: Rutgers University Press, 2020), 219.
65. Kaleem Aftab, "*Prevenge*'s Alice Lowe Interview: 'It Was Originally a Jokey Title but It Stuck,'" *The Independent*, February 7, 2017, https://www.independent.co.uk/arts-entertainment/films/features/prevenge-alice-lowe-interview-sightseers-beehive-the-mighty-boosh-horrible-histories-a7567076.html.
66. Aftab.
67. Aftab.

7. Feelings Hate You

1. Mark Fisher, *Capitalist Realism* (London: Zero Books, 2008), 2.
2. Fisher, 5.
3. Mark Fisher, "Good for Nothing," *The Occupied Times*, March 19, 2014, https://theoccupiedtimes.org/?p=12841.
4. Fisher, "Good for Nothing."
5. Anindya Bhattacharyya, "The Politics of Depression: Mark Fisher on Mental Health and Class Confidence," *RS21*, April 27, 2014, https://www.rs21.org.uk/2014/04/27/kpunk/.
6. Mark Fisher, *K-Punk: The Collected and Unpublished Writings of Mark Fisher* (London: Zero Books, 2018), 508. Fisher notes in this essay that "it would be facile to argue that every single case of depression can be attributed to economic of political causes," but also maintains that "most psychotherapy doesn't address the social causation of mental illness either" (508).
7. For instance, the Creature's death in *Frankenstein*, or the death of Reverend Jennings in Le Fanu's "Green Tea." On suicide's political economic role

in Romantic and Gothic literature, see Deanna Koretsky, *Death Rights: Romantic Suicide, Race, and the Bounds of Liberalism* (Albany: State University of New York Press, 2021).

8. Harry Benshoff, *Monsters in the Closet: Homosexuality and the Horror Film* (Manchester: University of Manchester Press, 1997), 103.

9. S. A. Bradley, *Screaming for Pleasure: How Horror Makes You Happy and Healthy* (San Leandro, Calif.: Coal Cracker Press, 2018), 257.

10. See Mathias Clasen, *Why Horror Seduces* (Oxford: Oxford University Press, 2017), and Coltan Scrivner, John A. Johnson, Jens Kjeldgaard-Christiansen, and Mathias Clasen, "Pandemic Practice: Horror Fans and Morbidly Curious Individuals Are More Psychologically Resilient during the COVID-19 Pandemic," *Personality and Individual Differences* 168 (January 2021), https://doi.org/10.1016/j.paid.2020.110397.

11. Sigmund Freud, *Beyond the Pleasure Principle*, trans. and ed. James Strachey (New York: W. W. Norton, 1961), 14.

12. Eva Illouz, *Saving the Modern Soul: Therapy, Emotions, and the Culture of Self Help* (Berkeley: University of California Press, 2008), 173.

13. David Church, *Post-Horror* (Edinburgh: Edinburgh University Press, 2021), 69. See also Richard Armstrong, *Mourning Films: A Critical Study of Loss and Grieving in Cinema* (Jefferson, N.C.: Macfarland, 2012).

14. Paul MacInnes, "The Babadook: 'I Wanted to Talk about the Need to Face Darkness in Ourselves,'" *The Guardian*, October 18, 2014, https://www.theguardian.com/film/2014/oct/18/the-babadook-jennifer-kent.

15. See Paul Mitchell, "The Horror of Loss: Reading Jennifer Kent's *The Babadook* as a Trauma Narrative," *Atlantis* 41, no. 2 (2019): 181.

16. See "The Babadook," *Rotten Tomatoes*, accessed December 26, 2023, https://www.rottentomatoes.com/m/the_babadook; "The Babadook," *Metacritic*, accessed December 26, 2023, https://www.metacritic.com/movie/the-babadook/critic-reviews; and "The Babadook," *The Numbers*, accessed December 26, 2023, https://www.the-numbers.com/movie/Babadook-The.

17. Karl Marx, *Capital*, vol. 1, translated by Ben Fowkes (London: Penguin, 1976), 449.

18. Braverman concisely defines scientific management as "an attempt to apply the methods of science to the increasingly complex problems of the control of labor in rapidly growing capitalist enterprises." Harry Braverman, *Labor and Monopoly Capital* (New York: Monthly Review Press, 1998), 59.

19. See Adam Smith, *The Wealth of Nations*, ed. Edwin Cannan (Chicago: University of Chicago Press, 1976), ii.302–5.

20. Braverman, *Labor and Monopoly Capital*, 58.

21. Braverman, 60.

22. Illouz. *Saving the Modern Soul*, 72.

23. Behaviorism found its earliest supporters not in the academy but in marketing, as the life of behavioral psychologist cum advertising executive John B Watson attests. See William Davies, *The Happiness Industry* (New York: Verso, 2015), 87–104.

24. Davies, 164.
25. See Davies, 164.
26. Davies, 146.
27. Illouz, *Saving the Modern Soul*, 173.
28. Illouz, 116; italics in original.
29. Illouz, 186.
30. It is also worth noting the educational level of these directors, given the import of film theory on their work. *Babadook* director Jennifer Kent has a degree in performing arts from Australia's National Institute of Dramatic Art. Ruth Paxton has an MA from Screen Academy Scotland and Kusama a BFA from New York University. Dolan graduated from IADT's National Film School. Aster earned an MFA from the AFI Conservatory. Severin Fiala says in interviews that he attended film school, and Garland studied the history of art at the University of Manchester. The two exceptions are Mattie Do and Keith Thomas, though neither are uneducated or untrained. Do worked informally with a Laotian film school after moving to Laos from Los Angeles (and works with her husband, who is a screenwriter), and Keith Thomas has a master's in religious education. On Do, see "Lao Horror, Lao Hopes: 10 Questions with Mattie Do." *Little Laos on the Prairie*, January 18, 2013, https://littlelaosontheprairie.org/2013/01/18/lao-horror-lao-hopes-10-questions-with-mattie-do/.
31. See MacInnes, "The Babadook." Drowning is a recurrent theme in allegorical horror. Most recently, Nikyatu Jusu's *The Nanny* (2022) uses drowning to allegorize the violence of capitalism's exploitation of careworkers and their families, using the drowning of a Senegalese careworker's child to represent the global North's oppression and exploitation of workers from the global South.
32. Adrienne Rich, *Of Woman Born* (New York: Norton, 1976), 24.
33. Rich, 24.
34. Linda Williams, "When a Woman Looks," in *The Dread of Difference*, 2nd ed., ed. Barry Keith Grant (Austin: University of Texas Press, 2015), 23.
35. Rich, *Of Woman Born*, 24.
36. Laura Mulvey, *Visual and Other Pleasures*, 2nd ed. (London: Palgrave, 2009), 35.
37. Mary Ann Doane, *The Desire to Desire: The Woman's Film of the 1940s* (Bloomington: University of Indiana Press, 1984), 19.
38. Doane, 95.
39. Doane, 180.
40. Doane, 180.
41. Mulvey, *Visual and Other Pleasures*, 208.
42. For a reading of the film's use of affect and community, see Cary Elza, "'Do You Feel Held?': Gender, Community, and Affective Design in *Midsommar*," *Journal for Cultural Research* 27, no. 3 (2023): 272–85, doi.10.1080/14797585.2023.2218629.
43. Beatrice Loayza, "Midsommar and the Legacy of Break-Up Horror Movies," *RogerEbert.com*, July 12, 2019, https://www.rogerebert.com/features/midsommar-and-the-horror-of-bad-breakups.

44. See Sonia Rao, "The Horrifying 'Midsommar' Is a Breakup Movie, According to Director Ari Aster," *Washington Post*, July 11, 2019, https://www.washingtonpost.com/arts-entertainment/2019/07/11/horrifying-midsommar-is-breakup-movie-according-director-ari-aster/.

45. Loayza, "Midsommar and the Legacy of Break-Up Horror Movies."

46. Jenni Miller, "The Stars of *Men* Unpack Its Mysterious Ancient Symbolism," *The Inverse*, May 19, 2022, https://www.inverse.com/entertainment/men-explained-sheela-na-gig-green-man-alex-garland.

47. Arlie Hochschild, *The Managed Heart*, 2nd ed. (Berkeley: University of California Press, 2012), 159.

48. On professionalism, see Hochschild, *Managed Heart*, 103. On the expansion of emotional management, see Hochschild, 160.

49. Richard Sennett, *Together* (New York: Penguin, 2012), 151.

50. See Luc Boltanski and Eve Chiapello, *The Spirit of New Capitalism*, new updated ed. (London: Verso, 2018).

51. Sennett, *Together*, 168.

52. Emotional labor's centrality to the modern cooperative workplace has led British journalist Rose Hackman to argue that capital should compensate it more equitably. On its face, Hackman's claim seems an extension of the call for wages for housework. However, Hackman isn't focused on building solidarity across gender and class lines. Instead, she calls for interventions in how employers evaluate and compensate emotional labor, including a call for "human resources departments ... [to] develop clear emotional-labor metrics based on amply available research and recognize the exponential value created from its performance." Should such ideas be implemented, I would expect no change in wages, only an increase in employer attempts to control how workers feel and express their feelings. No thanks. See Rose Hackman, "Emotional Labor at Work Is Work. It Should Be Compensated That Way," *Washington Post*, September 10, 2023, https://www.washingtonpost.com/opinions/2023/09/05/rose-hackman-emotional-labor-workplace-pay/, and Rose Hackman, *Emotional Labor: The Invisible Work Shaping Our Lives and How to Claim Our Power* (New York: Flatiron Books, 2023).

53. See M. Angelo Giardini, "Service Work as Affect Management: The Role of Affect-Related Competence" (PhD diss., Justus-Liebig-Universität, 2002), 52–53; Dieter Zapf, Christoph Vogt, Claudia Seifert, Heidrun Mertini, and Amela Isic, "Emotion Work as a Source of Stress: The Concept and Development of an Instrument," *European Journal of Work and Organizational Psychology* 8, no. 3 (1999): 371–400; Alicia A. Grandey, "Emotion Regulation in the Workplace: A New Way to Conceptualize Emotional Labor," *Journal of Occupational Health Psychology* 5, no.1 (2000): 95–110; J. Andrew Morris and Daniel C. Feldman, "Managing Emotions in the Workplace," *Journal of Managerial issues* 9, no. 3 (1997): 257–74. For an overview of occupational psychology's work on service workers' emotional labor, see Alicia A. Grandey and Robert C. Melloy, "The State of the Heart: Emotional Labor as Emotion Regulation Reviewed and Revised," *Journal of Occupational Health Psychology* 22, no. 3 (2017): 407–22.

54. Jennifer M. Silva, *Coming Up Short* (Oxford: Oxford University Press, 2014), 95.
55. Silva, 85.
56. Silva, 12 and 115.
57. This narrative turn seems to begin with the Belgian film *Man Bites Dog (C'est arrivé près de chez vous*, 1992) and was subsequently popularized by *The Blair Witch Project* (1999), *Paranormal Activity* (2007), and the host of found-footage films that followed. These ambiguous endings with their abrupt cuts from the action have entered the narrative lexicon of small-budget elevated-horror films such as *The Blackcoat's Daughter* (2014), *Bleed with Me* (2020), and *Blood Conscious* (2021).
58. Mckenzie Wark, *Gamer Theory* (Cambridge, Mass.: Harvard University Press, 2007), 11.
59. Fisher, "Good for Nothing."
60. Jordan Aldredge, "The Future of DIY Horror Is on the Internet: Jane Schoenbrun on 'We're All Going to the World's Fair,'" *No Film School*, July 22, 2021, https://nofilmschool.com/were-all-going-to-the-worlds-fair-interview.

Conclusion

1. On the Kentex fire, see Bibi van der Zee, "The Inside Story of the Kentex Disaster: 74 Workers Died but No One Is in Prison," *The Guardian*, July 20, 2015, https://www.theguardian.com/global-development-professionals-network/2015/jul/20/the-inside-story-of-the-kentex-disaster-74-workers-died-but-no-one-is-in-prison.
2. "Justice for Kentex Workers! Justice for All Filipino Workers!" *Migrante International*, May 19, 2015, https://migranteinternational.org/justice-for-kentex-workers-justice-for-all-filipino-workers/.
3. Ali Moosavi, "Nocebos and Placebos: An Interview with Lorcan Finnegan on *Nocebo*," *Film Int.*, November 6, 2022, https://filmint.nu/interview-with-lorcan-finnegan-nocebo-ali-moosavi/.
4. Nancy Fraser, *Cannibal Capitalism* (London: Verso, 2022), 17.
5. Fraser, 24.
6. Søren Mau, *Mute Compulsion: A Marxist Theory of the Economic Power of Capital* (London: Verso, 2023), 114.
7. Karl Marx, *Capital*, vol. 3, trans. David Fernbach (London: Penguin, 1991), 959.
8. Marx, *Capital*, 3:959
9. Marx, *Capital*, 3:959
10. For this idea in Marx, see also Karl Marx, *Grundrisse: Foundations of the Critique of Political Economy*, trans. Martin Nicolaus (London: Penguin, 1973), 699–727. For examples of contemporary accelerationist thought, see Nick Srnicek and Alex Williams, *Inventing the Future: Postcapitalism and a World without Work* (London: Verso, 2015), and Aaron Bastani, *Fully Automated Luxury Communism* (London: Verso, 2019).

11. As Alberto Toscano notes, Sartre's account in *Critique of Dialectical Reason* of Chinese deforestation amply makes this point. See Alberto Toscano, "Antiphysis/Antipraxis: Universal Exhaustion and the Tragedy of Materiality," *Mediations: Journal of the Marxist Literary Group* 31, no. 2 (2018): 129–48.

12. We can't imagine a world beyond capitalism if we refuse to think carefully about what capitalism is and isn't. As Katherine Gibson and Julie Graham, writing together under the nom de plume J.K. Gibson-Graham, explain, "Marxism has produced a discourse of Capitalism that ostensibly delineates an object of transformative class politics but that operates more powerfully to discourage and marginalize projects of class transformation." The assertion that capitalism is all-powerful, Gibson-Graham argue, keeps us from recognizing the noncapitalist relations and forms of production that occur inside or alongside it. J.K. Gibson-Graham, *The End of Capitalism (As We Knew It)* (Minneapolis: University of Minnesota Press, 2006), 252.

13. Fraser, *Cannibal Capitalism*, 18.

14. See C. Richard King, "The (Mis)Uses of Cannibalism in Contemporary Cultural Critique," *Diacritics* 30, no. 1 (Spring 2000): 106–23.

15. Fraser, *Cannibal Capitalism*, 21. Fraser here works from Karl Polanyi's influential account of the tension between market and nonmarket forces in *The Great Transformation*, in effect linking the mechanisms he describes to Moore's work on appropriation. I should note that, although Fraser includes racialization as one of her systems, her account of racialization is effectively one of its uses for the appropriation of land, labor, and resources, not as an autonomous system outside capitalist relations. This is likely why Fraser does not use "boundary struggles" to describe problems involving racialization.

16. See Vivek Chibber, *Postcolonial Theory and the Specter of Capital* (London: Verso, 2013), 14–19. See also Dipesh Chakrabarty, *Provincializing Europe* (Princeton, N.J.: Princeton University Press, 2000), and Lisa Lowe, *Immigrant Acts: On Asian American Culture Politics* (Durham, N.C.: Duke University Press, 1996).

17. Chibber, *Postcolonial Theory and the Specter of Capital*, 144; emphasis in original.

18. Søren Mau builds from Chibber's ideas to argue for the importance of difference to capitalism. See Mau, *Mute Compulsion*, 172.

19. This shouldn't be read as a *sub rosa* argument that class matters more than race or gender, or that difference is somehow "bad" and class politics "good." It simply means to show that Marxism can, should, and does account for difference's centrality for capitalist production and accumulation.

20. See Mau, *Mute Compulsion*, 305. For a defense of the falling rate of profit, see Andrew Kliman, *Reclaiming Marx's Capital* (Plymouth: Lexington Books, 2007). For recent proponents of the falling rate of profit thesis, see Aaron Benanav, *Automation and the Future of Work* (London: Verso, 2020), and Jason E. Smith, *Smart Machines and Service Work: Automation in an Age of Stagnation* (London: Reaktion Books, 2020).

21. Mau, *Mute Compulsion*, 310.

22. Quoted in Nancy Fraser, *The Old Is Dying and the New Cannot Be Born* (London: Verso, 2019), 29.
23. Dylan Rodriguez, *Forced Passages: Imprisoned Radical Intellectuals and the U.S. Prison Regime* (Minneapolis: University of Minnesota Press, 2006), 131.
24. See Martin Hägglund, *This Life: Secular Faith and Spiritual Freedom* (New York: Anchor Books, 2019).
25. Lynn Seagall, *Lean On Me: A Politics of Radical Care* (London: Verso, 2023), introduction.

INDEX

Abel, Marco, 6
abstract labor, 4, 17, 20, 28–30, 40, 49, 135, 164, 205
Adorno, Theodor, 83, 134
affect, 2–10, 25–26, 36–40, 44, 137, 173–75, 206, 217n6, 220n33, 224n92, 239n13, 247n42
Ahmed, Sara, 2
Alexander, Neville, 96–97
Althusser, Louis, 16, 221n53, 225n19
Altman, Rick, 9, 227n7
Anthropocene, 67–68, 89, 199
antiwork horror, 32–41
appropriation, 14–15, 47–48, 71–76, 103, 228n18
Asian American stereotypes, 40

Babadook, The (Kent), 175–78, 180–83
Baby, The (Gaymer and Robbins-Grace), 153
Balibar, Étienne, 16, 97
Banaji, Jarius, 17, 130–31, 225n15
Banquet, A (Paxton), 190–91
Basso, Luca, 127–28
behavioral psychology, 178–80, 246n23
Benjamin, Walter, 134–35, 218n13
Benning, James, 88
Benshoff, Harry M., 78, 174. *See also* cult film; psychedelic film

Boltanski, Luc, and Pierre Esquerre, 130–46, 240n30, 241n32
Bonneuil, Christophe, and Jean-Baptiste Fressoz, 67
Briefel, Aviva, 115, 155
British Board of Film Classification (BBFC), 55–57
Burke, Edmund, 6–7, 229n33
Burkett, Paul, 22, 73–74, 90, 223n73, 228n18, 230n9, 231n14

Candyman (DaCosta), 115–21
Candyman (Rose), 113–15
capitalism: as actively hostile to life, 14; affect and, 7–10; as always right, 57; critics on horror and, 4; destructive hierarchies and, 15–16; impersonal domination and, 17–18; managerial tactics of, 179. *See also* Marx, Karl
Capitalocene, 67–68, 230n9
care work, 36, 46, 62–65, 166, 229n34
Carroll, Noel, 5
Censor (Bailey-Bond), 55–61
Cherry, Brigid, 12
Chibber, Vivek, 204–5, 235n15
Church, David, 12, 152, 175
Clasen, Mathias, 1, 5, 174
class-structure horror, 38–39
Clover, Carol, 5–6, 9, 151, 219n18

Coleman, Robin R. Means, 98, 112, 114
commodity, 28–30, 36, 47, 89–90, 130, 133, 165, 203–4, 218n13, 218n14, 240n30, 241n32; asset form, 143–46; collection form, 139–42; effects on subjectivity, 123–24; fetishism, 3–4, 30–31, 128–29; frontiers of, 75; horrors of, 126–29; standard form, 89, 131–33; trend form, 134–38; uncanny and, 129, 131, 135
common sense, 10, 13, 118, 173, 199–200; as construction of hegemony, 10, 13, 21–23; that climate change is humanity's fault, 68; that commodification reduces to passive spectatorship, 124–25; that family is the normative ideal, 148–50, 160–61; that gentrification is inevitable, 93; that work is meaningful, 40, 43, 48, 57; that work is punishment, 26; that you should control your feelings, 175, 178–80
commoning, 163–66
Conference, The (Eklund), 34–35
Covid-19 pandemic, 2, 25–26, 44, 82, 126
critical horror, 6, 12–13, 77, 88–89, 98–100, 108–10, 113, 120–21
cult film, 78, 125–26
cults in horror, 158–63
cynicism, 36–39, 188–89. *See also* affect

Dalla Costa, Mariarosa, 47, 159, 227n9
Davies, William, 55, 180, 225n9, 229n28
Debord, Guy, 124–25, 140
degrowth, 90–91, 230n8
Demons (Bava), 125–26
depression in horror, 156, 174–82, 193–94, 245n7

Doane, Mary Ann, 183–84
domination: of abstract labor, 28; capital's impersonal social, 2–3, 17–19, 27–31, 41, 42, 67, 79, 202, 207; forms of, 15–16, 106, 138, 150, 162, 204, 231n16; in the Gothic, 32–33, 226n29; political, 225n12; by work, 33–41
Dracula (Stoker), 31–32
Drag Me to Hell (Raimi), 18–20, 36

ecofascism, 79–81, 83–84, 233n51
eco-horror, 69–71, 76–91. *See also* psychedelic eco-horror
eco-socialism, 68, 71–76, 202, 228n18, 230n8, 230n9, 231n14
elevated horror, 11–12, 23, 98–99, 116, 151–72, 175–77, 200, 242n20, 249n57
emotion work, 23, 175–76, 187–88, 193, 202, 228n21, 248n52
Engels, Friedrich, 74, 147–50
environmental uncanny, 70–71, 76, 78, 81–82, 86. *See also* eco-horror; irrealism; metaphor in horror; psychedelic eco-horror
experimental film, 88–89, 176

family: as attack on bodily autonomy, 166, 168; choice and, 160–61; neoliberalism and, 159–61; property and, 167–68
family abolition, 147–50, 162–66
Fanon, Frantz, 106, 114, 206
Federici, Silvia, 16, 45, 156–57, 227n9
feeling. *See* affect
feminist anticapitalist horror, 45, 49–52, 54, 61–65
Fisher, Mark, 25, 173–74, 193, 245n6
formalism, 10, 78, 88–89, 175, 183, 219n18
Foster, John Bellamy, 73, 90
found-footage horror, 49, 126–29, 191, 239n15, 249n57

Index | 255

Frank, Thomas, 125
Fraser, Nancy, 18, 21, 202–4, 206, 230n9, 250n15
fungal horror, 76–84, 232n41

Gaia (Bouwer), 78–81, 231n52
gender, 5–6, 9, 12–13, 40, 46, 48, 72, 80–81, 148–49, 159, 183–84, 189, 197, 221n47, 227n9, 248n52, 250n19
genre, 5–11, 98–100, 108–9, 111–15, 146, 222n62, 227n7, 239n13, 242n20
gentrification, 93–94, 96, 98–99, 102–7, 111–21. *See also* uneven development
Get Out (Peele), 101–4
Ghosh, Amitav, 68–69, 231n14
Gilmore, Craig, 116
Gilmore, Ruth Wilson, 16, 104, 116, 120–21
Glass, Rose, 62
Good Madam (Bass), 110–11
Gothic novels, 4, 13, 31, 113, 174, 221n51, 236n28
Grant, Barry Keith, 78, 125–26. *See also* cult film

Hägglund, Martin, 207
Hall, Stuart, 10, 104, 117, 125
Hardt, Michael, and Antonio Negri, 46
Harrison, Sheri-Marie, 13
Harvey, David, 72–73, 95, 236n17
Hatching (Bergholm), 192
hate, 2, 13–21, 25, 43, 67, 129, 207, 224n92
hegemony, 10
Heinrich, Michael, 3, 17, 29–30, 127, 225n15
Hereditary (Aster), 161–63
Hochschild, Arlie, 160, 187, 228n21
horror: aesthetics, 11–12, 23, 34, 80–81, 131–32, 151–56, 162–63, 167–68, 175, 192; affects of, 1–5, 8, 20–23, 69–70, 86–88, 101–4, 111, 120, 125, 201, 173–98, 225n9, 248n52; antiwork, 32–41; class-structure, 38–39; critical, 6, 12–13, 77, 88–89, 98–100, 108–10, 113, 120–21; depression in, 156, 174–82, 193–94, 245n7; ecological, 69–70; elevated, 11–12, 23, 98–99, 116, 151–72, 175–77, 200, 242n20, 249n57; feminist anticapitalist, 45, 49–52, 54, 61–65; found-footage, 49, 126–29, 191, 239n15, 249n57; masks in, 105, 240n22; masochism and, 5–6, 184, 219n29; mass-culture, 124–26, 130–46, 199; new Black, 13, 22, 98–121, 199, 206; pleasure and, 5–9, 26, 62–65, 100, 114, 125–26, 199, 201; therapeutic, 1–2, 9, 13, 23, 152, 155, 173–98, 200
horror comedy, 32, 33–34, 37, 108, 169–70, 220n43
Host (Savage), 126–29, 239n15
Huber, Matthew, 68
Huesera: The Bone Woman (Cevera), 153

I Blame Society (Horvat), 48–52
Illouz, Eva, 175–81, 189
In Fabric (Strickland), 131–33
I Saw the TV Glow (Schoenbrun), 197
In the Earth (Wheatley), 81–86
irrealism, 13, 26, 33, 100, 121, 135, 154, 158, 175, 177, 184, 189, 192. *See also* environmental uncanny; irrealism; metaphor in horror
Isaacson, Johanna, 8, 50–51, 153, 162, 228n21
Itoh, Makoto, 30, 225n15

Jameson, Fredric, 69, 94, 124, 221n51, 235n10
Jerng, Mark, 99
Jevons, William Stanley, 26
Jug Face (Kinkle), 158–59, 206

Kaplan, E. Ann, 69, 87
Kent, Jennifer, 175, 181–82
Kern, Leslie, 93–94, 96
Kornbluh, Anna, 218n8, 218n9

Lauro, Sarah Juliet, 49
Lazzarato, Maurizio, 16–17
Lewis, Sophie, 148–49, 164
Lipsitz, George, 22, 97
Loayza, Beatrice, 185–86
Long Walk, The (Do), 191
Lorde, Audre, 164
Lordon, Frédéric, 2, 44, 49
love, 39–40, 44–46, 48–49, 63, 65
Löwy, Michael, 13, 222n68
Lukács, Georg, 123–24

Malm, Andreas, 68, 75, 230n9
Marcuse, Herbert, 124
Marx, Karl, 3–4, 14, 15, 17, 20, 26, 27; on abstract labor, 28–29; on agents of circulation, 137; on boundaries and barriers of capital, 20; on capital's spectral agency, 2–3; on commodity fetishism, 3, 30–31, 36, 128–29, 134; on commodity form, 127; ecological thought of, 74–76; family abolition and, 148–50; on *Gallerte*, 4, 135; on labor-power, 28; on means of subsistence, 29–31, 133; on primitive accumulation, 15, 71–72, 156; on services, 46; on socially necessary labor, 29–30; on surplus labor, 27–29, 75; on surplus value, 14–15, 27–29, 47, 74, 137, 179; on theory of value, 27–33, 225n15, 228n18, 240n30
Marxist criticism, 4, 10
masochism, 5–6, 219n29
mass-culture horror, 124–26, 130–46, 199
Master (Diallo), 108–9
Mau, Søren, 18, 31, 206
Mayhem (Lynch), 33–41

McKittrick, Katherine, 103
McMillan, Jimmy, 93
McNally, David, 4
Men (Garland), 186–87
metabolic rift, 73–75
metaphor in horror, 22, 38, 52, 77, 98, 101, 109, 111, 120, 154–55, 175–76, 181. *See also* environmental uncanny; irrealism
Midsommar (Aster), 185–86
money, 17–21, 40, 43, 48, 127–28, 143, 224n88
Moore, Jason W., 21, 67, 73, 75, 223n73, 230n9, 250n15
Morris, William, 89–90
Mulvey, Laura, 183, 197, 219n29
Murder Party (Saulnier), 143–46
My Heart Can't Beat Unless You Tell It To (Cuartas), 154–55

Neocleous, Mark, 3, 96
neoliberalism: affects and, 36; ecofascism and, 79; effects on care work, 63; effects on commodification, 130; effects on communities, 116; effects on the family, 160; history of, 46, 55–59; as political project, 55–59, 229n27; and primitive accumulation, 72; waning hegemony and, 206;
new Black horror, 13, 22, 98–121, 199, 206
Ngai, Sianne, 7–8, 115
Nocebo (Finnegan), 200–201
Nosferatu (Murnau), 32, 226n29
NUM strike, 52–55

O'Brien, M. E., 148–50

Peele, Jordan, 99–107, 111, 237n34, 239n13
People Under the Stairs, The (Craven), 101
Personal Shopper (Assayas), 139–42
Petley, Julian, 56

plantation logic, 103
postcolonial theory, 235n15
postmodernity, 69
Postone, Moishe, 17
Power, The (Faith), 52–55
Prevenge (Lowe), 168–72
primitive accumulation, 4, 15, 47–48, 71–74, 94, 96, 156
psychedelic eco-horror, 70–71, 76–78, 86–88, 233n45
psychedelic film, 77–78. *See also* cult film

racial capitalism, 15–16, 75, 83–84, 96–97, 102–5, 110–17, 120–21, 199–200, 202
r/antiwork, 25–26
refusal of work, 25, 39–40, 43, 160, 224n2
reproductive work, 147–48, 160, 165–71, 227n9
revolution, 46, 69, 107, 147, 198
Reyes, Xavier Aldana, 5, 219n20, 220n46
Rich, Adrienne, 182–83
Roberts, William Clare, 71, 225n12
Robinson, Cedric, 15–16, 83, 96, 234n58
Ross, Andrew, 144

Saint Maud (Glass), 61–65
Saito, Kohei, 73–75, 230n1, 230n8, 230n9
Seagall, Lynn, 207
Sennett, Richard, 187–88
service work, 46, 63, 95, 139–43, 187–88, 227n11, 240n30
Seventh Victim, The (Robson), 174
Severance (Smith), 34–35
She Dies Tomorrow (Seimetz), 5, 12, 22, 70, 86–91
Shelley (Abbasi), 165–68
Shudder, 11, 33
Silva, Jennifer M., 181, 188–89
Simpsons, The, 32

Slaxx (Kephart), 135–38
Smith, Neil, 73, 94–95, 235n12
socially necessary labor, 29–30, 36
social reproduction theory, 7–8, 17, 21, 40, 45–48, 149–50, 153, 160, 171–72, 187, 202, 206, 227n11, 231n16, 231n18
Sohn-Rethel, Alfred, 17, 30, 127, 130
Soper, Kate, 90–91
spectatorship, 5–7, 9–10, 12, 78, 124–26, 129, 146, 183–84, 198, 239n13
Spinoza, Baruch, 20
Stuelke, Patricia, 45
Steven, Mark, 4–5
streaming, 11–12
sublime, 6–7, 220n33
surplus labor, 27–29, 75
surplus value, 14–15, 27–29, 47, 74, 137, 179
surrogacy, 164–68

Thatcher, Margaret, 55, 57
therapeutic horror, 1–2, 9, 13, 23, 152, 155, 173–98, 200
therapeutic narrative, 180–81, 189
Tsing, Anna Lowenhaupt, 77

Unearth (Lyons and Swies), 70
uneven development, 8, 16, 22, 72–77, 94–97, 99, 102, 110–11, 113–21, 199–202, 231n14, 235n12. *See also* gentrification; Harvey, David; Smith, Neil
Us (Peele), 105–7

value, 27–33, 225n15, 228n18, 240n30
video nasty controversy, 55–57, 61, 229n24
Vigil, The (Thomas), 189–90
Virno, Paolo, 36–37, 44, 226n35
von Trier, Lars, 175

Wages for Housework, 45–46, 159
Wark, Mckenzie, 193

We Are All Going to the World's Fair
  (Schoenbrun), 192–98
Weber, Max, 26
Weeks, Kathi, 25, 27
Weinstock, Jeffrey, 7
Wellington Paranormal, 108, 220n43
What We Do in the Shadows, 31–32
Wilderson, Frank, 100, 119–20
Williams, Linda, 9, 182–83, 219n18,
  219n25, 221n47, 227n7

Witch, The (Eggers), 155–58
woman's film, 45, 151, 183–84, 227n7
work: as meaningful, 43–44, 48–49,
  64–65; possession by, 45–55 as
  punishment, 25–26

Žižek, Slavoj, 30–31, 125
zombies, 34, 78, 125, 191, 228n19,
  232n41, 237n32
zombis, 49, 195, 228n19

JOSHUA GOOCH is professor of English at D'Youville University in Buffalo, New York. He is the author of *Dickensian Affects: Charles Dickens and Feelings of Precarity* and *The Victorian Novel, Service Work, and the Nineteenth-Century Economy*.